Policies and incentives for promoting innovation in antibiotic research

The European Observatory on Health Systems and Policies supports and promotes evidence-based health policy-making through comprehensive and rigorous analysis of health systems in Europe. It brings together a wide range of policy-makers, academics and practitioners to analyse trends in health reform, drawing on experience from across Europe to illuminate policy issues.

The European Observatory on Health Systems and Policies is a partnership between the World Health Organization Regional Office for Europe, the Governments of Belgium, Finland, Ireland, the Netherlands, Norway, Slovenia, Spain, Sweden and the Veneto Region of Italy, the European Commission, the European Investment Bank, the World Bank, UNCAM (French National Union of Health Insurance Funds), the London School of Economics and Political Science and the London School of Hygiene & Tropical Medicine.

Policies and incentives for promoting innovation in antibiotic research

Elias Mossialos, Chantal M Morel, Suzanne Edwards,
Julia Berenson, Marin Gemmill-Toyama, David Brogan

This study was commissioned and financed by the
Swedish Government

Keywords:
ANTI-BACTERIAL AGENTS
DRUG RESISTANCE, BACTERIAL
MOTIVATION
HEALTH POLICY
DRUG INDUSTRY – economics – manpower
DRUG DISCOVERY
BIOMEDICAL RESEARCH

© World Health Organization 2010, on behalf of the European Observatory on Health Systems and Policies

All rights reserved. The European Observatory on Health Systems and Policies welcomes requests for permission to reproduce or translate its publications, in part or in full.

> Address requests about publications to: Publications, WHO Regional Office for Europe, Scherfigsvej 8, DK-2100 Copenhagen Ø, Denmark
>
> Alternatively, complete an online request form for documentation, health information, or for permission to quote or translate, on the Regional Office web site (http://www.euro.who.int/pubrequest).

The designations employed and the presentation of the material in this publication do not imply the expression of any opinion whatsoever on the part of the European Observatory on Health Systems and Policies concerning the legal status of any country, territory, city or area or of its authorities, or concerning the delimitation of its frontiers or boundaries. Dotted lines on maps represent approximate border lines for which there may not yet be full agreement.

The mention of specific companies or of certain manufacturers' products does not imply that they are endorsed or recommended by the European Observatory on Health Systems and Policies in preference to others of a similar nature that are not mentioned. Errors and omissions excepted, the names of proprietary products are distinguished by initial capital letters.

All reasonable precautions have been taken by the European Observatory on Health Systems and Policies to verify the information contained in this publication. However, the published material is being distributed without warranty of any kind, either express or implied. The responsibility for the interpretation and use of the material lies with the reader. In no event shall the European Observatory on Health Systems and Policies be liable for damages arising from its use. The views expressed by authors, editors, or expert groups do not necessarily represent the decisions or the stated policy of the European Observatory on Health Systems and Policies.

ISBN 978 92 890 4213 0

Printed in the United Kingdom

Contents

List of tables, figures and boxes	vii
List of abbreviations	xi
Glossary	xiii
Foreword	ixx
Acknowledgements	xxi
10 key messages	xxiii

Introduction — 1

Chapter 1 Background on antibiotics — 9
1.1 What are antibiotics? — 9
1.2 Why antibiotics are important — 10
1.3 Externalities of antibiotics and AR — 11

Chapter 2 Background on AR — 15
2.1 What is AR? — 15
2.2 Severity of AR — 16
    2.2.1 AR trends in developed countries — 16
    2.2.2 AR trends in developing countries — 20
2.3 Clinical and economic impact of AR — 21
    2.3.1 Clinical outcomes — 21
    2.3.2 Costs of resistance — 23

Chapter 3 Causes of AR — 27
3.1 Misuse of antibiotics — 27
    3.1.1 Physicians and health-care providers — 28
    3.1.2 Livestock and agriculture — 31
3.2 Role of diagnostics in AR — 32
3.3 Role of vaccines in AR — 36
    3.3.1 Examples from Europe — 37
    3.3.2 Examples from the United States — 37
3.4 Lack of new antibiotics — 37
    3.4.1 The antibiotic market — 38
    3.4.2 Areas of unmet need — 43

Chapter 4 Reasons for limited innovation — 49
4.1 Antibiotic restrictions deter pharmaceutical investment in R&D — 49
4.2 Challenges in the antibiotics market – NPV — 50

4.3 Regulatory environment	53
4.4 Estimated cost of drug development	54
4.5 Scientific challenges	57

Chapter 5 Health system responses to AR — 59
- 5.1 Examples from Europe — 61
- 5.2 Examples from the United States — 63

Chapter 6 Analysis of opportunities and incentives to stimulate R&D for antibiotics — 67
- 6.1 Push incentives — 67
  - 6.1.1 Increasing access to research — 68
  - 6.1.2 Scientific personnel — 71
  - 6.1.3 Direct funding of research — 71
  - 6.1.4 Translational research — 77
  - 6.1.5 Tax incentives — 79
  - 6.1.6 PDPs — 83
- 6.2 Pull incentives — 89
  - 6.2.1 Monetary prizes — 89
  - 6.2.2 Advance market commitments — 95
  - 6.2.3 Patent buyout — 100
- 6.3 Lego-regulatory mechanisms — 100
  - 6.3.1 Clinical trials — 101
  - 6.3.2 Intellectual property mechanisms — 106
  - 6.3.3 Expedited regulatory review — 117
  - 6.3.4 Pricing and reimbursement — 121
  - 6.3.5 Liability protection — 126
  - 6.3.6 Antitrust laws — 127
  - 6.3.7 *Sui generis* rights — 127
- 6.4 Combined push-pull incentive models — 128
  - 6.4.1 Orphan drug designation — 128
  - 6.4.2 Call options for antibiotics model — 129

Chapter 7 Conclusions — 137
- 7.1 Rationale for intervention in the antibiotics market — 137
- 7.2 Preserving the effective life of existing and new antibiotics — 139
- 7.3 Key concepts in incentive design — 141
- 7.4 Conclusions on individual incentives — 147
  - 7.4.1 Direct public subsidy for basic research — 147

Appendix A. EU Council conclusions on innovative incentives — 159
Appendix B. US-EU joint declaration on creation of transatlantic taskforce on antimicrobial resistance — 161
Appendix C. Global vaccine research — 175
Appendix D. Possible funding mechanisms for a COA scheme — 177

References — 179

List of tables, figures and boxes

Tables

Table 3.1	Features and performance characteristics of commercial molecular assays for detection of MRSA	34
Table 3.2	Antibiotic launches since 2000	41
Table 3.3	New systemic antibacterial agents with new target or new MoA and in vitro activity based on actual data or assumed based on known class properties or MoA against the selected bacteria (n=15, as of 14 March 2008)	46
Table 4.1	Risk-adjusted NPV (US$ millions) for project therapeutic classes	51
Table 4.2	Top 13 oral drugs: patent expiry dates and 2007 revenues	54
Table 5.1	Susceptibility (S)/Resistance (R) results for *S. aureus* isolates in a selection of European countries, 2007	62
Table 6.1	Differences between EMEA accelerated review mechanisms	118
Table 6.2	Products with conditional and exceptional circumstance EMEA approvals to date	118
Table 6.3	Comparison of United States and EU orphan drug legislation and processes	129
Table 6.4	Length of time and estimated success per development phase	133
Table 7.1	Merits of push and pull mechanisms	144
Table A	New vaccines against infectious diseases: R&D status as of February 2006	175

Figures

Fig. 2.1	*S. pneumoniae*: proportion of invasive isolates nonsusceptible to penicillin, 2007	See colour section

Fig. 2.2	*S. pneumoniae*: proportion of invasive isolates resistant to erythromycin, 2007 .... See colour section
Fig. 2.3	*S. pneumoniae*: proportion of invasive isolates with dual nonsusceptibility to erythromycin and penicillin, 2007 .... See colour section
Fig. 2.4	*S. aureus* infections in ICUs in the NNIS system, 1987–1997 .... See colour section
Fig. 3.1	Total outpatient antibiotic use in 25 European countries, 2003 .... See colour section
Fig. 3.2	Correlation between penicillin use and prevalence of penicillin nonsusceptible *S. pneumoniae* .... See colour section
Fig. 3.3	ROC curve based on laboratory-based evaluation of 19 commercially available RDTs for TB (all patients = 355) .... See colour section
Fig. 3.4	Timeline of the rapid rate of resistance .... See colour section
Fig. 3.5	Discovery of new classes of antibiotic .... See colour section
Fig. 3.6	Ten-year trend in drug and biological submissions to the FDA .... See colour section
Fig. 3.7	New systemic antibacterial agents .... See colour section
Fig. 4.1	Antibiotic restrictions and the regulatory environment: impact on NPV	52
Fig. 6.1	8+2(+1) arrangements in the EU	112
Fig. 6.2	Call option price (US$ millions) as a function of development stage and Q	134

Boxes

Box 3.1	Coordinating prescribing practices with policies – lessons from the Medicare Product Quality Research Initiative in the United States	30
Box 3.2	Current status of diagnostic tests for detection of MRSA	33
Box 3.3	Case study – pneumococcal conjugate vaccine	36
Box 3.4	Main findings from the EMA/ECDC Joint Technical Report: *The Bacterial Challenge – Time to React*	42
Box 4.1	Regulatory experiences of five antibiotics recently reviewed by the FDA	55
Box 5.1	Literature on policies to guide appropriate antibiotic use	60
Box 6.1	The Structural Genomics Consortium	70

Box 6.2	The Wellcome Trust	72
Box 6.3	The Innovative Medicines Initiative (IMI)	73
Box 6.4	Project Bioshield	76
Box 6.5	Examples of promising drugs developed through PDPs	83
Box 6.6	Wellcome Trust: Technology Transfer division	85
Box 6.7	Institute of OneWorld Health (iOWH)	87
Box 6.8	Example of a prize for a diagnostic test, X PRIZE Foundation	90
Box 6.9	Ex-ante award calculation	92
Box 6.10	Stockpiling	99
Box 6.11	Using IP mechanism to inhibit development of resistance	113
Box 6.12	Broadening IP protection	114
Box 6.13	Health technology assessments (HTAs)	122
Box 6.14	ACE Programme proposal	124
Box 6.15	Health impact fund (HIF)	125

List of abbreviations

ABS	Antibiotic stewardship
ACE	Antibiotic Conservation and Effectiveness (Programme)
AMC	Advance market commitment
AR	Antibiotic resistance
BARDA	Biomedical Advanced Research and Development Authority
CA	Community acquired
CA-MRSA	Community-acquired MRSA
CDC	US Centers for Disease Control and Prevention
CGD	Center for Global Development
CHMP	Committee for Medicinal Products for Human Use (at EMA)
CMS	Centers for Medicare and Medicaid Services
CNS	Central nervous system
COA	Call Options for Antibiotics
COV	Call Options for Vaccines
DNA	Deoxyribonucleic acid
EARSS	European Antimicrobial Resistance Surveillance System
EC	European Commission
ECDC	European Centre for Disease Prevention and Control
EDCTP	European and Developing Countries Clinical Trials Partnership
EFPIA	European Federation of Pharmaceutical Industries and Associations
EIB	European Investment Bank
EIF	European Investment Fund
EMbaRC	European Consortium of Microbial Resources Centres
EMA	European Medicines Agency (previously European Agency for the Evaluation of Medicinal Products)
ESAC	European Surveillance of Antimicrobial Consumption
ESKAPE	*Enterococcus faecium, Staphylococcus aureus, Klebsiella* species, *Acinetobacter baumannii, Pseudomonas aeruginosa, Enterobacter* species
EU	European Union
FDA	US Food and Drug Administration
FDAMA	Food and Drug Administration Modernization Act
FP7	European Commission's Seventh Framework Programme
FRG	Functional resistance group
GAVI	Gavi Alliance (formerly Global Alliance for Vaccines and Immunization)
GDP	Gross domestic product
GIF	High Growth and Innovative SME Facility
GSK	GlaxoSmithKline
HHS	US Department of Health and Human Services

HIV/AIDS	Human immunodeficiency virus/Acquired immunodeficiency syndrome
ICU	Intensive care unit
IDSA	Infectious Diseases Society of America
IMI	Innovative Medicines Initiative
IP	Intellectual property
IV	Intravenous
MDG	Millenium Development Goals
MDR	Multidrug-resistant
MoA	Mechanisms of action
MRSA	Methicillin-resistant *Staphylococcus aureus*
MSSA	Methicillin sensitive *Staphylococcus aureus*
NCE	New chemical entity
NGO	Nongovernmental organization
NHSN	National Healthcare Safety Network
NIAID	US National Institute of Allergy and Infectious Diseases
NIH	US National Institutes of Health
NME	New molecular entity
NNIS	National Nosocomial Infection Surveillance
NPV	Net present value
NTD	Neglected tropical disease
ODA	Orphan Drug Act (USA)
OECD	Organisation for Economic Co-operation and Development
PCR	Polymerase chain reaction
PCV7	Heptavalent pneumococcal conjugate vaccine
PDP	Product development partnership
PhRMA	Pharmaceutical Research and Manufacturers of America
PIP	Paediatric investigation plan
PK/PD	Pharmacokinetics/Pharmacodynamics
PNSP	Penicillin-nonsusceptible *Streptococcus pneumoniae*
QALY	Quality-adjusted life year
R&D	Research and development
RDT	Rapid diagnostic test
RSFF	Risk Sharing Finance Facility
SARS	Severe acute respiratory syndrome
SGC	Structural Genomics Consortium
SME	Small and medium-sized enterprise
SMEG	SME Guarantee Facility
SPC	Supplementary protection certificate
TB	Tuberculosis
VRE	Vancomycin-resistant *enterococci*
WHO	World Health Organization
WT	Wellcome Trust

Glossary[1]

Antibiotic
In general, a compound or substance that either kills or inhibits the growth of a microorganism, such as bacteria, fungi and protozoa. Antibiotics have three major sources of origin: (i) naturally isolated; (ii) purely chemically synthesized; or (iii) semi-synthetically derived. In addition, they can be classified according to their effect on bacteria – those that kill bacteria are bactericidal; those that inhibit the growth of bacteria are bacteriostatic. Antibiotics are defined according to their mechanism for targeting and identifying microorganisms – broad-spectrum antibiotics are active against a wide range of microorganisms; narrow-spectrum antibiotics target a specific group of microorganisms by interfering with the metabolic process specific to those particular organisms.

Antibiotic resistance (AR)
Bacterium's ability to survive and even replicate during a course of treatment with a specific antibiotic. Failure to resolve an infection with the first course of antibiotic treatment may mean that the infection spreads; becomes more severe; and is more difficult to treat with the next antibiotic that is tried.

Intrinsic resistance: natural resistance of bacteria to certain antibiotics.

Acquired resistance: normally susceptible bacteria have become resistant as a result of adaptation through genetic change.

Multidrug resistance: corresponds to resistance of a bacterium to multiple antibiotics.

Attrition rate
Number of antibacterial agents moving out of development over a specific period of time.

Anti-infectives
Refers to antibacterials, antibiotics, antifungals, antiprotozoans and antivirals.

---

[1] This glossary is based on definitions drawn from published literature and around which there is broad consensus. Sources include: Canadian Institutes of Health Research; Centers for Disease Control and Prevention; Courvalin; Merriam Webster's *Medical Dictionary*; Last's *Dictionary of Epidemiology*; ECDC; EMA; Mosby's *Medical, Nursing, Allied Health Dictionary*; OECD; WHO.

However, many use the term antibiotic to refer to both natural and synthetic compounds which fight bacteria.

Antimicrobials
Medicinal products that kill or stop the growth of living microorganisms and include **antibacterial agents** (more commonly referred to as **antibiotics**) which are active against bacterial infections. Antimicrobials differ from antibiotics in that they can be either natural or synthetic substances which kill or inhibit the growth of viruses, fungi and parasites in addition to bacteria.

Bacteria
Microorganisms that can be divided into categories according to several criteria. One means of classifying bacteria uses staining to divide most bacteria into two groups (**Gram positive; Gram negative**) according to the properties of their cell walls.

Biofilm
Slimy layer formed when bacteria colonize foreign material such as intravascular or urinary catheters, orthopaedic devices and other implantable materials.

Call option
Option to buy an asset at a specified exercise price on or before a specified exercise date.

Clinical trial
A research activity that involves the administration of a test regimen to humans in order to evaluate its efficacy and safety.

Conjugation
Conjugation occurs when the cell surfaces of a donor and recipient bacterium come into contact to allow the transfer of circular DNA (plasmid) which contain genes which code for resistance.

Data exclusivity
Period during which drug regulatory agencies are not permitted to accept licensing applications for follow-on drugs. A form of market protection distinct from, but related to, the patent system.

Deadweight welfare loss
Result of allocative inefficiency, when the equilibrium for a good or service is not Pareto optimal. Common causes include monopoly pricing, externalities, taxes or subsidies.

Drug (antibiotic) formulation
Composition of a dosage form, including the characteristics of its raw materials

and the operations required to process it. Examples are **oral formulation** (by mouth) and **intravenous formulation** (by infusion into a vein).

Dual nonsusceptibility
Bacteria are resistant and thus not vulnerable to the therapeutic effects of two different classes of antibiotic drug, thus minimizing the options for treatment of infection.

Efflux pump
A channel that prevents the intracellular accumulation of antibiotic needed to kill the bacteria.

Externalities
Arise when an individual or a company's behaviour has positive or negative effects on another person who is not directly involved in the transaction. Hence, prices do not reflect the full costs or benefits in production or consumption of a product or service.

Positive externality: results in underprovision as the company does not obtain all of the benefits.

Negative externality: results in oversupply as the company does not account for the full external costs when producing the good.

First mover advantage
Market advantages gained by the first market entrant or occupant of a market segment.

Functional resistance groups (FRGs)
An antibiotic belongs to a particular FRG if the use of that antibiotic causes resistance to other antibiotics in the FRG but not resistance to antibiotics in other FRGs. Concept proposed by Laxminarayan et al. (2007)[2] because the current classification of antibiotics based on chemical classes is not in line with promoting the effectiveness of antibiotics. In particular, the use of a drug within one particular chemical class may lead not only to resistance to other drugs within that chemical class but also to resistance to drugs in other chemical classes.

Gram-negative bacteria
Gram-positive and Gram-negative bacteria are differentiated according to the chemical and physical properties of their cell walls. Gram negative are more problematic because they have outer cell walls which make them difficult to attack with antibiotics (Pray 2008). Encompass species such as *Escherichia coli*, *Helicobacter*, *Moraxella*, *Pseudomonas*, *Salmonella* and *Shigella*.

---

[2] Outterson and colleagues (Outterson 2005; Outterson et al. 2007) made a similar proposition.

Gram-positive bacteria
Gram-positive bacteria encompass species such as *Bacillus, Listeria, Staphylococcus, Streptococcus* and *Enterococcus*.

Horizontal gene transfer
Gene transfer from a resistant bacterium to a susceptible bacterium. Most resistance is obtained by this process.

Incentive
Any factor (financial or nonfinancial) that enables or motivates a particular course of action, or is a reason for preferring one choice over the alternatives.

Intellectual property (IP) protection
A type of legal monopoly whereby owners or inventors are granted certain exclusive rights in return for an invention with social value. Exclusive rights allow owners of IP to reap monopoly profits. These monopoly profits provide a financial incentive for the creation of IP, and pay associated R&D costs. In the case pf pharmaceuticals IP protection is exerted through the patent system.

Methicillin-resistant *Staphylococcus aureus* (MRSA)
Hospital pathogen, but can also occur in healthy individuals in the community. More than 10% of bloodstream infections in hospitals are due to MRSA. Patients with MRSA have worse outcomes than those with methicillin-sensitive *Staphylococcus aureus*.

Multidrug-resistant (MDR) bacteria
Bacteria can acquire resistance by genetic mutation and by accepting genes coding for resistance from other bacteria, resulting in MDR bacteria that are resistant to many different classes of antibiotic. Drugs with new mechanisms of action (MoA) are needed to be effective against MDR bacteria.

Net present value (NPV)
A project's net contribution to wealth – present value minus initial investment.

New chemical entity
A drug that does not contain an active moiety previously submitted to, or approved by, a drug regulatory agency. Distinguishes originator drugs from generic drugs.

Nosocomial (hospital-acquired) infection
Infection occurring in a hospital or another health-care facility, when the infection was not present or incubating at time of admission.

Orphan disease
Definition in the United States: a disease or condition affecting less then 200 000 people or which affects more than 200 000 people for "which there is

no reasonable expectation that a developer could recover its R&D investment through sales revenue".

Definition in the European Union: a life-threatening or chronically debilitating disease affecting a maximum of 5 in 10 000 people.

Open-source
A principle or broad range of tools for increasing access to knowledge, information and tools as a method of generating innovation.

Pharmacokinetics/pharmacodynamics (PK/PD)
Study of the rate of drug action (particularly with respect to the variation of drug concentrations in tissues with time) and the absorption, metabolism and excretion of drugs and metabolites.

Prophylactic
Medication used to prevent disease. Reduces risk of postoperative infection – without effective prophylactic antibiotics it may become dangerous to conduct many types of operation.

Product development partnership (PDP)
Class of public–private partnerships that focus on health product development; discrete organizations that largely (but not exclusively) coordinate collaboration between public (funding) and private (expertise, assets) contributors.

Push incentive
Subsidies to help to fund research. By reducing the costs of inputs and advancing the state of basic science, push mechanisms aim to make drug development cheaper.

Pull incentive
Offer of a financial reward upon delivery of a specified product.

Real option
Possibility to modify, postpone, expand or abandon a project.

Regulatory review
Process performed by a regulatory agency (i.e. FDA, EMA) to confirm that a health intervention is safe and efficacious for licensed (and therefore controlled) use within a population.

Reimbursement
Act of retrospective financial compensation for a cost incurred.

Selective pressure
Influence of antibiotic on natural selection to promote one type of organism. Antibiotics kill susceptible bacteria and allow resistant bacteria to continue to multiply.

Strike price
Exercise price of an option.

Systemic (or systemically administered) antibiotics
Compounds administered parenterally, for example intravenously.

Transduction
Process by which a virus can pass resistance between bacteria – resistant genes contained in the head of a virus are injected into bacteria that it subsequently attacks.

Transformation
Process by which bacteria take up DNA from dead bacteria in close proximity. The new genetic material, which has advantageous genes such as resistance, is incorporated into the bacteria's own DNA.

Foreword

The Swedish Government is concerned about the increasing frequency of bacterial resistance to currently available antibiotics. This poses a major threat to human health and causes significant morbidity and mortality in Europe and the rest of the world. A number of advanced interventions that we take for granted, for example surgery, cancer treatment, transplantation and care of premature babies, may be impossible when effective antibacterials are no longer available. For several decades, new classes of effective antibiotics were regularly developed, but since the 1970s very few have reached the market.

Antibiotic resistance was, therefore, one of the questions to which I assigned highest priority during the Swedish EU Presidency in autumn 2009. My main focus was to encourage research and development for new effective antibiotics. I hosted the expert conference "Innovative Incentives for Effective Antibacterials" in September in Stockholm 2009. The conference called on a unique mix of experts and spurred the establishment of an EU–US Task Force on Antimicrobial Resistance, and the EU decision in December 2009 to put together an action plan on antimicrobial resistance.

Policies and incentives for promoting innovation in antibiotic research has been a prerequisite for all the Swedish EU Presidency activities on how to encourage research and development for new effective antibiotics. The study was initially commissioned by the Swedish Government because I felt there was a failure to understand the issues surrounding the lack of new antibiotics and the possible methods to tackle these. It is my deepest wish that this study will be used as a basis for decisive action.

Göran Hägglund
Minister for Health and Social Affairs

Foreword

Acknowledgements

The authors would like to thank all the people who kindly took the time to speak with them in the process of putting together this study, including: George Quartz, Jerome A Donlon, Rebecca Lipshitz, Tom First (BARDA); David Pompliano (BioLeap LLC); Shelly Mui-Lipnik, Ted Buckley (Biotechnology Industry Organization); Kevin Outterson (Boston University); Rachel Nugent (Centre for Global Development); Barry Eisenstein, Mark Battaglini (Cubist Pharmaceuticals); Giulia Del Brenna, Martin Terberger, Martinus Nagtzaam, Tomas Jonsson (DG Enterprise); Anna Lonnroth, Irene Norstedt, Philippe Cupers (DG Research); Bernard Pecoul (DnDi); Miriam Gargesi (EDMA); Brendan Barnes (EFPIA); Gail Cassell (Eli Lilly); Bo Aronsson, Jordi Llinares Garcia, Patrick Le Courtois, Marie-Hélène Pinheiro (EMA); Shiva Dustdar (EIB); Edward Cox, Marta Wosinska, Dave Rader, John Farley, Michael Lanther, Nancy Booker (FDA); Paul Kim (Foley-Hoag LLP); Sophie Logez (Global Fund); David Payne, Linda Miller (GSK); Aaron Kesselheim (Harvard University); David Livermore (HPA); Padma Natarajan, Robert Guidos (IDSA); Julie Cheng (iOWH); Philippe Bey (formerly HMR); Ruth McNerney (London School of Hygiene & Tropical Medicine); Chris Colwell (McKenna Long & Aldridge LLP); Selina Namchee Lo, Tido von Schoen-Angerer (MSF); Anthony James (NHS Innovation Institute); Donald R Jaffe, John Quinn (Pfizer); Alan Goldhammer (PhRMA); Ramanan Laxminarayan (Resources for the Future); Birgit Kulik (Sanofi-aventis IMI Global Coordination Office); Patricia Noterman (Siemens/EDMA); Ellen 't Hoen (UNITAID); Ted Bianco, Catherine Quinn, Richard Seabrook (WT); Kathy Holloway, Paul Nunn (WHO); Amy Wong (X PRIZE Foundation). The authors would also like to thank those who provided feedback on all or part of the draft report: Kevin Outterson (Boston University); Brendan Barnes (EFPIA); Laura Freire-Moran (EMA); Irene Sacristan-Sanchez (DG Enterprise and Industry); Brad Spellberg (Harbor-UCLA Medical Center); Aaron Kesselheim (Harvard University); David Livermore (Health Protection Agency); and Jorge Mestre-Ferrandiz (Office for Health Economics).

The views presented in this study do not necessarily represent those of any of the above-mentioned individuals or organizations. Any errors remain those of the authors.

This study was commissioned and financed by the Swedish Government as part of its activities during the 2009 Swedish Presidency of the European Union, reflecting the importance of this issue across the European Union and the WHO European Region. It was carried out for the European Observatory on Health Systems and Policies by its Co-Director and a research team based at the London School of Economics and is published by the European Observatory as part of its study series.

The authors would also like to thank all those who helped with the preparation of the study: Bashar Hamad, Natasha Desai, Gregory Knapp, Priya Sharma and Amanda McDonnell.

Elias Mossialos, Professor of Health Policy, LSE Health (London School of Economics and Political Science)

Chantal M Morel, Research Fellow, LSE Health

Suzanne Edwards, Research Associate, LSE Health

Julia Berenson, Research Associate, LSE Health

Marin Gemmill-Toyama, Research Fellow, LSE Health

David Brogan, Resident Physician, Department of Orthopedic Surgery, Mayo Clinic, Rochester MN, United States

10 key messages

1. Bacterial resistance to currently available antibiotics is becoming increasingly frequent in both hospital and community settings. Resistance to entire antibiotic classes (e.g. beta-lactams, quinolones, tetracyclines, glycopeptides and macrolides) is emerging rapidly. Coupled with insufficient investment in new antibiotic treatments, this issue is becoming a pressing public health concern. In order to curb the growth of antibiotic resistance (AR) and prevent major morbidity and mortality from bacterial infections we must both address overuse and actively promote R&D for antibiotic medicines with novel mechanisms of action (MoA). This must be done through appropriately designed incentives for health and regulatory systems and through economic incentives that lure industry investment.

2. Resistance to antibiotics presents a major challenge in health care as resistant bacteria dramatically decrease the chances of effectively treating infections and increase the risk of complications and death (ReAct – Action on Antibiotic Resistance 2007). Within the EU alone, it is estimated that 2 million patients acquire nosocomial infections[3] each year (European Academies Science Advisory Council 2007), over half of which are drug-resistant (Vicente et al. 2006). Antibiotic resistant infections are associated with a 1.3 to 2-fold increase in mortality compared to susceptible infections (Cosgrove & Carmeli 2003).

3. AR imposes enormous health expenditure from higher treatment costs and longer hospital stays (Cosgrove 2006; Mauldin 2010; Okeke 2005; Roberts et al. 2009). However, resistance-related costs affect not only the health sector. Household income, government tax revenues and total national savings in the United Kingdom are estimated to fall by at least 0.3%, 0.35% and 2% respectively, due to MRSA alone (Smith et al. 2005)[4]. This has been calculated to produce a total loss of between 0.4% and 1.6% in real gross domestic product (Smith et al. 2005). In the United States, the cost of overall

---

[3] Nosocomial infections result from treatment in a hospital but are not the patient's primary condition.
[4] Smith et al. (2005) study estimate of the cost of antimicrobial resistance is based on MRSA in particular.

antimicrobial resistance has been preliminarily estimated at US$ 21–34 billion.[5]

4. A few key factors are causing underinvestment in R&D in antibiotics.

- Currently available, inexpensive, generic antibiotics are still (although to varying degrees) effective in treating the large majority of infections seen by health services.

- It is necessary for European public health authorities to emphasize rationing of existing antibiotics intended for severe infection (using generics as first-line therapies). However, this gives the impression that, if developed, new antibiotics will be kept as last resort treatments regardless of high levels of resistance to widely used antibiotics.

- Antibiotics do not appear profitable relative to drugs used for longer durations, e.g. for chronic diseases. One estimate suggests a risk-adjusted net present value (NPV) of 100 for antibiotics, compared with 300 for an anticancer drug, 720 for a neurological drug and 1150 for a musculoskeletal drug (Projan 2003).

- Current pricing and reimbursement policies do not prioritize drugs according to their ability to reduce morbidity or mortality. For example, cancer or central nervous system-related drugs attain much higher prices despite sometimes offering only a few months of additional life (Outterson 2005).

5. AR stems in part from overuse due to presumptive treatment in clinical settings. In large degree this is a consequence of the lack of rapid diagnostic tests (RDTs) that can tell physicians the nature of an infection quickly and accurately. Like antibiotics, RDTs for bacterial infections have received far too little investment. So far, few companies have taken interest despite the potential for widespread use of these devices in primary care settings and hospitals globally. However, unlike antibiotics, there are no inherent failures in the RDT market. Lack of communicated demand may stem from current health sector rationing incentives (e.g. systems in which physician budgets must cover point of care diagnostics while hospital budgets cover treatment of worsening infections) or lack of long-term cost–effectiveness analyses that properly account for the cost of bacterial resistance to the health service. Whatever the reason, timely, accurate diagnosis must become an explicit health system priority.

6. Antibiotics with novel MoA are needed in order to preserve efficacy over a longer time. New generations of existing antibiotics (product follow-ons)

---

5 Estimate from Foster (2010) extrapolating from Roberts et al. (2009).

are useful in staving off resistance to certain drug classes in the short term but longer-term solutions must focus on the development of antibiotics with novel MoA. However, the development of entirely new drugs does imply a significant amount of risk, which should be shared by the developer and the funder.

7. Incentives appeal to small and large developers to different degrees so an ideal scheme could consist of incentives that include some early funding to lower barriers to entry with a large and credible financial lure to carry an investigational product through the final stages of development. This may include an incentive that inherently combines push and pull elements or may offer the developer a range of incentive options.

8. Given the global nature of AR, an ideal incentive scheme would be implemented on a global level. Unfortunately, the difficulty in garnering such support is likely to prevent global solutions to urgent innovation needs for antibiotic drugs. In the immediate future the EU, alone or in conjunction with the United States, should make a concrete move to implement an incentive mechanism to promote R&D for new antibiotics.

9. Any chosen incentive mechanism must reward solely the development of drugs that are novel (against which it is predicted, to the extent possible, that no short- or medium-term resistance or cross-resistance will develop) and which treat infections for which there is no viable therapeutic alternative. The incentive should not reward the development of products that would otherwise have been developed within the normal market.

10. Specific endeavours to encourage the development of new antibiotics include: funding for training of new and experienced antimicrobial researchers; funding of translational research to bring more key academic research further towards product development; funding for open-access means of sharing R&D knowledge; the Call Options for Antibiotics (COA) model; a special designation for antibiotics; and the Antibiotic Conservation and Effectiveness (ACE) Programme proposal. However, it is likely that these proposals may bring new products to market at varying speeds. Whichever incentive mechanisms are chosen, they must be constructed with a long-term perspective, detaching any financial inputs from annual budgetary negotiations that risk putting them at the mercy of political whims, economic climates and other perpetually changing forces.

Introduction

Bacterial resistance to currently available antibiotics is becoming increasingly frequent in both hospital and community settings. We are even starting to see resistance to entire antibiotic classes such as beta-lactams, quinolones, tetracyclines, glycopeptides and macrolides. Resistance to antibiotics presents a major challenge in health care as resistant bacteria dramatically decrease the chances of treating infections effectively and increase the risk of complications and death (ReAct – Action on Antibiotic Resistance 2007). Within the European Union (EU) alone it is estimated that 2 million patients acquire nosocomial infections each year (European Academies Science Advisory Council 2007), over half of which are drug resistant (Vicente et al. 2006). Coupled with the lack of investment to discover new antibiotics, we are facing a potential health crisis. In response to this growing threat, in December 2009 the Council of the European Union called upon the European Commission (EC)[6] to:

> within 24 months, develop a comprehensive action-plan, with concrete proposals concerning incentives to develop new effective antibiotics, including ways to secure their rational use; and ensure that these proposals take account of the economic impact on the financial sustainability of healthcare systems.

Around the same time the United States joined forces with the EU to help tackle the issue through the formation of a transatlantic taskforce on antimicrobial resistance.[7] This book is intended to help shed light on some of the key policies and incentives proposed to tackle this problem.

Antibiotic resistance (AR)

The frequency and severity of AR is becoming evident worldwide. Resistance has been an isolated problem for hospitals and nursing homes but recently the proportion of community-acquired infections with bacteria resistant to antibiotics has increased (Frazee et al. 2005). In 2006, the European Antimicrobial Resistance Surveillance System (EARSS) reported that

---
6 See Appendix A.
7 See Appendix B.

pathogens resistant to the antibiotic penicillin occurred in up to 25% to 50% of isolates in France, Spain and Romania, indicating that penicillin is becoming obsolete in these three European countries (European Antimicrobial Resistance Surveillance System 2007 and 2008). EARSS also reported that MRSA bacteria were occurring in up to 25% to 50% of isolates in most of southern Europe, Ireland and the United Kingdom (European Antimicrobial Resistance Surveillance System 2007 and 2008).

Growth of resistance stems in part from overprescription of antibiotics. It is often wrongly accepted that infections encountered in hospital and especially in community practice are managed most effectively on the basis of clinical/empirical assessment (Finch 2007). Culture and sensitivity tests currently provide results within 36 to 48 hours (Boissinot & Bergeron 2002) therefore few infections are microbiologically confirmed sufficiently quickly to guide treatment decisions (Finch 2007). This presumptive treatment of patients means that viral infections are often misdiagnosed as bacterial infections, leading to inappropriately prescribed antibiotics. Risk aversion on the part of physicians, compounded by a mounting tendency for litigation in some countries, and ensuing overprescription of antibiotics will continue to amplify the growth of resistance until physicians have more sophisticated and effective RDTs that are quick and easy to use at the point of care.

Although specific recommendations for promoting R&D for RDTs lie outside the scope of this report, it should be underlined that both supply and demand side measures should be assessed to better understand and support the development of RDTs at the point of care to guide antibiotic treatment. From the supply side, inputs could take the form of targeted support for basic research and increasing access to enabling technologies – although from an economic perspective there is little justification for incentives comprising large financial subsidies. The demand side requires a major review of incentives within the health system structure; financing and reimbursement arrangements; the legal framework (including liability issues); and clinical guidelines. The alignment of incentive structures appears to hold the most promise for addressing AR through more targeted and informed prescribing and for signalling to the industry that there is a significant demand for good diagnostic products for bacterial infections. The tools used to help guide reforms should include the performance of long-term cost-effectiveness analyses comparing the economic costs and benefits of presumptive treatment with the use of RDTs at the point of care – given varying levels of pathogen resistance, varying diagnostic sensitivity and specificity, as well as varying price levels.[8] Such exercises would help to

---

[8] Similar analyses have been carried out for malaria, e.g. taking account of varying levels of absolute and growth rates of pathogen resistance, varying levels of diagnostic accuracy, varying treatment and diagnostic price levels, as well as a long-term perspective (Shillcutt 2008).

determine public purchasers' maximum price at which they would consider the procurement of RDTs to be cost-effective.

Beyond the development and use of RDTs, conservation of antibiotics will also require realignment of incentive structures in primary care services and hospitals as well as within the overall financing structures to ensure that prescribers are not perversely driven to overuse antibiotics. Policies relating to performance measurement and spending should take a longer-term perspective in weighing the risks and benefits of overuse. Financing systems also need to support infection control and antibiotic stewardship (ABS) to discourage practices that increase wasteful prescribing and the spread of resistance. It is crucial that policy-makers design *coordinated* policies that encourage physicians to meet quality care standards with support from diagnostic tools, where necessary, to determine the most appropriate treatment and use of antibiotics.

Antibiotics market

Despite the need, few new antibiotics are being developed. The industry pipeline has few late-stage candidates for drugs that can effectively combat the emergence and spread of drug-resistant bacterial strains (Pray 2008). In 2004, only 1.6% of the drugs in development among the 15 largest pharmaceutical companies were antibiotics – none from novel classes, none addressing multidrug resistant (MDR) Gram-negative infections (Spellberg et al. 2004). A 2009 report by the European Medicines Agency[9] (EMA) and the European Centre for Disease Prevention and Control (ECDC) warns of an almost empty pipeline with only two new drugs with a new mechanism of action or a new target to tackle MDR Gram-negative bacteria (European Medicines Agency and the European Centre for Disease Prevention and Control 2009), the cause of two thirds of MDR deaths.

The dearth of new antibiotics is partly due to the nature of the market. From an economic perspective (Rubin 2004), antibiotic use is generally associated with positive externality (public health) and a negative externality (AR)[10] that create failures in the market.

- Public health externality: when an individual uses an antibiotic as prescribed the individual is typically cured of an infectious and contagious disease which prevents the individual from spreading the disease to others.

---

9 Previously, European Agency for the Evaluation of Medicinal Products.
10 An externality exists when an individual's or a firm's behaviour, whether positive or negative, affects other individuals and those effects are not taken into account in the market price. A positive externality causes insufficient use of a good or service because private agents do not receive all of the benefits of the good or service. The converse is true for a negative externality.

- AR externality: when an individual uses an antibiotic a small number of bacteria become resistant to the treatment. The individual can transmit the resistant bacteria to other individuals who will eventually be unable to benefit from the use of the specific antibiotic to which the bacteria have become resistant (or from those against which there is cross-resistance). This also presents a negative internality as the patient consuming an antibiotic will herself/himself become more susceptible to subsequent infections (Outterson 2009).

Separate, yet related, to the externalities are the characteristics of the market that render it relatively unprofitable from the developers' perspective. First, generic antibiotics currently on the market are still (to varying degrees) effective in treating the majority of infections faced by health services. Second, EU public health authorities emphasise the importance of conserving existing antibiotics that are intended for severe infection by using generics as first-line therapy wherever possible. This signals to the industry that effective new antibiotics, when developed, will be dispensed infrequently and kept as last resort treatments even if there are high rates of resistance to widely-used antibiotics. Third, antibiotic regimes have a limited duration and fully curative nature, unlike drugs that mitigate the symptoms of chronic diseases. This increases marketing costs (to keep the product salient in the minds of potential prescribers) and decreases expected returns on investment. Therefore, relative to other therapeutic areas, antibiotics do not appear profitable. One estimate suggests a risk-adjusted NPV of 100 for antibiotics, compared to 300 for an anticancer drug, 720 for a neurological drug and 1150 for a musculoskeletal drug (Projan 2003). Fourth, an antibiotic that develops resistance rapidly theoretically has a shorter clinical lifespan therefore it is argued that developers who invest billions of dollars and significant time to develop new antibiotics may not reap the full benefits of their efforts (Power 2006). Fifth, the lack of appropriate assessment within pricing and reimbursement agencies means that the prioritization and corresponding price paid by public purchasers may not reflect an antibiotic's relative effectiveness in reducing morbidity and mortality. For example, much higher prices are paid for some drugs that offer only a few weeks or months of additional life – for example some cancer or CNS-related drugs (Outterson 2005).

Incentives to promote R&D of novel antibiotics

The potential for an impending health crisis due to the lack of new antibiotics, the inherent externalities in the market and the likely cost savings from improving treatment provide ethical and economic justification for a public body to undertake some intervention in the market. However, the result will be determined by the design of the incentive – timing and size of the reward, organizational driver and the target beneficiary.

Traditionally, incentives to encourage R&D have fallen into two main types – push and pull methods. Push incentives are financial injections that lower the financial risk to developers by reducing the cost of necessary inputs. These tend to impact the earlier stages of the development process (Sloan & Hsieh 2006) and includes examples such as grants or research-related tax breaks. Push incentives may come from both public and private sources such as venture capitalists or large philanthropic donors. In providing early funding, push mechanisms are particularly useful for attracting small and medium-sized enterprises (SMEs) that often operate with limited ready cash (Biotechnology Industry Organization 2009).[11] However, they are also fraught with difficulties. For example, developers paid through push mechanisms often lack the motivation to move on to the more applied phases of production. There is also the danger that eventual overpayment through push incentives will have a dampening effect on entrepreneurialism (Del Brenna 2009 [personal communication]). Push incentives also pose principal-agent problems in that researchers are compelled to show their work in the best light possible although this may not accurately reflect the merits of the investment. Thus, the funder bears most of the risk of product development funded through push mechanisms.

In contrast, pull mechanisms involve the promise of financial reward only *after* a technology has been developed. Examples include simple monetary prizes; the promise of tax credits to match eventual product sales; intellectual property (IP) extensions; or specified advance market commitments (AMCs). Pull incentives offer financial reward upon completion of technological advances in order to steer R&D investments in desired directions. Also, as profits increase with decreasing development costs they better align internal incentives to rectify inefficiencies. Finally, as pull mechanisms provide a reward only upon full product development and authorization, they provide researchers with the incentive to self-select the most promising products and thereby bypass many of the principal-agent problems inherent in push mechanisms. However, if the incentive relies only on the promise of rewards (as opposed to a fully earmarked existing sum), pull mechanisms are at the mercy of the changing political and economic (and associated budgetary) tides. It has also been suggested that pull mechanisms may corrode existing non-financial incentives to collaborate and slow the overall search for solutions. Finally, as financial rewards in pull mechanisms are reaped only following product development, the financial risk involved in all stages of R&D falls on the developer.

---

11 In the United States, BIO currently estimates that 120 (30% of all publicly traded biotech) companies are currently in this situation. However, funding drives in mid-2009 are believed to have been relatively successful.

Lego-regulatory mechanisms are pull incentives that use the market to determine reward size, in this case through higher prices or extended intellectual property protection. In this way they avoid some of the difficulty in extra-market calculations of reward size and better maintain the link between reward, eventual product usage and (arguably) quality that is broken in the case of most normal pull incentives. Within antibiotic development it may be all the more important to maintain this link given the difficulty of predicting the growth of resistance and hence the duration of product efficacy. Also, as lego-regulatory mechanisms do not require large financial sums outright they avoid the potential lack of credibility that can be associated with rewards promised by funding bodies that face political or budgetary volatility. However, the lego-regulatory mechanisms considered here (except pricing and reimbursement reforms) pose the risk of impeding competition to varying degrees.

The basic elements of push and pull mechanisms can also be combined within one incentive to create hybrid mechanisms or simply used in combination within an incentive package. Used together, or in hybrid incentives, push and pull mechanisms may help overcome many of their individual problems by covering (at least partially) developers' early R&D costs whilst providing the profit lure to accomplish full product development. Indeed, in a comparison of the ability of push, pull and hybrid incentive mechanisms to stimulate the development of effective treatments, the recent OECD report (Organisation for Economic Co-operation and Development 2009) supports Hsu and Schwartz's (2003) conclusion that a hybrid mechanism is the most viable. Incentive combinations may provide a crucial impetus to overcome developer reticence at the different (possibly key) stages of product development: early stage push funding provides greater financial space to explore early discovery ideas without needing to understand their full potential at the outset; the larger pull element entices the developer to undertake the latter phases of development, including expensive Phase III trials. The evolution between the respective incentive forces within a combination incentive (push to pull, small to large) is important as developers have been understood to respond more to profit incentives at the later stages of the research process (Finkelstein 2004). In addition, the combination of push and pull incentives also spreads risk between the funder and the developer.

New generations of existing antibiotics (product follow-ons) are useful in staving off resistance to certain drug classes in the short term but longer-term solutions require a focus on the development of antibiotics with these novel MoA. This presents a significant technical challenge and therefore incentives should allow for the risk to be shared to some degree between the public or non-profit funder and the investing developer. In isolation, pull mechanisms place the risk on the developer while push mechanisms place the risk on the funder – a combination of pull and push mechanisms will likely prove optimal for stimulating the market in the shortest term possible. This could be an incentive that inherently combines such elements or one that offers developers a range of incentive options. Specific endeavours to encourage the development of new antibiotics include: funding for training of new and experienced (former) antimicrobial researchers; funding of translational research to bring key academic research further towards product development; funding for open-access means of sharing R&D knowledge; the COA model; special designation for antibiotics; and the ACE Programme proposal. However, these respective proposals are likely to bring any new product to market at varying speeds.

Chapter 1
Background on antibiotics

1.1 What are antibiotics?

Antibiotics are chemotherapeutic agents that have revolutionized the treatment of infectious disease – turning life-threatening diseases into more manageable and treatable conditions. In addition to treating community-acquired infections, antibiotics have facilitated and improved the safety and outcomes of surgery and transplantation in hospitals and other health-care settings (Finch 2007). The combination of global immunization programmes; improvements in sanitation, housing and nutrition; and the use of such antimicrobial agents led to a significant fall in mortality from infectious diseases during the 20th century (WHO 2002).

In general, an antibiotic is a compound or substance that either kills or inhibits the growth of a microorganism, such as bacteria, fungi and protozoa. Antibiotics have three major sources of origin: (i) naturally isolated; (ii) purely chemically synthesized; or (iii) semi-synthetically derived. In addition, they can be classified according to their effect on bacteria – those that kill bacteria are bactericidal; those that inhibit the growth of bacteria are bacteriostatic. Antibiotics are defined according to their mechanism for targeting and identifying microorganisms – broad-spectrum antibiotics are active against a wide range of microorganisms; narrow-spectrum antibiotics target a specific group of microorganisms by interfering with the metabolic process specific to those particular organisms.

At the end of the 19th century and the beginning of the early 20th century, scientists began the search for new antibacterial agents for the treatment of infectious diseases. In particular, two groundbreaking events in the 1930s and 1940s catalysed the microbial drug era – Alexander Fleming's discovery of penicillin and Selman Waksman's discovery of streptomycin (Jayaraman 2009).

In fact, microorganisms have made significant contributions to medicine and drug discovery over the 80 years following these two discoveries (Demain & Sanchez 2009). For example, of the 25 top-selling drugs reported in 1997, 42% were natural products or their derivatives – 67% of these were antibiotics (Demain & Sanchez 2009). Following the discovery, development and successes of antibiotic therapies, the US Surgeon General William H Stewart declared in the 1960s that infectious diseases had been defeated and "the war against pestilence [was] won" (Spellberg et al. 2008a). However, the possibility of these "miracle drugs" successfully containing infectious diseases worldwide has recently been substantially undermined by the emergence of resistance to antibiotics.

1.2 Why antibiotics are important

The world faces urgent and emerging infectious disease threats that can be mitigated and controlled by effective and appropriate antibiotic therapy. However, trends in prevalence, incidence and global burden of disease indicate that we are far from conquering infectious diseases. More than one third of the world's population is likely infected by bacterial pathogens (Monaghan & Barret 2006). Despite the existence of antibiotic therapies, respiratory infections, tuberculosis (TB) and malaria continue to persist as major public health threats in the 21st century. For example, it is estimated that one third of the world's population is currently infected with TB and almost 9 million people have active disease (Monaghan & Barret 2006). The 2004 WHO report *Priority medicines for Europe and the world* states that infectious diseases rank as the highest total burden of disease worldwide as measured in disability-adjusted life years – 31% of the total burden (Kaplan & Laing 2004). In fact, infectious diseases were identified as the second leading cause of death in the world, with global mortality rates at 2.47 deaths per 1000 (slightly behind cardiovascular disease at 2.63 deaths per 1000) (Kaplan & Laing 2004). In 2004, infectious diseases accounted for more than one quarter of deaths at the global level (26.94%) (Kaplan & Laing 2004). Each year there are approximately 2 million fatalities from bacterial infections (Monaghan & Barret 2006). In particular, pneumonia and diarrhoeal diseases kill approximately 3.8 million children under 5 each year (WHO 2009).

Within the EU, infectious diseases do not rank amongst the top five groups accounting for the majority of burden of disease (Kaplan & Laing 2004). Indeed, infectious disease accounts for less than 7% of disease burden in the expanded EU (Kaplan & Laing 2004). Yet, resistant infections are increasingly posing major threats to health. This is also true in many developing countries where there have been recent concerns about possible outbreaks of extensively drug-resistant TB (Parmet 2007). Common bacterial pathogens have become rapidly resistant to previously effective antimicrobial therapy, undermining antibiotics' ability to treat illness. The recent rise of new strains of bacteria resistant to single and multiple classes of antibiotic has led to severe public health and economic consequences – higher treatment costs; longer duration of illness and hospital stays; increased risk of morbidity and mortality; and spread of disease (Cosgrove 2006; Okeke et al. 2005). Mortality rates and the spread of community and hospital-acquired infections resistant to antibiotics have escalated since the late 1990s. A recent study suggests that over 18 000 patients die each year in the United States as a result of MRSA (Klevens et al. 2007). Continuous investment in the search for new agents and drugs with novel MoA becomes necessary as resistance spreads and the global burden of infectious disease rises (see Chapter 2 for estimates of the prevalence, mortality, morbidity, costs and burden of AR).

1.3 Externalities of antibiotics and AR

The impact of antibiotic usage on population health can also be explained according to economic principles, particularly in terms of externalities (Laxminarayan et al. 2007; Rubin 2004). Following the Grossman model of health production, antibiotic treatment is a health-care good consumed by an individual to produce health (Grossman 1972). A patient experiences private benefits from consumption of appropriate antibiotics, primarily in the form of improved health outcomes, reduced risk of mortality and morbidity and shorter hospital stays. Conversely, a patient incurs private costs from antibiotic use – the bacteria in the patient's system not killed by the antibiotic will make it difficult for the patient to overcome future infections (Rubin 2004).[12] In addition to private benefits and costs, antibiotic consumption is associated with positive and negative externalities. An externality exists when an individual's behaviour has positive or negative effects on another person who is not directly involved in the transaction. Consequently, prices do not reflect the full costs or benefits of the production or consumption of a product or service. When a good has a positive externality, the private company will not produce enough of the product or service since the company does not obtain all of the benefits. Conversely, when a good has a negative externality then the private company will overproduce it as the company does not account for the external cost when producing the good.

---

12 Regardless of whether the antibiotics consumed are appropriate or inappropriate for the type of infection, patients have the harm of induced resistance in their microbial flora.

It is important to assess the positive and negative externalities of both antibiotic consumption and AR while considering the policy responses and options to contain AR.[13] In the case of antibiotics, a positive or public health externality exists – infection control and appropriate antibiotic usage help prevent and treat infections that otherwise could spread to the community (Rubin 2004; Saver 2008). Thus, the general public benefits when an individual consumes appropriately prescribed antibiotic therapy. According to economic theory, antibiotic developers will not produce enough antibiotics given that their companies do not obtain all of the benefits. In reality, discovery and development of new antibiotics has slowed dramatically over the past 25 years. In 2004, antibiotics made up only 1.6% of drugs in development amongst the 15 largest pharmaceutical companies (Spellberg et al. 2004). In addition, the industry pipeline has few late-stage candidates for antibiotics that can effectively combat the emergence and spread of drug-resistant bacterial strains (Pray 2008). Many experts argue that the pharmaceutical industry is not producing new antibiotics at a socially optimal level.

In contrast, a negative externality is associated with inappropriate antibiotic usage and AR – introduction of the antibiotic increases selection pressures for drug resistance in the environment as resistant bacteria can be transmitted to others, potentially reducing the effectiveness and benefits of the antibiotic medication to the public (Saver 2008). Also, as Laxminarayan (2002) argued, part of the problem stems from companies' failure to consider fully how their antibiotic sales affect future antibiotic effectiveness. This is attributed to the fact that antibiotic effectiveness is a common property resource (Laxminarayan 2002).[14] The tragedy of the commons that arises with AR means that the consumer and the supplier of antibiotics rarely experience the direct effects of AR, despite the fact that resistance negatively impacts the welfare of the public (Coast et al. 1998). Private companies have no incentive to take account of how their sales impact on future antibiotic effectiveness because of the cross-resistance across different antibiotics produced by various companies in the market (Laxminarayan 2002). Consequently, the market price of antibiotics does not adequately reflect the true social cost of AR and, therefore, too many antibiotics may be sold to achieve a socially optimal level of consumption. It is important to note that as time progresses and resistance increases, the positive externality associated with reduced transmission may be reduced (Coast et al. 1998). Consequently, the negative externality associated with AR may diminish the public health benefits of antibiotic consumption. Laxminarayan and Brown

---

[13] For further reference see the Coast et al. (1998) study. The authors develop an extensive economic model to represent the positive and negative externalities of antibiotics.
[14] Saver (2008) notes the open debate on whether antibiotics are truly analogous to common pool assets. Common goods can be renewed and replaced over time. However, the number of effective doses of an antibiotic may be finite and thus antibiotics could be characterized as what Outterson (2005) calls a "potentially exhaustible resource".

(2001) argued that the current problem of AR is attributable to the absence of economic incentives that encourage individuals to take account of the negative impact on social welfare caused by their use of antibiotics. Hence, it may be necessary to address AR's tragedy of the commons and create incentives for antibiotic developers to internalize the costs of resistance.

In addition to the tragedy of the commons problem, resistance is intergenerational and thus likely to be incurred by our descendants (Coast et al. 1998). Individuals and companies do not consider how their current consumption impacts on future stocks – use of antibiotics in the current period diminishes the effectiveness of antibiotics in future periods. Economic theory holds that consumers discount costs that occur in the future since they value a current dollar more than a future dollar, when adjusting for inflation (Reed 2002). If AR occurs in the future, the present cost of resistance would be less. Coast et al. (1998) note that the time frame and the discount factor impact the degree to which reducing resistance will result in overall benefit for society. They explain that where time frames are long and discount rates are small, reducing resistance is likely to result in positive benefit to society. By comparison, where time frames are short and/or discount rates large, there may be an overall cost to society if policies are aimed at reducing resistance.

When designing policies that internalize the costs of resistance and thus aim to reduce resistance, it is necessary to consider AR's interregional nature – resistance can cross country borders and travel far distances (Coast et al. 1998). Coast et al. (1998) noted that two countries may each be both the source and the victim of resistance but the transfer and spread of resistance may be unequal. Additionally, they argue that policies aimed at reducing antibiotic usage within a particular country may not work in another country, given that local epidemiological factors impact the spread of resistance mechanisms (Coast et al. 1998). According to this logic, policies to combat resistance are more likely to result in positive benefit to society when local level rather than global epidemiological factors are taken into consideration.

Last, the negative externality of AR is further exacerbated by the fact that a principal-agent relationship exists between the physician and the patient. The less informed principal (patient) relies upon the fully informed agent (doctor) to act on his/her behalf and maximize his/her utility or welfare in the form of health. Therefore, physicians direct the course of therapy, such as prescribing of antibiotics. According to Reed, Saver and others, physicians face few incentives to withhold antibiotics from patients (Reed 2002; Saver 2008). Reed argued that physicians perceive each individual prescription's impact on resistance to be so small that the potential cost of not prescribing the antibiotic outweighs the uncertain costs associated with resistance. Applied to the individual patient rather than to society, the Hippocratic ethos contributes to this weighing of options leading to treatment. Also, physicians frequently prescribe antibiotics when uncertain of diagnosis because of the high cost of liability in the event of treatment failure (Reed 2002). Physicians do not consume the antibiotics that they prescribe and do not generally incur the costs associated with inappropriate prescribing practices. Consequently, Saver suggests that in order to internalize costs appropriately, either physicians should theoretically bear some of the resistance costs associated with antibiotic consumption or the costs borne by patients and their physicians should be coordinated (Saver 2008).

The positive public health and negative AR externalities associated with antibiotic consumption represent market failures in that antibiotic developers, patients, physicians and other consumers of antibiotics do not directly reap the full benefits of antibiotic consumption nor incur the full costs of resistance. Therefore, many experts recommend that policies that aim to curb the rapid spread of AR need to create incentives that internalize either the costs of resistance or the benefits of antibiotic drug discovery and development.

Chapter 2
Background on AR

In order to understand why resistance to antibiotics presents such a threat to public health, it is necessary to understand how and why resistance develops and what can be done to curtail the ongoing spread.

2.1 What is AR?

Resistance became a major challenge to the treatment of infectious diseases shortly after the introduction of antibiotics. These were originally of natural origin, developed from bacteria or fungi (Demain & Sanchez 2009). In 1928, Alexander Fleming first discovered antibiotics after isolating penicillin from the fungus *Penicillium notatum* (Deasy 2009).[15] By 1940, penicillin was developed as the first antibiotic on the market and demand grew as antibiotics were seen as miracle drugs providing a rapid cure of infection. However, clinical cases of penicillin-resistant *Staphylococcus aureus* infections were reported three years after the initial use of the drug and more than 60% of hospital *S. aureus* infections were resistant by the end of the first decade of widespread use of penicillin (Pray 2008).

AR results from the use and misuse of antibiotics; it is a complex process by which bacteria change and develop properties that render ineffective the drugs used to kill them (Bancroft 2007). The use of antibiotics kills susceptible bacteria but those that resist the drug survive and multiply, replacing the eradicated bacteria (Centers for Disease Control and Prevention 2008). This is an example of a selective pressure exerted by antibiotics – resistant bacteria continue to grow and spread resistance (Alliance for the Prudent Use of Antibiotics 1999).

Bacteria gain resistance through various methods: some bacteria make an antibiotic ineffective before the drug can kill them; some strains alter the drug attack site so that the antibiotic becomes ineffective; some rapidly pump out

---
[15] Howard Walter Florey, Ernst Chain and Norman Heatley completed development of the penicillin antibiotic following Fleming's discovery of the fungus.

the antibiotic – antibiotic efflux (Centers for Disease Control and Prevention 2008). The efflux pump is a channel that prevents the intracellular accumulation of antibiotic needed to kill the bacteria (Webber & Piddock 2003); resistance due to antibiotic efflux is an increasing problem worldwide (Davin-Regli & Pegis 2007). Some bacteria have a natural resistance to antibiotics but others become resistant through genetic mutation or by acquiring resistance from another bacterium (Alliance for the Prudent Use of Antibiotics 1999).

Genetic transfer of resistance occurs most often through conjugation, transformation and transduction. Conjugation occurs when the cell surface of a resistant bacterium and a recipient bacterium come into contact and transfer DNA plasmids that contain genes coding for resistance (Food and Drug Administration 2005; Moritz & Hergenrother 2007). Transformation occurs when bacteria take up DNA from dead bacteria in close proximity and incorporate the new genetic material, which may have advantageous genes such as resistance, into their own DNA (Derbyshire & Bardarov 2000). Transduction is the process by which genes contained in the head of a virus are injected into bacteria that it subsequently attacks (Alliance for the Prudent Use of Antibiotics 1999).

Since bacteria can acquire resistance by both genetic mutation and by accepting genes coding for resistance from other bacteria, they can become resistant to multiple classes of antibiotic. This results in MDR bacteria. Most resistance is obtained by gene transfer from a resistant bacterium to a susceptible bacterium through horizontal gene transfer (European Parliament 2005). This type of spread can occur easily on the skin surface or in the gut, where different bacteria mix.

2.2 Severity of AR

AR poses a major challenge to local, national and global public health. Resistant bacteria dramatically reduce the possibility for effective treatment of infectious diseases and infections. In addition, AR increases patients' risk of complications, morbidity and mortality (ReAct – Action on Antibiotic Resistance 2007). The problem is further complicated and risks are escalated as resistance to entire antibiotic classes (e.g. beta-lactams, quinolones, tetracyclines, glycopeptides and macrolides) emerge.

2.2.1 *AR trends in developed countries*

Within Europe, AR is more prevalent in the south than in the north (European Parliament 2005). In particular, the prevalence of AR is lowest in Scandinavia and highest in the Mediterranean countries. Resistance may be higher in southern European countries due to differences in health systems, such as policies that allow antibiotics to be dispensed over the counter. Southern, Mediterranean and eastern countries also tend to have higher overall usage of antibiotics (defined by daily doses/1000 inhabitants) relative to northern European countries (Goossens et al. 2006). Numerous studies confirm that increased antibiotic consumption is associated with the emergence of AR worldwide (Goossens 2009).

Several national, continental and international surveillance systems have been developed to track the spread of hospital- and CA-AR, raise awareness of the problem and stimulate governments to take action through policy interventions (European Antimicrobial Resistance Surveillance System 2008). In the EU, the EARSS collects data on the prevalence and spread of major invasive bacteria relevant to AR throughout participating European countries (European Antimicrobial Resistance Surveillance System 2008). In the United States, the Centers for Disease Control and Prevention's National Healthcare Safety Network (NHSN) has some of the same responsibilities.[16] In addition to surveillance systems, a wealth of information on trends in resistance has been provided by studies conducted over the past several decades on particular pathogen isolates for hospital and CA infection cases. The following discussion provides an overview of the trends in resistance for particular pathogens that pose a challenge to public health.

Streptococcus pneumoniae

S. pneumoniae is a common cause of disease in Europe, particularly for young children, elderly people and patients with compromised immune functions. Upper airway infections (e.g. sinusitis and otitis media), pneumonia, invasive bloodstream infections and meningitis are the most common clinical manifestations of this bacterium. Pneumonia, an acute respiratory infection, remains the most common killing disease worldwide (Alliance for the Prudent Use of Antibiotics 2005). Approximately 3 million people per year die of pneumococcal infections (European Antimicrobial Resistance Surveillance System 2008).[17] The following discussion provides an overview of the data on the trends of *S. pneumoniae* resistance from the *EARSS Annual Report 2007* (European Antimicrobial Resistance Surveillance System 2008).

---

16 It should be noted that the NHSN took over only a subset of the surveillance responsibilities previously borne by the (now defunct) National Nosocomial Infections Surveillance system. Some experts argue that the NHSN's current antimicrobial resistance surveillance activities are dangerously insufficient.
17 For other bacterial pathogen resistance trends in Europe, see the *EARSS annual report 2007*: http://www.rivm.nl/earss/Images/EARSS%202007_FINAL_tcm61-55933.pdf, accessed 24 May 2010.

S. pneumoniae *resistance to penicillin*

In 2007, 1198 (10%) of the 11 606 *S. pneumoniae* isolates were nonsusceptible (resistant) to penicillin in 30 countries (see Fig. 2.1 in the colour section). However, penicillin-nonsusceptible *S. pneumoniae* (PNSP) varies across Europe. In the majority of northern European countries, PNSP levels were below 5%; the exceptions were Belgium (9%), Finland (13%) and Ireland (17%). Levels of PNSP were substantially higher in southern and eastern Europe, reaching over 25% in Cyprus, France, Israel, Poland, Romania and Turkey. In particular, in 2007 the EARSS concluded that the level of PNSP in Finland and Turkey was rising significantly and the proportion of fully resistant *S. pneumoniae* isolates was rising in Ireland, Slovenia and Turkey. However, the EARSS also reported promising findings – the three countries with the highest levels of PNSP in 2006 (Spain, France and Israel) demonstrated more than 10% reductions in PNSP in 2007.

S. pneumoniae *resistance to erythromycin*

According to the EARSS Annual Report 2007 (European Antimicrobial Resistance Surveillance System 2008) 1708 (16%) of the 11 014 *S. pneumoniae* isolates were nonsusceptible to erythromycin (see Fig. 2.2 in the colour section). Reports of erythromycin nonsusceptibility have risen – in 2006, five countries reported erythromycin nonsusceptibility levels less than or equal to 5%; in 2007, Estonia and Latvia were the only two countries reporting such low levels of nonsusceptibility. In 2007, nonsusceptibility proportions were 5% to 10% in 8 countries and 10% to 25% in 12 countries. The greatest proportions were reported in Cyprus, France, Finland, Hungary and Italy – all reached nonsusceptibility levels over 25%. In particular, Finland demonstrated significant increases in erythromycin nonsusceptibility – from 6% in 1999 to 26% in 2007. Spain, France, the United Kingdom, Croatia and Belgium made positive progress, experiencing significant decreases in the proportion of isolates nonsusceptible to erythromycin. In addition, fewer countries reported very high levels of erythromycin nonsusceptibility – in 2006, six countries reported over 30% erythromycin nonsusceptibility in *S. pneumoniae* isolates; in 2007 only three countries (France, Hungary, Italy) remained at this level.

S. pneumoniae *dual nonsusceptibility to penicillin and erythromycin*

In 2007, trends of dual nonsusceptibility varied across Europe (European Antimicrobial Resistance Surveillance System 2008). Dual nonsusceptibility remained below 5% for 13 countries and between 5% and 10% for 8 countries (see Fig. 2.3 in the colour section). However, high dual nonsusceptibility levels of 10% to 20% were reported in six countries. In 2007, Cyprus and

France reported the highest dual nonsusceptibility levels at 20% and 29%, respectively. The data highlight another worrying trend – despite low relative numbers of dual nonsusceptible isolates, three low-endemic countries (Norway, Germany, the Netherlands) showed a continuously significant increasing trend of dual nonsusceptible isolates. In addition, dual nonsusceptibility levels rose in Ireland, Finland and Turkey. However, there are also signs of improving trends for some European countries with previously high dual nonsusceptibility levels. Dual nonsusceptibility levels fell significantly in Belgium and Spain – in the latter levels halved from 2001 to 2007.

S. pneumoniae resistance is dynamic and thus surveillance systems like the EARSS are necessary to reveal significant changes in resistance trends that may threaten public health. Five countries (three of which had the highest PNSP proportions in 2006) experienced significant decreases in PNSP levels but nonsusceptibility increased in Finland and Turkey. In addition, despite the fact that several countries witnessed a drop in the prevalence of erythromycin nonsusceptibility, an equal number of countries experienced a rise in nonsusceptibility in 2007. Finally, dual nonsusceptibility increased in the majority of European countries. Belgium and Spain were the exceptions, showing decreases in dual, PNSP and erythromycin nonsusceptibility.

S. aureus *and MRSA*

Infections caused by the *S. aureus* pathogen, particularly MRSA infections, are a major cause of illness and death worldwide. *S. aureus* is a leading cause of hospital-acquired infections and is becoming increasingly prevalent in CA infections too. MRSA has spread rapidly in Europe – in 2006, methicillin-resistance occurred in up to 25% to 50% of isolates in most of southern Europe, Ireland and the United Kingdom (European Antimicrobial Resistance Surveillance System 2007). In the United States, MRSA is now the most commonly isolated antibiotic-resistant pathogen (Lodise & McKinnon 2007). Klein et al. (2007) report that the estimated number of *S. aureus*-related hospitalizations in the United States increased by 62% (294 570 – 477 927) and the estimated number of MRSA-related hospitalizations more than doubled (127 036 to 278 203) between 1999 and 2005. *S. aureus* manifests itself in numerous clinical outcomes – as the primary cause of lower respiratory tract infections and surgical site infections and the second leading cause of nosocomial bacteraemia, pneumonia and cardiovascular infections (Klein et al. 2007).

The *S. aureus* pathogen is extremely difficult to treat and is associated with greater complications, mortality and morbidity because of its evolving resistance to antibiotics (see Fig. 2.4 in the colour section). According to Lowy (2003), more than 80% of CA and hospital-acquired *S. aureus* isolates were resistant to penicillin by the late 1960s. In particular, *S. aureus* isolates from intensive care units (ICUs) have rapidly become resistant to a greater number of antibacterial agents over the past several decades. The (now defunct) NNIS System collected nosocomial infection surveillance data on hospitals in the United States from 1970. A report published in 2004 reported a continuing increase in antibacterial resistance in American hospitals (National Nosocomial Infections Surveillance System 2004). The data demonstrated that nearly 60% of *S. aureus* isolates were resistant to methicillin, oxacillin or nafcillin in 2004. In addition, the NNIS System found that MRSA increased by 11% amongst nosocomial infections in ICU patients (calculated as the 2003 rate compared with mean rate of resistance from the previous five years). Increased resistance means that fewer existing antibiotics can effectively treat such hospital-acquired infections. In Fig. 2.4 (see colour section), Lowy (1998) used data from the NNIS System to demonstrate the gap between the number of infections and the percentage of infections sensitive and resistant to antibacterial agents.

Morbidity and mortality due to MRSA have become an unfortunate reality for many patients as more infections have become insensitive to available antibiotics. With MRSA, studies have found the risk of mortality to be double that of nonresistant strains of the bacteria (Cosgrove et al. 2003). An estimated 2 million patients in American hospitals are infected with MRSA during hospital stays, accounting for 90 000 deaths; resistant bacteria are the primary cause of death in 70% of these deaths (Laxminarayan et al. 2007). Similarly, in the EU it is estimated that 2 million patients every year acquire nosocomial infections and that these account for 175 000 deaths (European Academies Science Advisory Council 2007).

Studies have also demonstrated a dramatic increase in the number of methicillin-resistant strains found in the community. Early studies of CA-MRSA focused on particular patient groups, such as those with a history of injection drug use and other high-risk patients with serious illnesses, previous antibiotic therapy or residence in a nursing home. However, Moreno et al. (1995) demonstrated that CA-MRSA was becoming present in patients with general and non-high risk profiles on admission to an American university hospital participating in the 21-month study. In addition to identifying the spread of MRSA amongst the general population, Moreno et al. determined the frequency of CA-MRSA compared with nosocomial MRSA. They found that 58% of MRSA cases were CA, 28.5% were nosocomial and 13.5% were transfers (Moreno et al. 1995).

2.2.2 *AR trends in developing countries*

Although levels of resistance are still high in developed countries, they are most alarming in developing counties (European Parliament 2005).

In developed countries a prescription is usually required for antibiotics; in developing countries antibiotics are often available over-the-counter, leading to self-medication and inappropriate use. A study found that rates of neonatal hospital-acquired infections in developing countries were 3 to 20 times higher than in developed countries. In low- and middle-income countries, 70% of nosocomial neonatal infections could not be treated by the WHO-suggested regimen of ampicillin and gentamicin, due to resistance (Zaidi et al. 2005). Resistance in developing countries often leads to death because of a lack of access to more affordable and effective antibiotics (Levy 1998).

2.3 Clinical and economic impact of AR

The impact of AR can be assessed from the perspective of the hospital, a third-party payer, the patient and society (McGowan 2001). The majority of studies assess the impact of resistance from a hospital perspective as data regarding in-hospital morbidity, mortality and the costs associated with resistance are relatively easy to retrieve (Cosgrove & Carmeli 2003). Studies from the patient perspective typically determine the short-term direct effect of resistance on those affected in terms of mortality and length of hospitalization. The indirect and long-term consequences of antibiotic-resistant infections in patients should also be measured but such data are often difficult to gather. A few studies have assessed the impact of AR from the social perspective. Evidence collected so far suggests that AR leads to increased morbidity, mortality and prolonged hospital stays and thus imposes major financial outlays for health systems and patients. Cosgrove and Carmeli (2003) report that the majority of published studies have shown an association between AR and adverse outcomes – patients with resistant infections show higher mortality, morbidity and costs (1.3 to 2-times higher) than those with susceptible infections. However, the full economic impact of AR is difficult to quantify due to differing perspectives and to the numerous potential externalities that need to be considered. There is also a great deal of uncertainty surrounding the effect of current drug consumption on future resistance and whether this should be included in cost estimates (Laxminarayan 2002).

2.3.1 Clinical outcomes

Many studies conclude that antibiotic-resistant infections are associated with greater mortality than antibiotic-susceptible infections. For example, Cosgrove et al. (2003) reported that patients with MRSA have double the risk of death compared with patients with nonresistant strains of the bacteria. In a more recent and extensive report using meta-analysis of data from various studies with relevant mortality data published between 1980 and 2000, Cosgrove (2006) also determined that a significant increase in mortality is associated with MRSA bacteraemia, relative to methicillin-susceptible *S. aureus* (MSSA) bacteraemia (OR 1.93, P<0.001). Engemann et al. (2003) evaluated patients with *S. aureus* surgical site infections. Their study determined that the presence of MRSA in a surgical wound increased the adjusted 90-day postoperative mortality risk 3.4-fold compared with the presence of MSSA and by 11.4-fold compared with the absence of infection. In the most recent study identified, Roberts et al. (2009) determined that antimicrobial-resistant infections in general had an attributable mortality of 6.5% and were associated with an excess duration of hospital stay of between 6.4 and 12.7 days.

Various treatment-related factors are associated with the increased risk of morbidity, mortality and length of hospital stay for patients with resistant infections. Cosgrove and Carmeli (2003) concluded that antibiotic-resistant pathogens affect patient outcomes in three different ways. First, resistant genes may alter the fitness of a bacterial pathogen, making the pathogen more or less virulent. Second, the presence of resistance in a bacterial pathogen can lead to a delay in the administration of appropriate antibiotic therapy. Third, the antibiotic therapies required to treat resistant pathogens may be toxic or inadequate (Cosgrove & Carmeli 2003). In terms of the second effect, patients with resistant infections are at risk of receiving delayed administration of effective antibiotic therapy. For example, approximately 43% of patients with MRSA did not receive appropriate therapy within 45 hours of onset of *S. aureus* compared with only 9.8% of patients with susceptible methicillin-resistant infection (Lodise et al. 2003). Such a delay in adequate treatment is concerning as it increases the risk of poor clinical outcomes for patients. Lodise et al. (2003) determined that patients with nosocomial *S. aureus* bloodstream infections who faced treatment delays exceeding 45 hours had a three-fold increase in their risk of mortality. In addition, they found that delayed treatment increased the length of hospital stay – from 14.3 days for patients treated effectively within 45 hours of onset of nosocomial *S. aureus* bloodstream infections to 20.2 days for patients with delayed treatment (Lodise et al. 2003).

Antibiotic class, activity and dosage also impact the clinical outcomes of patients infected with resistant bacteria. Cosgrove and Carmeli (2003) note that infections caused by antibiotic-resistant pathogens may require more toxic therapy which can lead to adverse outcomes. For example, Levin et al. (1999) demonstrated that the use of colistin for treatment of highly resistant *Pseudomonas* or *Acinetobacter* infections is associated with renal dysfunction. Other studies demonstrate that some antibiotic agents commonly used to treat resistant pathogens may in fact be less effective than other agents used to treat susceptible strains. For example, research has demonstrated that vancomycin (a cornerstone of therapy for serious methicillin-resistant infections) may in fact be inferior to antistaphyloccal beta-lactams for treating infections with elevated bactericidal activity, in terms of minimum inhibiting concentrations (Sakoulas et al. 2004). Finally, in a more recent study, Cosgrove et al. (2003) propose another treatment-related factor that may affect patient outcomes. They suggest that patients with severe cases of antibiotic-resistant infection often require an increased frequency of surgical interventions to control infection (Cosgrove 2006). Therefore, early detection and diagnosis, timely treatment and adequate dosage and class of antibiotic therapy are essential to improve clinical outcomes for patients with resistant bacterial infections.

2.3.2 Costs of resistance

In general, the total cost of resistance comprises three components: (i) direct medical costs – e.g. longer length of hospital stay, increased costs within services, isolation and infection control measures, increased frequency of surgical intervention and other complications; (ii) organizational and infrastructure costs – e.g. those associated with maintaining surveillance programmes and central reference laboratories; and (iii) indirect costs – e.g. lost earning potential from morbidity and mortality amongst those with drug-resistant infections.

Numerous studies have been conducted to compare the morbidity, mortality and costs associated with susceptible and resistant bacteria in hospitals. In 1992, the Office of Technology Assessment in the United States conducted a study to estimate the hospital costs of AR resulting from hospital-acquired infections (US Congress, Office of Technology Assessment 1995). It was estimated that the extra cost of hospitalizations resulting from antibiotic-resistant infections was approximately US$ 1.3 billion in 1992. In 2009, the Chicago Antimicrobial Resistance Project estimated the cost attributable to antimicrobial-resistant infections to range between US$ 18 588 and US$ 29 069 per patient for medical costs alone (Roberts et al. 2009). Canadian studies have also estimated direct costs associated with hospital care. In comparison with drug-susceptible infections, Bryce and Kerschbaumer (2000) report that drug-resistant infections add approximately 10 000 to 20 000 Canadian dollars to the cost of each hospital stay in terms of per diem room costs, case detection, prevention of cross-transmission and other indirect costs. Maragakis et al. (2008) estimate that patients with infections due to antimicrobial-resistant organisms have significantly higher costs (US$ 6000–30 000) than patients with infections susceptible to antimicrobial treatment.

Some studies have sought to estimate the costs associated with certain conditions. For example, in the United States the annual cost associated with antibiotic-resistant ear infections is US$ 20 million (Howard 2004). In the United Kingdom, patients with drug-resistant urinary tract infections are 70% more expensive to treat at the general practitioner level than those with drug-susceptible infections (Fasihul et al. 2009). In particular, many experts have responded to a growing public health concern with MRSA by estimating the direct medical costs associated with this pathogen. In a study conducted by Engemann et al. (2003), patients with MRSA infection had mean attributable excess hospital charges of US$ 13 901 and US$ 41 274 in comparison with patients with MSSA infection and patients without infection, respectively.

However, studies have drawn contradictory conclusions on the clinical and economic impacts associated with susceptible and resistant bacteria. Such differences may be explained by the fact that factors other than drug resistance may explain the association between resistant infection and higher mortality, morbidity and costs. Methodologies may vary, particularly when measuring the impact of resistance. These may include controlling for length of stay; selection of the control group; adjustment for severity of illness; timing of the onset of infection; timing of the measurement of the severity of the underlying illness; defining mortality and morbidity; and the approaches used to measure costs associated with AR (Cosgrove & Carmeli 2003). Howard et al. (2003) argue that a key factor underlying such differing results is patient severity of illness and how it is used to measure the effect of hospital-acquired infections on patient outcomes. In addition, Lodise and McKinnon (2007) note that certain medical and co-morbid conditions predispose patients to MRSA infection and that such clinical factors may independently contribute to adverse clinical outcomes, leading to inherent selection bias in some studies. Finally, the varying treatment and prescribing practices across hospitals can influence study results (Howard et al. 2003). Despite these arguments, two meta-analyses studies that adjusted for severity of illness and co-morbid conditions demonstrated that the mortality rates were significantly higher for MRSA than for MSSA infection and the difference in mortality could not be explained solely by patient factors (Cosgrove et al. 2003; Whitby et al. 2001).

Many studies estimating the direct cost of resistance consider only the costs to the health sector, such as hospital length of stay, treatment, clinical complications, morbidity and mortality. These may severely underestimate the true costs of resistance for patients and society. First, estimates of the direct cost of resistance on the health sector rarely consider the additional costs associated with physicians changing their prescribing patterns to counter resistance. For example, Howard et al. (2003) assert that studies that examine only the costs of treatment failure in patients with infections due to resistant pathogens may understate the burden of resistance because local susceptibility patterns may influence the physician's empirical treatment of patients with infections. Specifically, physicians in areas where AR is prevalent may prescribe drugs other than those that, in the absence of resistance, would be preferred on the basis of cost, dosing schedule or side effect profile. Howard et al. (2003) argue that the excess drug costs, inconvenience and side effects experienced by patients when physicians switch empiric therapies should be included when measuring the burden of AR. Second, many studies do not incorporate a societal perspective when estimating the direct cost of resistance and thus do not consider the impact across all sectors of the economy. Smith et al. (2005) argue that the majority of cost estimates do not account for the impact of resistance on non-health sectors and economic indicators such as national income, labour supply and economic growth. The authors use a computable general equilibrium model to take into account the economy-wide impact of antimicrobial resistance.[18] According to their model, the real gross domestic product (GDP) falls by between 0.4% and 1.6% (equivalent to a £5-21 billion loss in the United Kingdom). In addition, household income, government tax revenues and total national savings fall by up to 0.3%, 0.35% and 2%, respectively. The authors also estimate that British consumers would be willing to pay about £8 billion to avoid the impact of MRSA. According to Smith et al. (2005), the model demonstrates that resistance affects not only the health-care sector but also the wider economy. Thus, the costs and the social impact of resistance are severely underestimated and hence policies to contain resistance are frequently undervalued.

Phelps (1989) also attempts to account for the non-health sector externalities associated with antibiotic consumption as a consequence of resistance in the United States. In his calculation, Phelps considered the costs of prescribing more expensive drugs, additional hospital days and premature death. He estimated that the national cost of resistance in 1989 ranged from US$ 100 million to US$ 35 billion, depending on the rate of resistance growth and probability of death following infection. Such a wide range of cost estimates demonstrates the difficulty of obtaining sufficient information to calculate the burden of resistance. Elbasha (2003) modified this model to calculate the deadweight loss to society from resistance net of any benefit resulting from antibiotic treatment. This paper reported an annual loss of between US$ 378 million and US$ 18.6 billion, with US$ 225 million attributed to amoxicillin use alone (Elbasha

---

18 Smith et al. (2005) lay out an economic model to explain how resistance impacts non-health sectors and the wider economy. They argue that increasing mortality and morbidity attributable to resistance amongst the population of working age will lead to a fall in the labour supply and labour productivity. This will produce a fall in national output since this is a direct function of the quantity (labour supply) and quality (productivity) of physical and human inputs. Such a decline in national output translates into reductions in national income, national savings, welfare and investment in capital – further diminishing the productive capacity of the economy. Therefore, as the marginal costs of production rise, firms' profitability falls and unemployment increases. Such effects lead to a reduction in overall social welfare. Smith et al. (2005) incorporate such non-health sector impacts into their calculation of the costs associated with resistance.

2003). In the EU, estimates of costs associated with antibiotic consumption in 2001 were €9 billion, with the costs associated with MRSA infections totalling €117 million (European Parliament 2005). More comprehensive estimates of the social cost of AR are anticipated in the forthcoming Burden of Resistance and Disease in European Nations (BURDEN) project. Commissioned by the Directorate-General for Health and Consumers, it is expected that this will be completed in 2010.

Chapter 3
Causes of AR

The cause of the growth in AR is largely twofold: (i) how antibiotics are used in practice; and (ii) insufficient investment in research for diagnostics and antibiotics.

3.1 Misuse of antibiotics

Antibiotic consumption and prescribing patterns vary within Europe, depending on the incidence of CA infections; cultural and social determinants; the pharmaceutical market; regulatory practices; public knowledge about antibiotics and resistance; and the health-care system, structure and resources (Ferech et al. 2006). The European Surveillance of Antimicrobial Consumption (ESAC) project is an international network of national surveillance systems that collects data on antibiotic consumption in ambulatory care and hospital settings from 34 European countries. Fig. 3.1 (see colour section) provides a summary of the ESAC's data on total outpatient antibiotic use in 25 European countries in 2003 (Ferech et al. 2006). The southern, Mediterranean and eastern European countries tend to have greater seasonal variation in antibiotic usage (demonstrating inappropriate consumption of antibiotics during seasons with high rates of cold viruses) as well as higher overall usage (defined by daily doses/1000 inhabitants) than northern European countries (Goossens et al. 2006). In addition to volume differences, there is also variation in the choice of therapy between European countries – more broad-spectrum antibiotics tend to be prescribed in Mediterranean countries (Coenen et al. 2001).

It is important to compare antibiotic consumption trends with rates of AR in order to determine whether or not policies that encourage reduction of antibiotic consumption can slow the rapid spread of resistance. Numerous studies confirm that increased antibiotic consumption is associated with the emergence of AR worldwide (Goossens 2009). For example, the study of Goossens et al.

(2005) – collecting data from the EARSS, the PROTEKT[19] surveillance study and a pan-European project (Kahlmeter 2003) – demonstrated a positive correlation between resistance and antibiotic consumption. Fig. 3.2 (see colour section) shows the study's conclusion that a positive correlation exists between penicillin use and the prevalence of PNSP (Goossens et al. 2005). Higher rates of resistance were observed in European countries with moderate to high antibiotic consumption.

Several actors in the health-care system may contribute to the inappropriate prescribing of antibiotics that has facilitated the rapid spread of resistance – pharmaceutical companies that market their antibiotics to the general public; patients who insist on antibiotics; physicians who do not have time to wait for diagnostic culture test results and/or to explain why antibiotics are not necessary; and physicians who are overly cautious (Arnold & Straus 2005). For example, studies have found that physicians in developed countries often overprescribe antibiotics in an attempt to eliminate all risk (Charles & Grayson 2004). Pharmaceutical marketing often targets physician insecurity, encouraging harmful overprescribing with broad-spectrum drugs (Charles & Grayson 2004). In many cases such marketing practices are counter-productive as antibiotics are ineffective against viral infections and broad-spectrum antibiotics also kill the good bacteria that aid natural function (Levy 1998). The problem is confounded by the fact that third-party coverage and inexpensive generics make antibiotics inexpensive for the patient.

3.1.1 *Physicians and health-care providers*

AR poses a challenge for health-care providers amongst whom physicians are generally the predominant prescribers. Effective treatment of infectious diseases while limiting the emergence and spread of AR will require health-care providers to change their evaluation, diagnosis, treatment and prescribing methods.

Frequently, health-care providers diagnose inappropriately and prescribe antibiotics for infections caused by viruses such as the common cold. A 2001 study in the United States estimated that 55% of all antibiotics prescribed for upper respiratory infections were unnecessary (Taubes 2008). Rapid antigen-based diagnostic tests, such as those for influenza and pharyngitis, can facilitate the evaluation process and help eliminate unnecessary prescribing of antibiotics (Deasy 2009). However, lack of readily available and timely diagnostic testing contributes to cost- and time-related misuse. Health-care providers infrequently test for whether a patient has a viral or bacterial pathogen before prescribing antibiotics because rapid, real-time, reliable, point-of-care diagnostics are not always available and the cost of such advanced diagnostics

---

19 Prospective Resistant Organism Tracking and Epidemiology for the Ketolide Telithromycin.

can be prohibitive (Finch 2007; Finch & Hunter 2006). Therefore, health-care providers need improved and lower-cost diagnostic tools to facilitate diagnosis and thus reduce such unnecessary prescribing.

In addition to ensuring accurate diagnosis, it is also important to improve prescribing practices once the health-care provider has identified that an infection requires antibiotics. A combination broad-spectrum antibiotic (kills a wide variety of bacteria) is often prescribed when a single narrow-spectrum antibiotic (kills specific bacteria) would treat the infection more accurately and effectively (Arnold & Straus 2005). In theory, before initiating antibiotic therapy, health-care providers should perform culture and sensitivity testing (C&S) to determine the most likely causative bacteria for a site of infection and thus use the most narrow-spectrum antibiotic as possible (Deasy 2009). For example, the CDC currently recommends culture and sensitivity testing of purulent wounds for routine infection management in patients (Deasy 2009). However, most health-care providers will not wait for a pathogen to be cultured when a patient is seriously ill and in many cases resort to broad-spectrum antibiotics (failing to narrow their treatment choice even when results become available). In addition to culture and sensitivity testing testing to determine the initial antibiotic therapy, a health-care provider should also take account of a patient's risk for less common or resistant pathogens based on the individual's medical and travel history (Deasy 2009).

The duration of antibiotic therapy is not usually based on clinical evidence and the majority of health-care providers follow general recommendations that err on the side of caution. Few randomized controlled trials establish the necessary duration of antibiotic therapy prescribed for different infections. Among the few existing studies the consensus appears to be that short-course therapy is just as effective as long-course therapy in the treatment of bacterial infections (Taubes 2008). However, the optimal duration of therapy is still under debate.

A final important factor to consider on inappropriate prescribing is that health-care providers respond to different incentives which often encourage excess antibiotic prescribing. One example of such an incentive is the Medicare quality improvement initiative which focuses on early antibiotic therapy for patients with lower respiratory tract infections (see Box 3.1).

The CMS example provides insight into the importance of embracing a whole system perspective and aligning the incentives of various stakeholders when creating benchmarks for performance. Targets linked to pay-for-performance do encourage health-care providers to follow particular evidence-based procedures that can lead to improved health outcomes. However, when the time interval for achieving a benchmark excludes the possibility of performing diagnostic

Box 3.1 *Coordinating prescribing practices with policies – lessons from the Medicare Product Quality Research Initiative in the United States*

The CMS conducts the Medicare Product Quality Research Initiative programme of performance measurement to improve the quality of care for Medicare beneficiaries. This uses clinical care pathways to achieve health-care practitioner compliance with recommended guidelines for quality care (McDonnell Norms Group 2008). The clinical pathways approach draws upon evidence-based recommendations for processes and provides assessable quality measures such as timelines. For patients with particular diseases or health conditions, hospital providers are expected to meet benchmarks for time intervals from emergency room arrivals to diagnostic and/or therapeutic procedures. In particular, the CMS records clinical pathways for Medicare patients presenting with lower respiratory tract infections and admitted to hospitals. The CMS focuses on patients with lower respiratory tract infections because pneumonia accounts for a significant number of hospitalizations of Medicare beneficiaries – more than 60 000 fee-for-service Medicare hospitalizations each year (Houck et al. 2004). Timing of antibiotic therapy for Medicare patients admitted to hospital with lower respiratory tract infections has been an audited performance measure. The CMS focuses on this particular performance measure because timely administration of antibiotic agents to hospitalized Medicare patients with pneumonia is associated with improved survival. Reports demonstrate reduced mortality and improved health outcomes for Medicare patients and cost savings for hospitals when patients received antibiotics within four hours of presentation (Houck et al. 2004). Current CMS guidelines recommend that health-care providers administer antibiotic treatment to patients with lower respiratory infections within four hours of admission to hospital.

Hospitals and health-care providers face increasing pressure to meet the CMS-recommended guideline for antibiotic therapy since the performance measure is used as a basis for public reporting and pay-for-performance programmes. When the CMS sets benchmarks for the time interval in which providers administer antibiotics, providers and hospitals report and measure when antibiotics are prescribed. The CMS provides health-care providers with the incentive to administer antibiotics as quickly as possible in order to meet the benchmark and thus there are no incentives to withhold antibiotics, even if inappropriate. However, existing diagnostic technology limits health-care providers from having relevant evidence within the four-hour time interval to determine whether a patient actually needs antibiotics. Conventional culture techniques take two days to confirm the presence of a bacterial pathogen (McDonnell Norms Group 2008). New molecular techniques such as gene amplification take approximately four to six hours to quantify pathogenic organisms but such techniques are expensive and not suited for use in hospital (McDonnell Norms Group 2008).

> The CMS performance measure thus presents a challenge as providers do not have the tools to diagnose patients properly within the timescale to meet the target. The CMS target for timely antibiotic administration further complicates the process of diagnosis because health-care providers are not penalized for inappropriate administration of antibiotics for viral upper respiratory tract diseases (McDonnell Norms Group 2008). Indeed, attempts to achieve a performance target of 100% for antibiotic administration may encourage inappropriate antibiotic usage (Metersky et al. 2009). Consequently, many emergency departments initiate antibiotic therapy on Medicare patients who might present signs of respiratory infection without regard to the specific location or the causative agent of infection (McDonnell Norms Group 2008). Such behaviour is problematic since elderly patients with pneumonia present with atypical signs and symptoms (Metersky et al. 2009). A recent study determined that Medicare patients with a hospital discharge diagnosis of pneumonia present in an atypical manner that could lead to a diagnostic uncertainty (Metersky et al. 2009). Inappropriate diagnosis and antibiotic administration can lead to AR and divert limited resources from patients actually in need of antibiotics (Metersky et al. 2009).

examinations, health-care providers have no incentive to perform diagnostic examinations on patients presenting with atypical signs and symptoms. In the case of antibiotics, health-care providers have the incentive to engage in excessive prescribing without proper diagnosis. Therefore, policy-makers must design coordinated policies that encourage health-care providers to meet quality care standards while also using discretion and diagnostic tools to determine the most appropriate treatment and use of scarce health-care resources.

3.1.2 *Livestock and agriculture*

In addition to inappropriate prescribing and overconsumption of antibiotics, antibiotic use for growth promotion and treatment of infection in animal livestock contributes to the acceleration of AR. More than half of all antibiotics produced globally are used in animals (European Academies Science Advisory Council 2007; Laxminarayan 2002). A large quantity of antibiotics are purchased for growth promotion in livestock but this market has a much smaller value than that for antibiotics used in humans because the latter are sold at a higher price (Laxminarayan 2002). For example, in 1992, Bayer's €300 million sales of the human antibiotic ciprofloxacin (Cipro) far exceeded the €2 billion sales of the animal growth promoter antibiotic Baytri, although they are the same class of antibiotic (Laxminarayan 2002).

Generally, the livestock industry uses antibiotics for two purposes: (i) to improve feed efficiency and rate of weight gain; and (ii) to prevent and treat disease (Laxminarayan 2002). Animals are given antibiotics in low doses over a long period to promote growth but this practice drives resistance through long-term exposure (Levy 1998). However, antibiotics have only a minor effect on animals' growth and the EU banned their use for this purpose in 2006 (European Parliament 2005). The United States allows antibiotics in animals but the Center for Veterinary Medicine (CVM) and the Food and Drug Administration (FDA) closely scrutinize this use (Levy & Marshall 2004). However, during an infectious outbreak farmers commonly treat all the stock rather than singling out the infected animal(s), thereby increasing the risk of AR.

3.2 Role of diagnostics in AR

The ability to identify targeted pathogens with RDTs could greatly improve the use of antibiotics as well as reduce the cost and time needed to conduct clinical trials (Infectious Diseases Society of America 2004). Although RDTs for certain bacteria are becoming more widely available (see Box 3.2), currently the most accurate and widespread identification of bacterial infections entails culture methods and biochemical assays within a laboratory setting. These methods are slow, taking 36 to 48 hours to provide results (Boissinot & Bergeron 2002), thereby deterring doctors in both hospitals and general practice from waiting for results before treating patients or even sending tests to the laboratory at all. Thus, viral infections are often misdiagnosed as bacterial infections, leading to inappropriately prescribed antibiotics. Unnecessary use of broad-spectrum antibiotics is also widespread as the lack of appropriate RDTs hinders practitioners from determining the precise cause of infection (Boissinot & Bergeron 2002). Risk aversion on the part of physicians and ensuing overprescription of antibiotics will continue to amplify the growth of resistance until doctors have more sophisticated and effective diagnostics that are quick and easy to use at the point of care and with easy maintenance.

Some of the technical barriers to the development of RDTs have been lifted in recent years. For example, patents on key platform technologies (e.g. those surrounding polymerase chain reaction – PCR) are expiring to the point where academics no longer perceive significant technical barriers to their development. The persistent time-lag in RDTs reaching the market as well as the general underprovision by the market suggests that a bottleneck exists somewhere in the market itself. It has been proposed that developers are uncertain whether the use of complementary diagnostic tests will increase or decrease the corresponding antibiotic market share (Meurer 2003).

RDT market demand is significantly impacted by demand side determinants including the health system structure; health system incentives; health

> **Box 3.2** *Current status of diagnostic tests for detection of MRSA*
>
> A recent review (Carroll 2008) looked at currently available RDTs for MRSA detection (nasal and blood specimens). This focused on amplification and probe-based assays, the former demonstrating how multiplexing (detection of more than one marker from a mixture) and rapid detection directly from positive blood cultures has become standard due to the advent of real-time PCR platforms and improvements in DNA-extractions methods. See Table 3.1.

financing and reimbursement mechanisms; the legal framework; clinical guidelines; and the level of resistance (Meurer 2003). Systems that impose the cost of both diagnosis and treatment for worsening infection on the same party should achieve proper alignment of incentives for fostering demand for diagnostics. This alignment should not be challenging for financing systems based on comprehensive private insurance, national health systems or social insurance systems that cover primary care visits but decentralized budgeting and rationing policies may work against the incentives for proper diagnosis. For example, if physicians' budgets include RDTs but not the treatment of more acute infections deriving from inappropriate treatment (including treatment with ineffective antibiotics), they will be less inclined to use or stress the need for RDT procurement. However, even those financing structures that would normally promote the use of RDTs seem to lack foresight – some industry representatives simply ascribe the lack of RDTs to the lack of perceived demand from health services. The industry also cited concern about the eventual uptake and diffusion of a developed RDT as a barrier to development (Noderman 2009 [personal communication]). Long-term cost-effectiveness analyses that take account of the prolonged misuse of antibiotics are urgently needed.

In addition to the health system limitations, resistance adds to the difficulty of producing adequate RDTs. Even if the bacterial infection can be identified, the pathogen's susceptibility to available antibiotics must also be known if the RDT is to guide treatment decisions. Short of running full susceptibility tests using multicompound plates in the laboratory, a better understanding and ability to detect gene variants would greatly improve the use of point-of-care diagnostics.

Current push funding for RDTs is covered by the EC's Seventh Framework Programme (FP7) for research and technological development. The programme's third call for research, published in December 2008, identified a key priority to be: "confronting the increasing emergence and spread of antibiotic drug resistant pathogens in Europe". One of the three translational research projects for AR is currently focusing on point-of-care diagnostics and the three-year €4.2 million project to establish the European Consortium of Microbial

Table 3.1 Features and performance characteristics of commercial molecular assays for detection of MRSA

	Test/developer	Clinical characteristics	Comments
Molecular assays	BacLite 3M, UK		Non-molecular assay
	BD GeneOhm MRSA BD GeneOhm CA, USA	Sensitivity 88–96.1% Specificity 93.5–99% PPV 61.1–94% NPV 97–99.7% Targets: SCCmec	Amplifies some mecA-negative *S. aureus*; does not amplify SCCmec type V; false-positive rate as high as 5%; inhibition as high as 0.7–6%
	GeneXpert Cepheid, CA, USA	Sensitivity 86.3–96.5% Specificity 90.4–94.9% PPV 80.5–90.4% NPV 96.6–99.6% Targets: SCCmec	No external peer-reviewed publications as of 2008 Likely to have similar issues as other assays that amplify targets in SCC*mec* insertion site
	Hyplex StaphyloResist BAG Health Care, Gerrmany	Sensitivity 91.5–97.6% Specificity 77.2–90% PPV 26.2–31.4% NPV 99.5–99.7% Targets: various (with hybridization)	No internal control and not available in United States
	GenoQuick Hain Lifescience, Germany	Sensitivity 100% Specificity 99.4% PPV 96% NPV 100% Targets: various	No external peer-reviewed publications as of 2008
Non-amplified probes	PNA FISH EVIGENE AdvanDx, MA, USA	Unlike PNA FISH, EVIGENE is able to distinguish MRSA from MSSA. Both are rapid, simple and have demonstrated an impact on patient outcomes	
Nucleic acid amplification	BD GeneOhm StaphSR Assay BD Diagnostics CA, USA	Sensitivity 100% Specificity 98.4% PPV 92.6% NPV 100% Targets: *S.aureus* primers and probes; SCC*mec* target sequences	FDA approval for positive blood cultures; FDA approval pending for nasal swabs, wounds; likely to have similar issues as other assays that amplify targets in SCC*mec* insertion site
	LightCycler Staphylococcus Research Use Only Kit MGRADE Roche Diagnostics, Switzerland	Sensitivity and specificity 100% For coagulase-negative staphylococci (CoNS): sensitivity 72%, specificity 92% Targets: ITS 16S-23S mecA gene for its ITS assay	Two separate non-FDA-cleared assays available for investigational use only; possible problem with mixed bloody cultures containing MSSA and MR CoNS

Source: Adapted from Carroll 2008.

Notes: The availability of these tests undoubtedly holds much promise, not least as effective tools for infection control programmes. The more rapid turnaround times (2-4 hours as opposed to the 3 days required by culture-based mechanisms), high negative predictive value of the assays and their ability to distinguish coagulase-negative staphylococci from MRSA and MSSA are significant developments. The consistently high sensitivities and specificities are in contrast to currently available TB diagnostics (see Fig. 3.3 in colour section) indicating the different technical challenges presented by different pathogens.

Resource Centres (EMbaRC) should also contribute to greater innovation in RDTs. Also, the EC is providing funding for the Ultra-Sensitive Diagnosis for Emerging Pathogens (USDEP) consortium. This includes ApoH Technologies, the Robert Koch Institute, the Institut de Recherches pour le Développement and the Pontificia Universidad Católica de Chile. The consortium is exploiting a single technology apolipoprotein H (ApoH) which may improve the detection threshold (sensitivity) for diagnosis of emerging pathogens, regardless of the molecular techniques used (Ultra-Sensitive Diagnosis for Emerging Pathogens 2007).

3.3 Role of vaccines in AR

As with antibiotics, the pharmaceutical industry does not produce vaccines at a socially optimal level. The positive externalities of vaccines and antibiotics are in part related to the infectious nature of the diseases they target. Kremer and Snyder (2003) highlight not only that informational asymmetries are greater in the vaccines market than for drugs (predicting future demand is more challenging for a preventative product) but also how vaccine use may limit the size of its own market in the future. It is argued that this further reduces revenue and certainty relative to drugs and likely reinforces the dogma that vaccines are necessarily low-margin, single (or limited-use) products (Milstien et al. 2006). However, vaccine development is reportedly both quicker (<10 years) (Struck 1996) and less expensive than drug development. Previous estimates which placed vaccine development costs at approximately US$ 200 million (André 2002) are now being challenged (Light et al. 2009).

The presence of these market failures has contributed to years of underprovision – the vaccine market represents only 1.5% of pharmaceutical sales (Warner 2005). However, industry analysts have recently described vaccine R&D as a "high-growth area", increasing 26% between 1999 and 2003 (Datamonitor 2003). WHO has described some vaccine-pipelines as "crowded" (WHO 2006), including some for the most resistance-affected pathogens (see Appendix C). The reasons for this growth have not been analysed systematically but likely they include increased availability of funding; increased regulatory certainty; improved supply infrastructures (Milstien et al. 2006); technological advances; and the focus on newer high-value products, i.e. Prevenar® (see Box 3.3), which offer the possibility of reduced reliance on high-volume immunization schedules (Datamonitor 2003). For funding specifically, the involvement of public and philanthropic donors (albeit largely for developing world vaccines) in combination with the introduction of market-related incentives such as the Vaccine Fund/GAVI FUND, AMCs and the International Finance Facility for

> **Box 3.3** *Case study – pneumococcal conjugate vaccine*
>
> Conjugate vaccines such as Wyeth's heptavalent[1] pneumococcal vaccine (PCV7) Prevenar have been shown to be effective in curtailing drug-resistant *S. pneumoniae*:
>
> - decreased proportion of these infections in immunized children in the United States – from a peak of 45% in 2001 to 33% in 2002 i.e. incidence reduction of 85% in Atlanta between 1999 and 2002;
> - lower incidence within the wider community due to herd-immunity effects, evidence shows a risk-ratio reduction in toddler-to-infant transmission of 0.46–0.49;
> - PCV7 prevented 35 antibiotic prescriptions per 100 children vaccinated in a Californian study of 37 868 children (from first dose to 3.5 years), suggesting 1·4 million antibiotic prescriptions could be prevented annually in the United States;
> - 77% decrease in invasive pneumococcal disease amongst children aged <5 years and 39% decrease in hospital admissions for pneumonia amongst children aged <2 years (Grijalva et al. 2007).
>
> Launched in 2000, PCV7 vaccine is already in widespread use globally and forms part of the national immunization programme in 26 mature markets[2] (as of August 2008). It has been widely reported that the vaccine's impact on drug-resistant *S. pneumoniae* is eroded over time by increasing the proportion of those (especially penicillin-intermediate resistant *S. pneumoniae*) within non-vaccine serotypes.
>
> 1 Wyeth's Prevenar 13 (13-valent) received first regulatory approval in July 2009 and is currently undergoing FDA fast-track review.
> 2 In 2006, the GAVI Alliance (GAVI) made funding available through 2015 for pneumococcal conjugate vaccine introduction in the 72 countries with the lowest GNP per capita (<US$ 1000 per capita) in 2003.
>
> *Source*: Dagan & Klugman 2008.

Immunization (Olesen et al. 2009) may partly explain the resurgence in private sector interest.

Vaccines offer the potential to reduce demand for antibiotics and slow the spread of AR. For example, in a United States' study of more than 37 000 children, the use of heptavalent pneumococcal conjugate vaccine (PCV7) reduced first-line antibiotic prescriptions by 5.7% and second line by 13.3%. From the first dose to age 3.5 years PCV7 prevented 35 antibiotic prescriptions per 100 children vaccinated. Authors suggest that this translates into an overall reduction of 1.4 million antibiotic prescriptions annually in the United States (Fireman et al. 2003). These findings were corroborated by a similar study in France that demonstrated a decrease in antibiotic treatment for acute otitis media from 51.8% to 40.09% over two years (Kaplan et al. 2004). The importance of including resistance-susceptible serotypes in newly developed vaccines is now widely acknowledged.

3.3.1 *Examples from Europe*

Interestingly, two thirds of global vaccine R&D is conducted by European companies and almost 90% of vaccine production takes place in Europe (Galambos 2008). A number of significant EU programmes – such as the EC's 36-month €1.7 million NOVAFLU project (Novel Vaccination Strategies and Vaccine Formulations for Epidemic and Pandemic Influenza Control) and the 48-month €3.3 million PANFLUVAC project (Efficacious Vaccine Formulation System for Prophylactic Control of Influenza Pandemics) – were launched in response to threats from severe acute respiratory syndrome (SARS) and avian influenza in 2002 and 2003, respectively. The EC's Sixth Framework Programme (FP6) reportedly had 581 research groups from 52 countries participating in the ongoing vaccine research projects (Olesen et al. 2009), with more than 40% of the total EC contribution to basic vaccinology being attributed to four projects: MUVAPRED, Savin MucoPath, MUNANOVAC and EPIVAC.[20]

3.3.2 *Examples from the United States*

Despite substantial and prolonged funding commitments and regulatory easing (less stringent data requirements under certain circumstances detailed in the BioShield legislation), the known pipelines for vaccines against biothreats remain relatively sparse. However, there has been a recent increase in public agencies seeking to commercialize avenues for their more successful projects (Levine & Sztein 2004).

3.4 Lack of new antibiotics

In addition to the misuse of antibiotics and deficiencies of available diagnostic tools, the lack of sufficient development of new classes of antibiotic challenges current efforts to slow the rise of AR. Over the billion years of their existence, bacteria have encountered a wide range of naturally occurring antibiotics and thus developed resistance mechanisms to survive (Demain & Sanchez 2009). In 2004, over 70% of pathogenic bacteria were estimated to be resistant to at least one of the currently available antibiotics (Demain & Sanchez 2009). A timeline of antibiotics facing rapid emergence and spread of drug resistance is provided in Fig. 3.4 (see colour section) (Pray 2008). Following the launch of an antibiotic agent, resistance in the targeted bacteria begins to develop (European Medicines Agency and the European Centre for Disease Prevention

---

20 MUVAPRED – Mucosal Vaccines for Poverty Related Diseases; Savin MucoPath – Developing Vaccines for Enteric and Pulmonary Infections; MUNANO VAC – Mucosal Nano Vaccine Candidate for HIV; EPIVAC – Development of a Multi-step Improved Epidermis Specific Vaccine Candidate against HIV/AIDS.

and Control 2009) and new agents need to be developed continually to keep pace with pathogenic bacteria acquiring resistance.

3.4.1 *The antibiotic market*

With sales of US$ 79 billion per year, the anti-infectives market is the third largest pharmaceutical market globally, after the CNS and cardiovascular markets (IMS LifeCycle™ 2008). The antibiotic market itself generates sales of US$ 37 billion per year and accounts for 48% of anti-infectives and 5% of the global pharmaceutical market. In 1997, the sales value of the antibiotics market was 10% of the global pharmaceutical market. Subsequently, this share has declined year on year as the growth in the antibiotics market has been outpaced by the growth of other parts of the pharmaceutical market. Annual sales growth in the antibiotics market now stands at 1% to 2% in comparison with 10% and 23% for antivirals and vaccines, respectively (IMS LifeCycle™ 2008).[21]

Fig. 3.5 (see colour section) provides a timeline of the discovery of new classes of antibiotic. The pharmaceutical industry produced sufficient new antibiotics from the 1940s until the late 1980s (European Medicines Agency & European Centre for Disease Prevention and Control 2009), several of which were of novel classes with new MoA. However, antibiotic developers have launched few new antibiotic molecules that can address the problems caused by resistance since the early 1990s. Fig. 3.6 (see colour section) presents a visual representation of the significant fall in antibiotic production over the past two decades.

It should be noted that this trend is not specific to the antibiotics market. There has been a decline in activity across all therapeutic classes, especially recently. The decreasing number of submissions to the FDA across all therapeutic classes in the 10-year period from 1993 to 2003 is shown in Fig. 3.6 (see colour section).

The number of large pharmaceutical companies funding and maintaining internal capacity for R&D of antibacterial therapies has declined dramatically over the past three decades. Many experts argue that such a decline in antibacterial drug discovery and development is due to pharmaceutical companies' decisions to shift R&D resources to more profitable therapeutic areas, for example musculoskeletal and CNS drugs (Finch & Hunter 2006; Projan 2003). Power (2006) states that the current situation is a result of downsizing antibiotic R&D programmes during the 1970s and 1980s. In addition, Chopra et al. (2008) note that pharmaceutical company mergers and takeovers since the late 1990s have led to a loss of research groups with expertise in antibiotic drug discovery. Despite the rise of MRSA and vancomycin-resistant *Enterococcus faecium* (VRE)

---

21 The growth of the antibiotic market peaked in 2003 (11% on the previous year) due to the launch of Cubicin.

Fig. 2.1 S. pneumoniae: *proportion of invasive isolates nonsusceptible to penicillin, 2007*

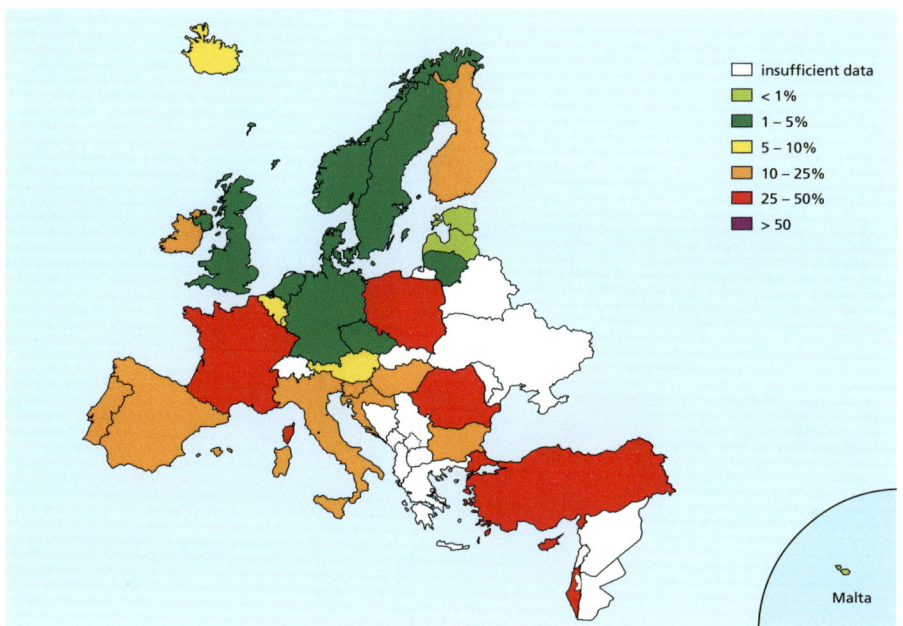

Source: Adapted from the European Antimicrobial Resistance Surveillance System 2008.

CS2 Policies and incentives for promoting innovation in antibiotic research

Fig. 2.2 S. pneumoniae: *proportion of invasive isolates resistant to erythromycin, 2007*

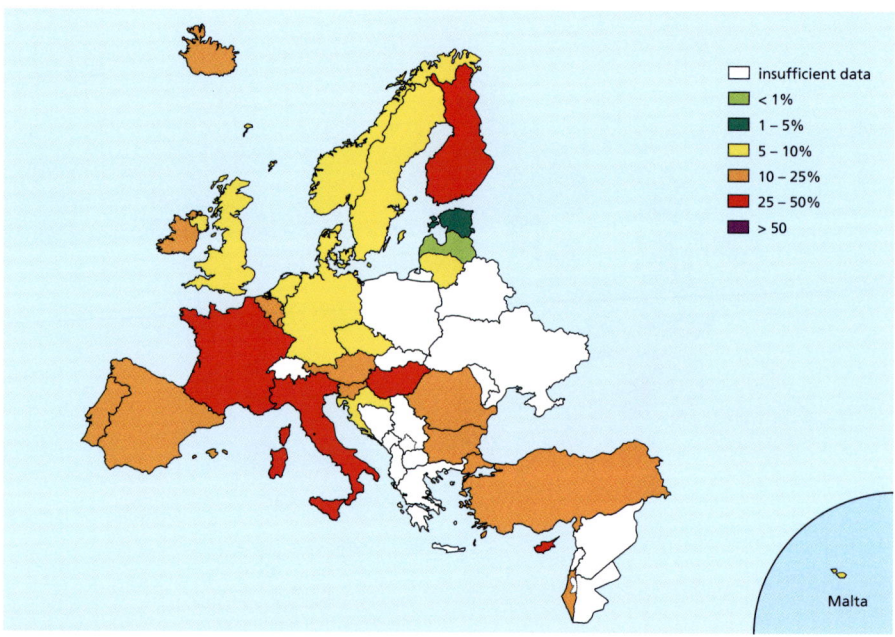

Source: Adapted from the European Antimicrobial Resistance Surveillance System 2008.

Fig. 2.3 S. pneumoniae: *proportion of invasive isolates with dual nonsusceptibility to erythromycin and penicillin, 2007*

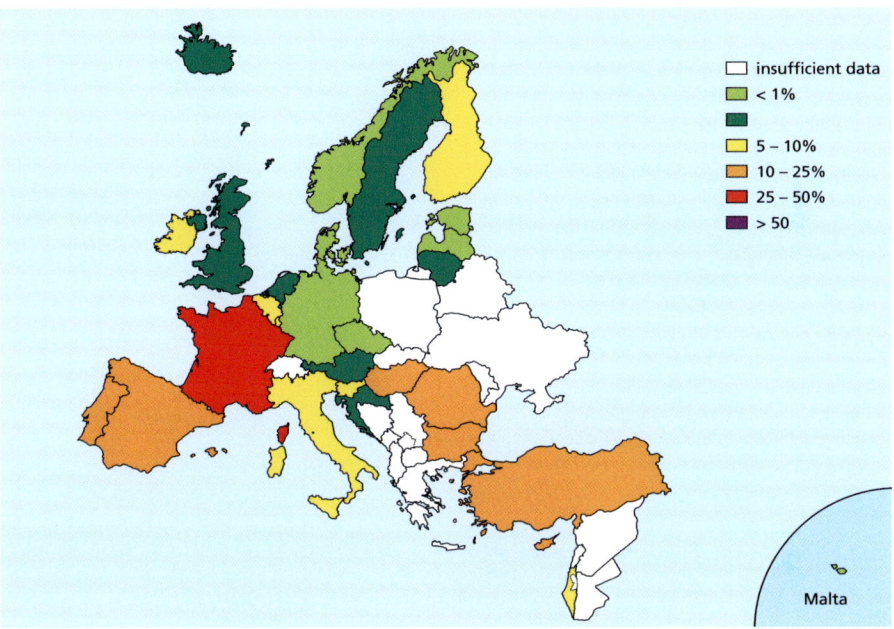

Source: Adapted from the European Antimicrobial Resistance Surveillance System 2008.

CS4 Policies and incentives for promoting innovation in antibiotic research

Fig. 2.4 S. aureus *infections in ICUs in the NNIS system, 1987-1997*

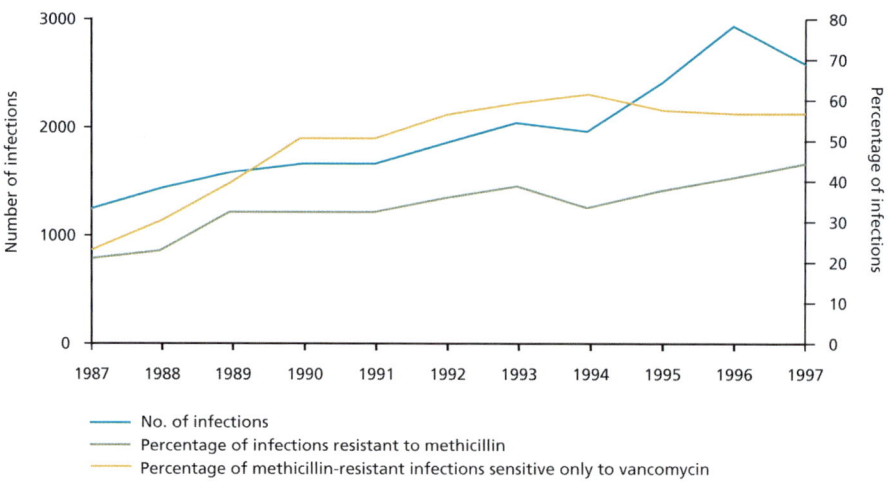

— No. of infections
— Percentage of infections resistant to methicillin
— Percentage of methicillin-resistant infections sensitive only to vancomycin

Data include total infections, infections with methicillin-resistant strains and infections with methicillin-resistant strains sensitive only to vancomycin. Isolates were tested for sensitivity to the following antimicrobial agents: gentamicin, tobramycin, amikacin, ciprofloxacin, clindamycin, erythromycin, chloramphenicol, trimethoprim–sulfamethoxazole and vancomycin. Some hospitals did not test for susceptibility to all these antibiotics.

Source: Lowy 1998.

Fig. 3.1 Total outpatient antibiotic use in 25 European countries, 2003

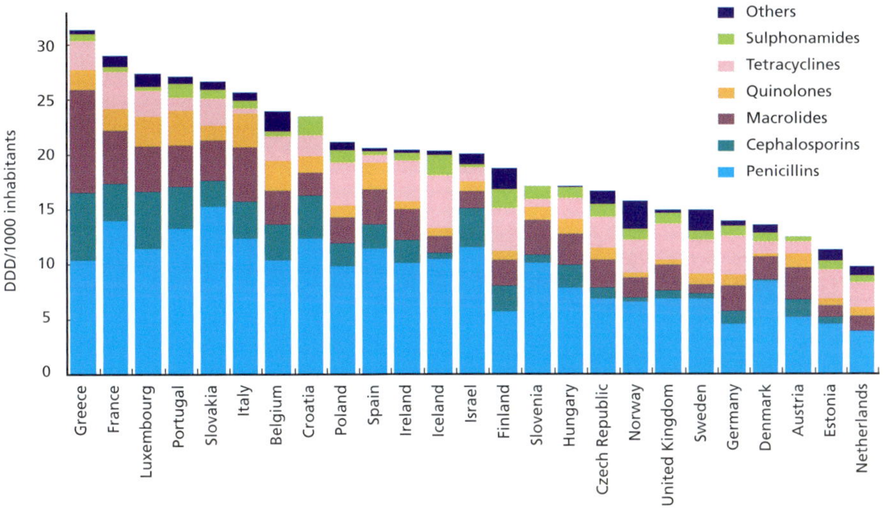

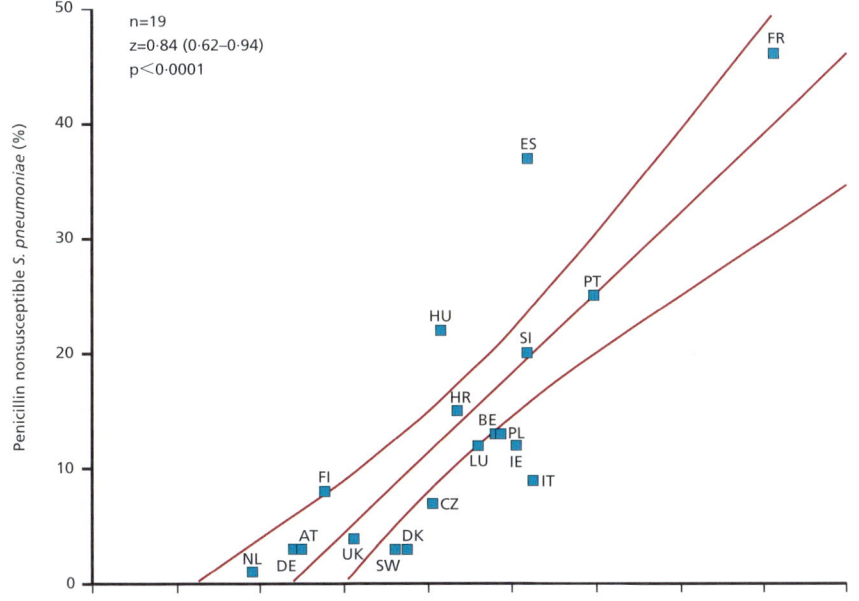

Source: Ferech et al. 2006.

Fig. 3.2 Correlation between penicillin use and prevalence of PNSP

n=19
z=0.84 (0.62–0.94)
p<0.0001

AT, Austria; BE, Belgium; HR, Croatia; CZ, Czech Republic; DK, Denmark; FI, Finland; FR, France; DE, Germany; HU, Hungary; IE, Ireland; IT, Italy; LU, Luxembourg; NL, Netherlands; PL, Poland; PT, Portugal; SI, Slovenia; SW, Switzerland; ES, Spain; UK, England only.

Source: Goossens et al. 2005.

Fig. 3.3 ROC curve based on laboratory-based evaluation of 19 commercially available RDTs for TB (all patients = 355)

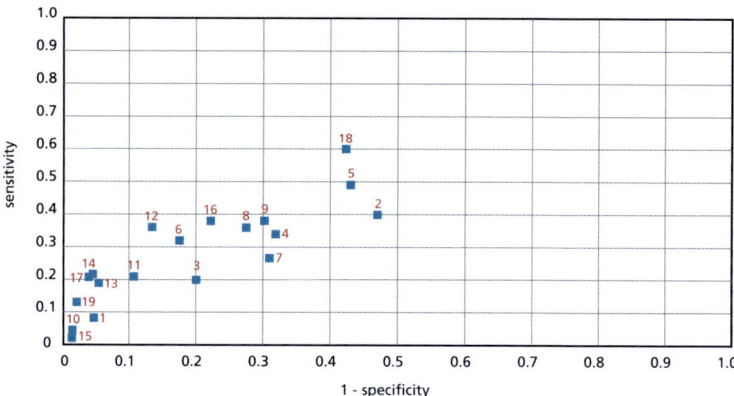

Source: Special Programme for Research & Training in Tropical Diseases 2008.

Note: The remaining challenges appear to be largely practical. For example, laboratories must consider whether they have the resources to use these platforms as intended, e.g. in real-time mode as opposed to daily batch testing. Also, clinical success in reducing the number of MRSA infections has thus far been proven only in the ICU (Carroll 2008), not yet in the community.

Fig. 3.4 Timeline of the rapid rate of resistance

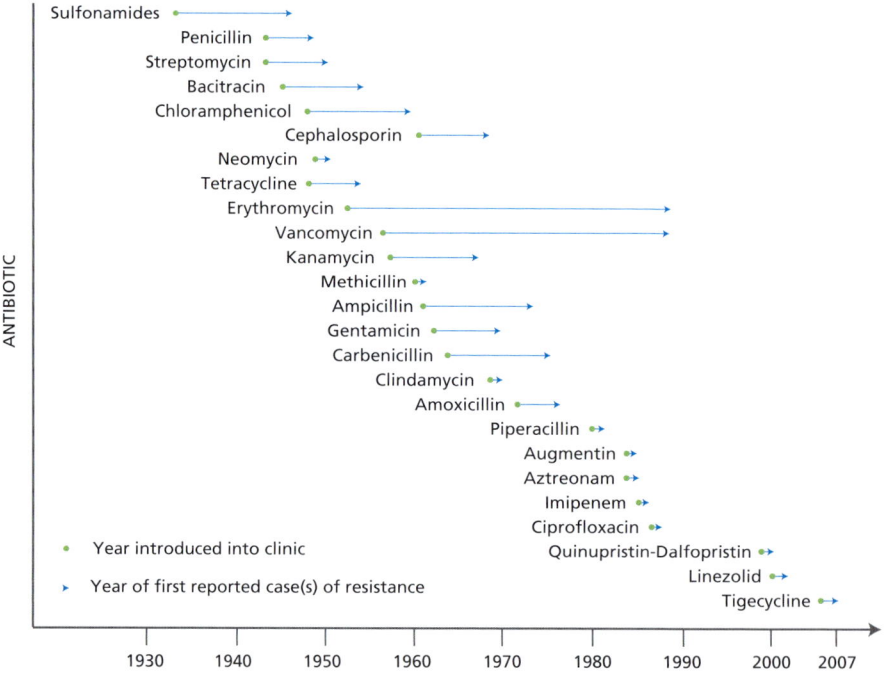

Note: Some of the dates are estimates only.

Source: Pray 2008.

Fig. 3.5 *Discovery of new classes of antibiotics*

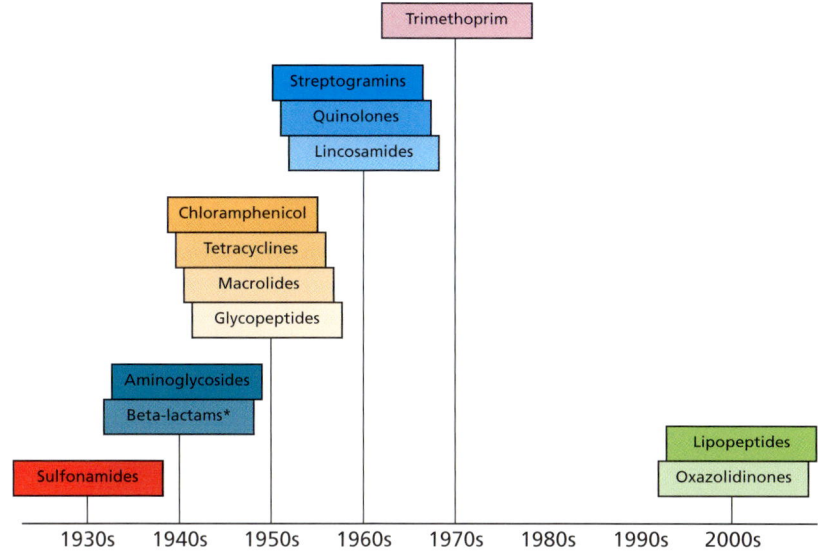

Note: Penicillins were the first beta-lactams. Other frequently used agents of the beta-lactam class include cephalosporins and carbapenems, developed in the 1960s and 1980s, respectively (European Medicines Agency & European Centre for Disease Prevention and Control 2009).

Sources: Figure based on the findings of Levy 2002; Nordberg et al. 2004; Singh & Greenstein 2000 – constructed and provided courtesy of EMEA.

Fig. 3.6 *Ten-year trend in drug and biological new molecular entity submissions to the FDA*

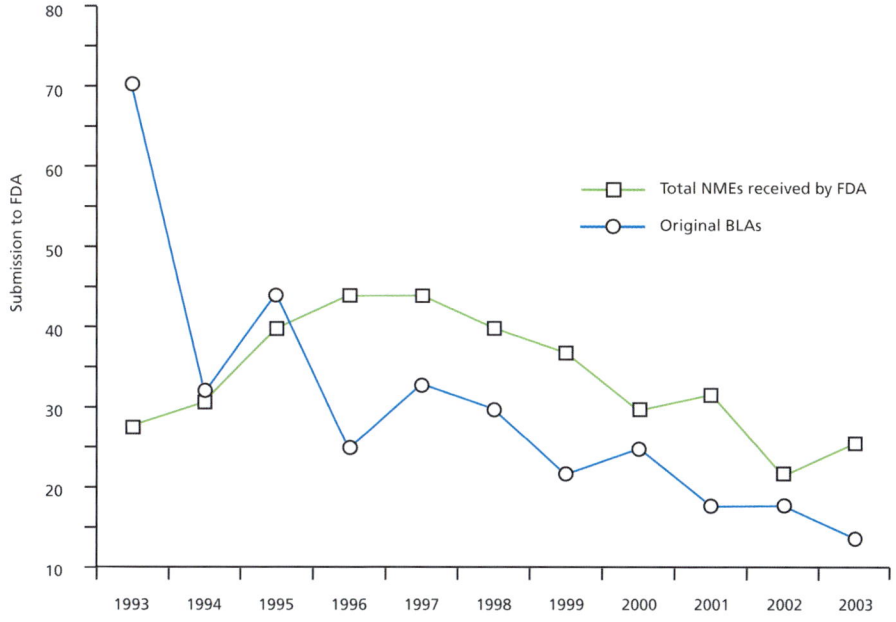

Source: Powers 2004.

CS8 Policies and incentives for promoting innovation in antibiotic research

Fig. 3.7 *New systemic antibacterial agents*

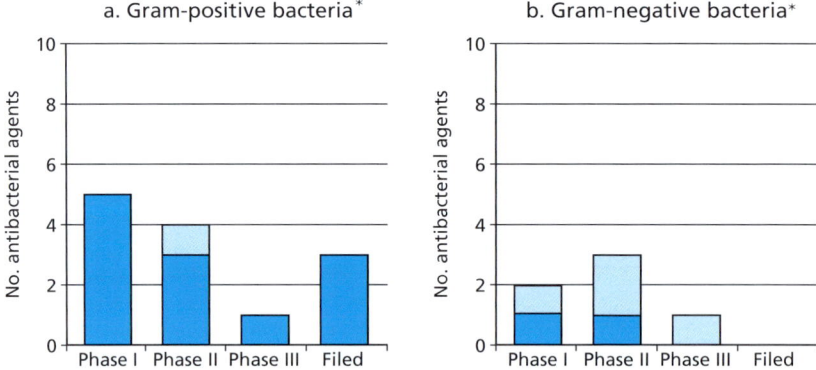

Note: In vitro activity based on actual data is depicted at the bottom of each column in darker colour. Assumed in vitro activity based on class properties or MoA (where applicable) is depicted in a lighter colour at the top of each column (n=15).

* Two carbapenems have been omitted from Fig. 3.7b since they are no more active against Gram-negative bacteria than earlier carbapenems. The relative novelty of these agents was based on a better profile of activity against antibiotic-resistant Gram-positive bacteria and therefore included in Fig. 3.7a.

Source: European Medicines Agency and the European Centre for Disease Prevention and Control 2009, provided courtesy of EMEA.

epidemics in the early 1990s, Pray (2008) points out that pharmaceutical companies' return to the field of antibiotic R&D was only a temporary resurgence. By 1991, approximately 50% of large pharmaceutical companies had stopped or reduced funding for infectious disease research programmes (Shlaes et al. 1991). By 2005, only eight pharmaceutical companies maintained in-house R&D capacity for antibiotics (Power 2006). Since the mid 1990s, three major pharmaceutical companies – Aventis, Eli Lilly and Bristol-Myers Squibb – have discontinued all R&D efforts in the field of antibiotics (Power 2006).

More positively, in 2000 Roche span its anti-infectives R&D unit into a separate company called Basilea Pharmaceutica (Sellers 2003) and a handful of pharmaceutical companies (including GlaxoSmithKline – GSK, Pfizer, Johnson & Johnson) continue to fund antibacterial research. Wyeth[22] discontinued its anti-infective discovery programme but the company continues to fund the development of a few promising anti-infective drugs. In addition to funding antibacterial research, GSK has been developing potential novel treatments with the work of its Infectious Diseases Center of Excellence for Drug Discovery. In fact, Payne and colleagues (2007) argue that GSK has developed more potential novel treatments in the past four years than over the previous 20 years due to the complete DNA sequencing of a bacterial genome. However, Taubes suggests that GSK's sequencing and evaluation of 300 "canonical" bacterial genes, thought to be essential to the viability of bacteria, have fallen short of expectations (Taubes 2008). GSK spent seven years and more than US$ 70 million evaluating these genes to find only five leads – four- to five-fold less than for other therapeutic areas (Taubes 2008). Consequently, none of GSK's antibacterial products have yet made it to market, as demonstrated in Table 3.2 below.

Biotechnology companies and smaller pharmaceutical companies, the SMEs, have stepped in to fill some of the void in antibiotic development. Chopra and colleagues (2008) argue that smaller companies are engaging in antibiotic R&D, particularly for the development of agents for health-care associated infections. As highlighted by Box 6.5, a number of the molecules are being or have been developed by small pharmaceutical companies, alone or in partnership with other companies. This shift is likely because large pharmaceutical companies require annual sales of US$ 500–800 million to recoup R&D costs, whereas many SMEs need substantially lower annual sales to recoup investments, perhaps US$ 100–200 million per year (Monnet 2005). It has been suggested that SMEs and other research bodies (e.g. universities) are more interested in innovative research than "blockbuster" research.

---

22 Wyeth was bought out by Pfizer in early 2009.

Chopra et al. (2008) point out that most of the products currently being developed by SMEs were originally in-licensed from larger companies that were downsizing their commitments to antibiotic discovery. Thus, SMEs focus efforts on developing and bringing to market previously discovered molecules rather than discovering new targets in-house. For example, Cubist Pharmaceuticals acquired the rights to daptomycin from Eli Lilly in 1997 and obtained marketing authorization from the FDA in 2003 (Monnet 2005). Chopra and colleagues (2008) note that SMEs endure high costs when taking a new drug to market and thus have limited financial resources left to invest in new drug discovery efforts or basic research programmes. Barrett (2005) asserts that no SME has been able to sustain itself on internal research and discovery programmes. In addition, many SMEs face other significant financial pressures and barriers to entry (Projan 2003). They often lack the financial stability or the cash flows required to enter the antibiotics market, which is associated with substantial uncertainty concerning return on investment. Biotechnology investment in the field began falling in the late 1990s due to funding problems (Barrett 2005) and most smaller companies must rely on investors and government funding for drug development. Table 3.2 lists the pharmaceutical and biotechnology companies that have launched antibiotics since 2000. It demonstrates the significance of SMEs' involvement in developing antibiotics.

In 2004, the Infectious Diseases Society of America (IDSA) conducted an analysis of pipelines of 15 major pharmaceutical companies and 7 biotech companies. The findings were published in the report *Bad bugs, no drugs* (Infectious Diseases Society of America 2004). The authors found that the pharmaceutical companies and biotech companies had only four antibiotics in Phase II or III clinical development. This compared with 67 drugs for cancer, 34 for metabolic/endocrine disorders, 33 for inflammation/pain and 32 for pulmonary diseases. In a recently updated report, the IDSA concluded that the number of antibacterials in Phase II or III of clinical development remained minimal four years after the previous study (Boucher et al. 2009). Interviews with leaders of anti-infective development at Abbott, AstraZeneca, Bayer, GSK, Eli Lilly, Merck, Novartis, Ortho McNeil/Johnson & Johnson, Pfizer, Roche, Sanofi-aventis, Schering-Plough and Wyeth revealed that only three new compounds were in advanced clinical development: (i) ceftobiprole; (ii) dalbavancin; and (iii) PTK 0796.[23] The study concluded that currently there are no antibiotics in advanced development that have activity either against purely Gram-negative bacteria or against other bacteria already resistant to all currently available antibiotics (see Fig. 3.7 in the colour section). A recent EMA/ECDC Joint Technical Report provides current evidence of the lack of antibacterial drug development to tackle multidrug resistance (European Medicines

---

23 7-Dimethylamino - 9 - (2,2 dimethylpropyl) - aminomethylcycline.

Table 3.2 *Antibiotic launches since 2000*

Brand	Ingredient	Class code	Launch year	Country	Company
Zyvox	Linezolid	J1X	2000	USA	Pfizer
Ketek	Telithromycin	J1F	2001	Germany	Aventis
Invanz	Ertapenem	J1P	2002	USA	Merck & Co.
Omegacin	Biapenem	J1P	2002	Japan	Meiji Seika
Q-Roxin	Balofloxacin	J1G	2002	South Korea	Choong Wae
Pazucross	Pazufloxacin	J1G	2002	Japan	Mitsubishi Pharma
Sword	Prulifloxacin	J1G	2002	Japan	Meiji Seika
Factive	Gemifloxacin	J1G	2003	South Korea	LG Chemical
Cubicin	Daptomycin	J1X	2003	USA	Cubist Pharma
Tygacil	Tigecycline	J1X	2005	USA	Wyeth
Finibax	Doripenem	J1P	2005	Japan	Shionogi
Geninax	Garenoxacin	J1G	2007	Japan	Taisho: Toyama Kagaku
Gracevit	Sitafloxacin	J1G	2008	Japan	Daiichi Sankyo

Source: IMS LifeCycle™ 2008.

Agency and the European Centre for Disease Prevention and Control 2009). This indicates a general lack of agents that act on new targets or possess new MoA. Box 3.4 summarizes the conclusions.

Despite general agreement that key antibiotics (e.g. for Gram-negative infections or those termed the ESKAPE[24] pathogens) are underdeveloped, there are varied perceptions of the magnitude of the wider problem. There is much debate over the definition of a novel antibiotic given that it is not completely clear what differentiates a new antimicrobial class from structurally-related relatives. This leads to different counts of the number and novelty of drugs currently on the market and in the pipeline. Some experts argue that only two novel classes of antibiotics have been introduced over the past 30 years – the oxazolidinones in 2000 and the cyclic lipopeptides in 2003. They argue that all other antibiotic agents launched[25] in the past decade are derivatives of old classes, with limited therapeutic value due to growing resistance. Charles and Grayson (2004) suggest that several of the antibiotics classified as novel were actually discovered in the 1980s. Poor initial results and issues with toxicity forced many pharmaceutical companies to cease development of antibacterial agents. For example, the antibiotic daptomycin was shelved in the early 1990s due to toxicity but was later reassessed at a lower dose (Charles & Grayson 2004). Monnet (2005) contends that ketolides and glycylcyclines originate from existing classes and notes that the majority of novel molecules

---
24 *Enterococcus faecium*, *S. aureus*, *Klebsiella* species, *Acinetobacter baumanii*, *P. aeruginosa* and *Enterobacter* species.
25 Received marketing approval from a regulatory agency.

> **Box 3.4** *Main findings from EMA/ECDC Joint Technical Report:* The bacterial challenge –time to react
>
> The EMA/ECDC study assessed the current state of the antibacterial drug development pipeline by collecting data from the two commercial databases (Adis R&D Insight and Pharmaprojects) on antibacterial agents in clinical development. The main results from this analysis are detailed below.
>
> There is a gap between the burden of infections due to MDR bacteria and the development of new antibiotics to tackle the problem.
>
> - Resistance to antibiotics is high amongst Gram-positive and Gram-negative bacteria that cause serious infections in humans, reaching 25% or more in several EU Member States.
> - Resistance is increasing in the EU amongst certain Gram-negative bacteria e.g. as recently observed for *Escherichia coli*.
> - In the EU, about 25 000 patients per annum die from an infection with the selected MDR bacteria.
> - In the EU, infections due to these selected MDR bacteria result in extra health-care costs and productivity losses of at least €1.5 billion each year.
> - Fifteen systemically administered antibacterial agents with a new MoA or directed against a new bacterial target were identified as being under development with a potential to meet the challenge of MDR. Most were in early phases of development and primarily developed against bacteria for which treatment options are already available.
> - There is a particular lack of new agents with new targets or MoA against MDR Gram-negative bacteria. Two such agents with new or possibly new targets and documented activity were identified, both in early phases of development.
> - A European and global strategy to address these gaps is needed urgently.
>
> *Source*: European Medicines Agency and the European Centre for Disease Prevention and Control 2009

introduced since 1980 are part of the two antibiotic classes, cephalosporins and fluoroquinolones (see Table 3.3 below). Outterson and colleagues (2007) argue that three (five if ketolides and glycylcyclines are included)[26] new antimicrobial classes can be counted since 1999.

Charles and Grayson (2004) highlight that the antibiotic market is crowded with me-too antibiotics, drugs from the same class developed by competing companies. Although the discovery of new drugs is essential to curb the spread

---
26 Spellberg et al. (2004) challenged the characterization of ketolides and glycylcyclines as novel as they are related to existing classes.

of resistance, Chopra and colleagues (2008) warn against the development of me-too analogues of existing antibiotics, arguing that the development of me-too drugs is counter-productive given that pre-existing resistance mechanisms may evolve rapidly to confer resistance to the derivative antibiotic. They advise pharmaceutical companies and SMEs to select molecular strategies that minimize the potential for future selection of resistance to new agents.

3.4.2 Areas of unmet need

The literature shows some disagreement over which areas constitute the greatest unmet need but this section aims to simply summarize the main themes. The need for new treatments can be broken down by whether bacteria are Gram positive or Gram negative and by biofilm resistance. Barrett and Barrett (2003) consider that the re-emergent Gram-negative pathogens and MRSA rank amongst the top problem pathogens found in hospital settings. However, in the past few years the FDA has approved a small number of drugs active against MRSA. Rice (2006) recently labelled the ESKAPE pathogens to highlight the fact that they currently cause the majority of hospital infections in the United States and effectively "escape" the effects of antibacterial drugs (Boucher et al. 2009; Rice 2006). Although existing effective treatment options are available for most common infections, there is now general agreement that the most significant needs are for drugs to treat MDR Gram-negative bacterial infections or the set of ESKAPE pathogens (several of which are Gram-negative).

Gram-positive bacteria

Agents from several antibiotic classes are available to treat Gram-positive bacteria but emerging resistance to existing antibiotics has led to the development of new antibiotics to treat MRSA and VRE, including daptomycin, linezolid, quinupristin-dalfopristin and tigecycline (Rice 2006). However, these treatments have important limitations – particularly that none is proven to work better than vancomycin against MRSA; and linezolid and quinupristin-dalfopristin have some toxic side-effects (Arias & Murray 2009). Other Gram-positive pathogens with unmet need are *S. epidermidis*, VRE, *Enterococcus faecalis* and mycobacteria. In the past five years only four agents that have clinical activity against these bacteria have been approved: daptomycin, gemifloxacin, telithromycin and tigecycline (Projan & Bradford 2007).

In addition, the emergence of CA infections that are resistant to existing antibiotic therapies raises concern. The virulence of the newly identified MRSA strains, including CA-MRSA, is another area of unmet need (Moellering 2006). MRSA is an increasingly common pathogen in all forms of pneumonia (Kollef & Micek 2005) and studies indicate that there are indications of a possible outbreak of widespread CA-MRSA infections (Nordmann et al. 2007). This trend is already visible in the United States where CA-MRSA infections are the leading cause of identifiable skin and soft tissue infections in emergency rooms (Arias & Murray 2009). Treatments for CA-MRSA infections are available or in the pipeline but MDR strains are beginning to emerge (Arias & Murray 2009). In addition, uncertainty surrounds best clinical practices for treatment of CA-MRSA. In particular, there is a consensus that additional studies are needed to define the optimal antibiotic choices for the treatment of MRSA pneumonia (Kollef & Micek 2005).

Gram-negative bacteria

Gram-negative bacteria have a long history of taxonomic changes, moving from one family to another (Bradley et al. 2007), and express a variety of modifying enzymes that reduce the activity of antibiotics once they have entered the cell. Scientists also face the challenge of breaching the Gram-negative cell wall. Therapies for Gram-negative organisms are associated with lower rates of successful bacteriological and clinical outcomes, together with increased toxicity, likely contributing to the lack of sufficient R&D in this area (Richet & Fournier 2006). Gram-negative organisms (including *Acinetobacter baumannii*, *Pseudomonas aeruginosa* and *Stenotrophomonas maltophilia*) are frequently MDR and are considered to be the primary cause of infections in immunocompromised patients, especially in ICUs.

Antibiotics in the pipeline for the treatment of serious Gram-negative bacterial infections include ceftarolin, ceftobiprole and the cephalosporins. Also, tigecycline has the potential to treat some MDR Gram-negative organisms. Other potential compounds include doripenem and faropenem (Vergidis & Falagas 2008); antibiotic peptides and efflux pump inhibitors are two new classes of agents under development. While traditionally considered to be toxic, polymyxins are old antibiotics that are being used because of their activity against resistant Gram-negative organisms.

Biofilms

Another problematic form of resistance is the formation of biofilms, discussed further in Section 4.5. The development of antibiotic agents that have activity against biofilm bacteria with proven efficacy in treating infections without device removal would be a major advance in antibiotic therapy (Rice 2006).

Evolution of resistance

Initially, newer antibiotics generally show low susceptibility to resistance but the fact that most antibiotics are either natural products or derived from natural products indicates that resistance is inevitable for all antibiotics (Rice 2003). Knowledge of how multiple efflux pumps remove antibiotics across the cell surface indicates that some organisms (e.g. *P. aeruginosa* which has a multitude of efflux pumps) will always develop resistance to antibiotics. Novel treatments will always be necessary in these situations and researchers need to aim for individual new molecular entities (NMEs), not necessarily new antibiotic classes, that have no cross-resistance with existing antibiotics.

Usability of existing treatments

The availability of highly active, once-daily intravenous (IV) antibiotics such as ceftriaxone and potent broad-spectrum oral agents such as fluoroquinolones provided many opportunities for early discharge of patients who required prolonged antibiotic administration. However, there are concerns that the dosing schedules of some other antibiotic agents are incompatible with administration outside of hospital and inconvenient for community treatments, thereby requiring prolonged hospitalizations and increasing the risk for further infection. This indicates an unmet need for developing newer oral agents that can be administered in the community setting and IV agents with better dosing schedules.

Safety issues that caused four drugs to be withdrawn from some markets also indicate the need for better antibiotics. Temafloxacin was withdrawn from sale in the United States shortly after approval in 1992 because of serious adverse reactions that resulted in three deaths (Food and Drug Administration 1992). Due to the risk of hepatotoxicity, trovafloxacin was withdrawn from the EU market in 1999 (European Agency for the Evaluation of Medicinal Products 1999) and in the United States in 2003. Grepafloxacin was withdrawn worldwide due to the effect of lengthening the QT interval on the electrocardiogram, leading to cardiac events and sudden death (Ball 2000). In 2007, approval for two of telithromycin's three indications was withdrawn (acute bacterial sinusitis and acute exacerbation of chronic bronchitis) in the United States due to hepatotoxic effects, four cases having been fatal (Ross 2007). It was withdrawn from the EU market in 2008, for all indications (European Medicines Agency 2008).

MDR pathogens

Although most pathogens are susceptible to at least one antibiotic, pathogens are increasingly resistant to multiple antibiotics (Rice 2003). In particular, Boucher and colleagues (2009) argue that MDR Gram-negative bacteria constitute a major challenge for the future. Table 3.3 from the EMA/ECDC report summarizes new systemic antibacterial agents by degree of novelty, phase

Table 3.3 New systemic antibacterial agents with new target or new MoA and in vitro activity based on actual data or assumed based on known class properties or MoA against the selected bacteria (n=15, as of 14 March 2008)

Name of agent	Mechanism of action (MoA)	Degree of novelty	Route of administration[a]
WAP-8294A2	Membrane integrity antagonist	New MoA	IV, Top
PZ-601[c]	Cell wall synthesis inhibitor	New target	IV
ME 1036[c]	Cell wall synthesis inhibitor	New target	IV
NXL101	DNA gyrase inhibitor/ DNA topoisomerase inhibitor	New MoA	IV, PO
Friulimicin B	Cell wall synthesis inhibitor	New MoA	IV
Oritavancin	Cell wall synthesis inhibitor Membrane integrity antagonist	New target	IV, PO
Telavancin	Cell wall synthesis inhibitor Membrane integrity antagonist	New target	IV
Ceftobiprole medocaril[F]	Cell wall synthesis inhibitor	New target	IV
Ceftaroline fosamil[F]	Cell wall synthesis inhibitor	New target	IV
Tomopenem[‡]	Cell wall synthesis inhibitor	New target	IV
hLF1-11	Chelating agent / immunomodulation	New MoA	IV, PO
Lactoferrin	Chelating agent / immunomodulation	New MoA	IV, PO
Talactoferrin alfa[b]	Chelating agent / immunomodulation	New MoA	PO, Top
Opebacan[b]	Membrane permeability enhancer/immunomodulation	New MoA	IV
NXL104/ ceftazidime[§]	Beta-lactamase inhibitor + cell-wall synthesis inhibitor	New target	IV

a Information on routes of administration is uncertain in early drug development.

b Agents with only assumed in vitro activity.

c Are no more active than earlier carbapenems against Gram-negative bacteria. Relative novelty of these agents was based on a better profile of activity against antibiotic-resistant Gram-positive bacteria.

F Reported MRSA activity suggests a different binding profile to PBPs than currently licensed cephalosporins.

‡ Reported activity against bacteria resistant to earlier carbapenems might not actually represent a different target range but could be due only to evasion of resistance mechanisms by the new agent.

§ Ceftazidime is a licensed cephalosporin. Only the beta-lactamase inhibitor NXL104 displays additional enzyme inhibition resulting in a broader range of activity than earlier agents.

Source: European Medicines Agency and the European Centre for Disease Prevention and Control 2009, provided courtesy of EMA.

of clinical development, new target or new MoA and route of administration (European Medicines Agency and the European Centre for Disease Prevention and Control 2009). The table helps to demonstrate whether new antibacterial agents fill an unmet need – demonstrating that the majority of the investigational agents identified by the searches were directed against the same target and had the same MoA as at least one licensed agent (European Medicines Agency and the European Centre for Disease Prevention and Control 2009). The EMA/ECDC report found that "of the four with activity against Gram-negative bacteria based on actual data, two acted on new or possibly new targets and none via new mechanisms of action"(European Medicines Agency and the European Centre for Disease Prevention and Control 2009). In addition, the table shows that there is only one new systemic antibacterial agent with activity against Gram-negative bacteria displaying a new MoA.

Although there are hundreds of antibiotics on the market, Barrett and Barrett (2003) report that these represent derivatives of only a small handful of structural classes. In particular, although many of the new candidate compounds close to launch attempt to fill unmet medical need, none is likely to meet the need for a new antibiotic that fights MDR pathogens. Barrett and Barrett (2003) raise the need for novel ways of identifying new bacterial targets for the discovery of novel inhibitors and additional useful classes for pharmaceutical intervention. They support the expansion of the field of microbial genomics – the use of bioinformatics to catalogue the entire metabolic mechanisms of microbes and identify all essential functions. Future antibiotics will not be able to respond to therapeutic needs unless scientists focus their efforts on identifying novel bacterial targets against emerging resistant pathogens.

Chapter 4
Reasons for limited innovation

Numerous factors explain pharmaceutical companies' declining interest in R&D of new antibiotic therapies. Several are discussed below.

4.1 Antibiotic restrictions deter pharmaceutical investment in R&D

In order to slow the rapid spread of AR, policy-makers and organizations worldwide have been funding and operating campaigns that teach providers and patients about the issue. Several countries are adopting regulations, public campaigns and policies that encourage appropriate use of antibiotics and target various stakeholders within health-care systems – patients, health-care providers, health insurance companies, pharmacists and pharmaceutical companies. National education campaigns to encourage the general public in appropriate antibiotic use have been conducted in Australia, Belgium, France and the United Kingdom (Goossens et al. 2006). For example, the Belgian Government has generated public awareness through booklets, leaflets, television and radio advertising and a web site (Power 2006). It has also implemented policies aimed at changing physicians' prescribing practices – family practitioners receive feedback on their prescribing habits (Power 2006). Evaluations of the nationwide campaign in Belgium conclude that it appears to have been successful in reducing high rates of antibiotic consumption – during the 2000/2001 and 2001/2002 December to March periods of the campaign total antibiotic sales decreased by 11.7% and 9.6% (in defined daily doses), respectively (Bauraind et al. 2004). Data from Japan, Finland, Hungary and Iceland suggest that national policies promoting the restriction of antibiotic usage not only reduce consumption but also can result in decreased levels of drug-resistant bacterial infections (Pray 2008). Although no nationwide educational campaign has been implemented in the United States, the CDC has funded campaigns in 28 states and is expanding the Get Smart[27] programme incrementally (Goossens et al. 2006). Studies demonstrate that educational campaigns in the United States have contributed to a recent decline in oral antibiotic prescription rates for children (Edgar et al. 2009). However, despite encouraging prescription rate declines, survey data from a recent national study showed that there is continuing misunderstanding about the appropriate use of antibiotics amongst the general population in the United States – 44% of individuals surveyed who had used an antibiotic within the past year reported skipping doses; 45% of individuals surveyed who had used an antibiotic within the last year believed that antibiotics can effectively treat viruses (Edgar et al. 2009). Recently, the FDA has moved to warn patients about overconsumption of antibiotics by issuing a regulation requiring more thorough labelling.

Many industry experts argue that public health measures to limit antibiotic use act as disincentives, deterring pharmaceutical companies from investing in antibiotic R&D (Power 2006; Rubin 2004; Spellberg et al. 2008a). This is often called the supply-side externality of antibiotics – policies that encourage more prudent use of antibiotics decrease pharmaceutical profits, slow innovation and investment, reduce development and thus leave the public dependent on existing antibiotics that may not be very effective (Rubin 2004). Such a situation creates conflict between the two necessary means of controlling resistance – restricting the use of antibiotics and developing new antibiotics.

4.2 Challenges in the antibiotics market – NPV

Pharmaceutical companies have large yet finite financial resources that require difficult economic trade-offs. NPV is a key parameter in identifying which competing therapeutic area to choose for investing capital for discovery and development of novel therapies (Projan 2003). Pharmaceutical companies calculate the NPV to evaluate an investment decision, compare investment strategies and determine the viability of specific products within the market (Power 2006). In general, the NPV provides an estimate of the projected costs and potential returns of a development programme, according to current values and in terms of cash flow (Power 2006). More technically, the NPV is the expected value of a given project after projecting expenses and revenues into the future and discounting for the potential investment value of financial resources spent on the project (Projan 2003). In addition, companies calculate the NPV by incorporating risk assessment and adjustment to model the combined risks at different points in the development process and evaluate the likelihood of obtaining regulatory approval (Power 2006). Table 4.1 gives examples of

---

27 Further information can be found at: http://www.cdc.gov/getsmart/, accessed 26 April 2010.

risk-adjusted NPVs calculated for various project therapeutic classes in 2003 (Projan 2003). Projan (2003) and Power (2006) both argue that NPVs for antibiotics are lower than for other pharmaceutical treatments. According to such NPV estimates, Projan argues that antibacterial agents are not an attractive therapeutic investment.

Table 4.1 *Risk-adjusted NPV (US$ millions) for project therapeutic classes*

Project therapeutic class	Risk-adjusted NPV (US$ millions)
Musculoskeletal	1150
CNS	720
Oncology	300
Vaccines	160
Injectible antibiotic (Gm+)	100
AS-psoriasis	60
Liver transplant	20
Oral contraceptive	10

Source: Projan 2003.

Power (2006) argues that policy restrictions and resistance both negatively impact the NPV for antibiotics as policies encouraging minimal use of antibiotics (e.g. labelling antibiotics with warnings against their use) reduce the cash flow and thus the potential profit of a pharmaceutical company investing capital in antibiotic R&D. Further, increased regulatory measures also increase development costs, limit the number of indications or diseases for which a drug can be recommended as standard treatment and thus reduce the chances of obtaining a satisfactory return on investment (Power 2006). Power demonstrates how resistance can have a negative effect on the NPV. Antibacterial agents that develop resistance rapidly have a shorter clinical lifespan and are useful for only a few years, therefore a pharmaceutical company that invests billions of dollars and takes over a decade to develop a new antibiotic may not reap the full benefits of such efforts. Consequently, Power (2006) asserts that the NPV for an antibiotic falls when resistance to a drug develops and spreads amongst the general population.

Other conditions unique to the antibiotics market result in lower NPVs and thus fewer revenues for pharmaceutical companies.

First, the majority of antibiotics treating infectious diseases and bacterial pathogens are administered to patients for short courses of therapy. Conversely, patients with chronic conditions take medications for prolonged periods and therefore therapies for these conditions are often more profitable. The

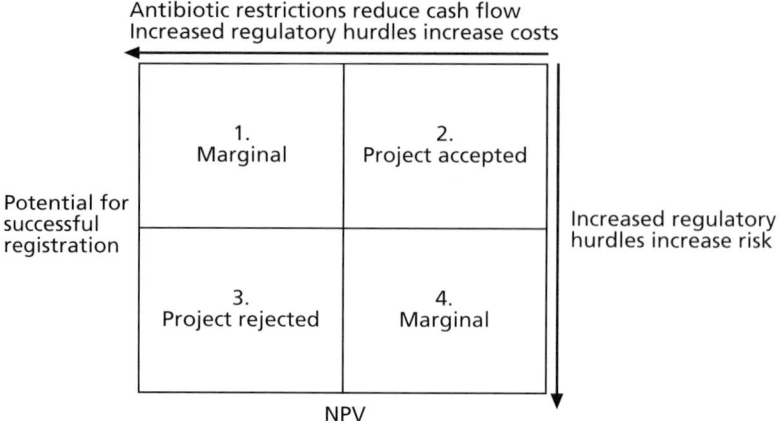

Fig. 4.1 *Antibiotic restrictions and the regulatory environment: impact on NPV*
Source: Power 2006.

NPVs of antibiotics are significantly lower than for drugs treating chronic conditions (see Table 4.1). Currently, the most profitable antibiotic (Pfizer's Zithromax®) has sales of approximately US$ 2 billion per year, much less than for drugs taken for chronic conditions, e.g. Lipitor's annual revenues are about US$ 9 billion (Rubin 2004). Power (2006) and Projan (2003) therefore infer that pharmaceutical companies that use NPV estimates to rank drug development priorities will rank antibiotic drugs as a lower priority than therapies for chronic conditions. Hence, pharmaceutical companies are shifting their focus to R&D of drugs for chronic conditions.

Second, generic pharmaceutical manufacturers dominate the antibiotics market. Two of the largest selling and most widely used antibiotics are generic forms –amoxacillin/clavulanate (Augmentin) and ciprofloxacin (Cipro) (Projan 2003). Power (2006) contends that pharmaceutical companies have difficulty competing against generic manufacturers because the latter do not bear the risks of drug development. This allows them to set extremely low drug prices in comparison to innovator companies and thereby gain a large share of the market once originator patents expire.

Third, the numerous challenges unique to the antibiotics market have significantly reduced the market revenues for pharmaceutical companies investing in this therapeutic area. Most antibiotics generate annual revenues of only US$ 200–300 million, while the costs of bringing any drug to market have been estimated to be as high as US$ 400–800 million per approved agent (DiMasi et al. 2003) (see Section 4.4 for discussion of these estimates). Projan (2003) shows that recently launched antibiotics developed to target resistance (notably linezolid and quinipristin-dalfopristin) have not captured as much of the market share as anticipated. Some argue that small market shares have encouraged pharmaceutical companies to shift R&D resources from antibacterial drug discovery to more profitable therapeutic areas (e.g. musculoskeletal and CNS drugs) (Finch & Hunter 2006; Projan 2003).

Other authors present opposing views. Pray (2008) argues that global antibiotic sales are quite significant and several antibiotics have reached blockbuster status, reporting the example of GSK's Augmentin® for which sales totalled approximately US$ 1 billion in 2007. Yet while asserting that there is money to be made in the antibiotics market, Pray (2008) acknowledges that the financial risk associated with involvement in antibiotic R&D acts as a disincentive. Branded antibiotics have achieved blockbuster status but many pharmaceutical companies are not willing to bear the economic risk. It could be argued that the profitability of other competing therapeutic areas will decrease due to impending patent expiry. Table 4.2 lists the 13 top-selling oral drugs, 11 of which will reach their patent expiry dates by 2012. Lower foreseeable profits in chronic condition drug development could help to stimulate pharmaceutical companies into viewing investment in R&D for antibiotics as more valuable in the years to come.

4.3 Regulatory environment

Regulatory requirements for proving the efficacy and safety of NMEs have led to greater uncertainty and risk in the market authorization process for antibiotics. A major area of uncertainty relates to noninferiority, particularly the requirements for demonstrating relative efficacy within tighter statistical parameters (Projan 2003). These stricter statistical parameters and approval requirements have had the unintentional effect of substantially increasing costs for pharmaceutical companies and thus eliminating incentives to invest in antibiotics R&D (Power 2006). The drug approval process has been further complicated as regulatory agencies are less prepared to accept adverse side effects with antibiotics than with other classes of therapeutic agents (Chopra et al. 2008). Also, incentives to invest in antibiotic discovery and development are reduced by the lack of guidelines from regulatory agencies regarding the type of clinical trial (e.g. placebo-controlled versus noninferiority clinical trials) and evidence acceptable for demonstrating the safety and efficacy of new antibiotics (Spellberg et al. 2008a). The significant debate surrounding noninferiority versus superiority and diverging messages from the FDA and EMA also create uncertainty for the industry, greatly contributing to disincentives for antibiotic R&D (Spellberg et al. 2008b). Section 6.3 covers the various regulatory requirements and how such regulations impact drug development.

Table 4.2 Top 13 oral drugs: patent expiry dates and 2007 revenues

No.	Product	Company	US patent expiration date	2007 US revenues (US$ billion)
1	Lipitor	Pfizer	Mar-2010	8.1
2	Nexium	AstraZeneca	May-2014	5.5
3	Plavix	Bristol-Myers Squibb	May-2012	3.9
4	Vytorin/Zetia	Merck/Schering-Plough	Apr-2017	3.7
5	Seroquel	AstraZeneca	Sept-2011	3.5
6	Singulair	Merck	Aug-2012	3.4
7	Prevacid	Takeda	May-2009	3.4
8	Actos	Takeda	Jan-2011	2.9
9	Effexor XR	Wyeth	Jun-2010	2.9
10	Lexapro	Forest	Mar-2012	2.6
11	Risperdal	Janssen	Jun-2008	2.6
12	Protonix	Wyeth	Jan-2011	2.5
13	Zyprexa	Eli Lilly	Oct-2011	2.4

Source: compiled from various sources.

Difficulties in conducting antibiotic clinical trials are another reason why developers are reluctant to invest in R&D. The major challenges include the difficulty of recruiting a sufficient number of patients with the appropriate indications; a lack of RDTs to identify and recruit appropriate patients; and a high degree of regulatory scrutiny. Box 4.1 outlines some experiences that developers of antibiotics seeking FDA approval have faced in recent years.

4.4 Estimated cost of antibiotic development

The cost of drug development is a topic of much debate. The oft-cited estimate of US$ 802 million in 2000 comes from a 2003 study by DiMasi and colleagues (2003). This is an updated and slightly amended version of their original 1991 study, based on industry self-reported data. The study covered the R&D costs of drugs that were approved, for the most part, during the 1990s. The authors estimated the average pre-tax cost outlay (expected costs divided by clinical approval success rates) per new drug to be US$ 403 million. Inclusion of opportunity (capitalized) costs to the point of regulatory approval using an assumed real discount rate of 11% led to the total cost estimate of US$ 802 million (excluding any post approval costs such as post-marketing surveillance or further clinical studies). The study was based on data from 68 randomly selected investigational NME compounds from the (proprietary) Tufts Center for the Study of Drug Development (CSDD) database. R&D costs came from 10 multinational pharmaceutical companies participating in

Box 4.1 *Regulatory experiences of five antibiotics recently reviewed by the FDA*

1. **Faropenem.** Developer (Replidyne) performed comparative noninferiority trials sought by the FDA for various community respiratory tract infection indications. Upon submitting results, company was informed that requirement had been changed post hoc – superiority trials were the new requirement.

2. **Dalbavancin.** Developer (Pfizer) performed one Phase III trial as required by the FDA. FDA later decided that two trials would be needed so compound was passed to Duranta (a venture capital start up) to continue development. Given that the drug has less than five years of patent life left in the United States, it is difficult to see how it can be raised to a viable proposition, allowing the cost and time required for such a trial.

3. **Ceftobiprole.** Product developed to Phase II by Basilea Pharmaceutica, then licensed to Johnson & Johnson. Following Phase III trials, a licensing application was filed with the FDA in 2007. Issues have arisen surrounding data quality at one or more sites and both FDA and EMA licenses are consequently delayed. Regardless of the potential seriousness of these issues (accounts vary), the procedures to deal with the matter are very slow (now two years) to resolve. Basilea Pharmaceutica, a promising new company (spun off by Roche) is now financially strained, has laid off research staff and is now the subject of a legally binding arbitration case with Johnson & Johnson.

4. **Oritavancin.** Having bought this compound from Eli Lilly, Targanta took it to the FDA Advisory Committee in November 2008 with two rather old Lilly Phase III trials. The Advisory Committee voted against it, demanding trials with more MRSA. Many believe this to be a perverse demand given that there were many *S. aureus* infections in the trials and the compound is equally active against both methicillin-susceptible and methicillin-resistant staphylococci. It is reported that Targanta has since laid off staff (Oritavancin has been bought by the Medicines Company).

5. **Iclaprim.** Developed by Arpida. FDA Advisory Committee voted against this product in November 2008, largely because it narrowly failed to meet a 10% delta in skin and skin structure infections compared with linezolid. Arpida has since laid off most of its staff. It is argued that, at the very least, iclaprim would have represented a further option against staphylococcal infections and may have proved useful if these developed resistance to other new agents.

Source: Livermore 2009 [personal communication].

a confidential survey. Calculations account for the probability that a randomly chosen investigational compound would enter each respective development phase; the reported cost associated with each phase; the duration of each phase; and the probability of approval (all probabilities deriving from the wider CSDD database). The costs of compounds abandoned during testing were also included through linkage with costs of approved compounds.

Adams and Brantner of the Federal Trade Commission in the United States replicated the DiMasi study in 2006 using the latter's published cost estimates along with information on success rates and durations from a publicly available dataset – Pharmaprojects (Adams & Brantner 2006). Their sample was not restricted to NMEs and was based on drugs entering human clinical trials for the first time between 1989 and 2002 for which they had an entry date and at least one additional piece of information after entry. The Adams and Brantner (2006) study used the same spending information as the DiMasi study but the Pharmaprojects dataset overall derived higher probabilities of drugs entering Phase III and thus higher expected costs for that crucial phase.[28] Their results suggest that the expected cost of developing a drug could be between US$ 521 million for one large developer and US$ 2119 million for a similarly large developer. They suggest that the difference implies that some of the estimated costs could be attributable to the strategic decisions of the individual drug firms. Their estimates are based on observed success rates and durations of actual drugs but there is a concern that these numbers are affected by many factors, including endogenous factors under the control of the firms developing the drugs.

The DiMasi et al. (2003) methodology (and hence that also used by Adams and Branter) has been challenged by several groups: the *Public Citizen's Congress Watch* (2002) refers to the "US$ 802 million myth." Many groups believe the prices and rates of return in the prescription drug market to be supra competitive, often citing the accounting rates of return of around 18% that were used in the late 1990s (Frank 2003). Love (2003) argues that the "average" size of the trials used to calculate costs in the DiMasi study is considerably larger than those that the FDA cites in its approval letters; and that the costs per patient are significantly higher than those that the National Institutes of Health or the WHO reported for trials they support, and in comparison to a number of private estimates of the costs of outsourced clinical trials. He also highlights the fact that the cost data underlying the DiMasi estimates (collected from 10 large pharmaceutical companies) were never disclosed, arguing that the costs of clinical trials reported in the Tufts study may be overstated or at least not representative of the average product approved by the FDA. Love (2003) suggests that many of the underlying assumptions in the Tufts report may not be reasonable when applied to particular situations, for example for products licensed from third parties; products that have benefited from

---

28 For more detailed explanation of differences see Adams & Brantner 2006.

government support; orphan products; or products that have received fast-track regulatory approval. He is especially critical of the way in which many groups use the estimates to represent actual company outlays on a particular product, suggesting that a firm needs to return multiples of the higher number as reward for risk and investment return. This would entail double counting given that both the risk (cost of failures) and the opportunity cost of capital (11% real) have already been included – and these are the main drivers of the high estimates. Finally, Love (2003) points to the skewed interpretation of the estimate, given that 26% of all preclinical and clinical research (US$ 140 million of US$ 543 million) and 33% of all outlays on clinical trials (US$ 140 million of US$ 422 million), are assumed to be spent on post-approval clinical studies. Many of these are related to product marketing, therefore they are expenses for drugs that are already on the market and lack a clinical or public health objective (Love 2003).

Funded by the US National Institute of Allergy and Infectious Diseases (NIAID), the TB Alliance study estimated the cost of TB drug development to be between US$ 115 million and US$ 240 million. This includes the costs of failures (Global Alliance for TB Development 2001). Indeed, DiMasi and colleagues (2004) agree that the development costs for such indications would typically be well below the average for all drugs. The TB Alliance study used some of the DiMasi 2003 assumptions but also contained important differences such as lower cost estimates for clinical trials. The study assumed one pivotal clinical trial and provides numerous examples of actual and possible clinical trial costs, with detailed explanations of the fixed and variable costs for the different types of trial. The base case calculation assumes the total number of patients to be equivalent to approximately one quarter of the average found in the DiMasi study. The TB Alliance study calculated the cost per approved indication, not the cost per approved drug (many drugs are investigated for multiple indications prior to their first marketing approval).

4.5 Scientific challenges

No doubt the scientific difficulties of antibiotic development have influenced the lack of investment in R&D for infectious diseases. Scientists face a key challenge to find a lead compound – a substance that can act as an antibacterial agent (Royal Society 2008). Any lead compound then needs to be screened and refined to see whether it can be a candidate drug. It has been estimated that, on average, 20 candidate drugs are required to yield 1 marketable drug. Scientists can take different routes to discover lead compounds, including screening natural sources for antibacterial properties; screening synthetic compounds against isolated cellular targets; or employing novel methods of modifying older molecular targets (Royal Society 2008). As it was felt that developing antibiotics from natural sources was inefficient and time-consuming, many pharmaceutical companies have recently switched to methods involving combinational chemistry and target-based genomic approaches.[29] However, it has been suggested that these new approaches are costly and inefficient and have not yet resulted in any new antibiotic discoveries (Finch & Hunter 2006; Payne et al. 2007). It may be that screening lead products has not led to many candidate drugs because synthetic chemical screening libraries have a bias towards molecules for mammalian targets rather than bacterial targets (Royal Society 2008).

Scientists are increasingly recognizing that some of these scientific difficulties are due to the fact that bacteria have intrinsic means of resistance (Payne et al. 2007) in which biofilms and efflux pumps are two of the most important contributors. The problem with bacterial resistance in biofilms appears to be some change in the bacterial characteristics that make them less susceptible to antibiotics. Also, there appear to be multiple resistance mechanisms that work simultaneously (Stewart & Costerton 2001). Other properties of biofilms mean that antibiotics are unlikely to be able effectively to target all cells in the biofilm. Efflux pumps, which decrease the intracellular concentration of antibiotics, are also important contributors to resistance.

Part of the scientific difficulty in developing antibiotics is due to a lack of good data on chemical compounds. The classic screening of compound libraries in the search for new antibiotics was not producing results and some suggest that this resulted in pharmaceutical companies developing me-too drugs instead of novel therapies (Poupard 2006). This pushed many companies to funnel resources into more cutting edge technologies such as genomics, combinational chemistry and rapid throughput screening (Finch & Hunter 2006). These technologies have identified new targets but have not yet resulted in marketable drugs.

---

29 Target-based genomic approaches involve comparing the genome sequences of different pathogenic species to determine the genes that most of the species have in common (Royal Society 2008).

Chapter 5
Health system responses to AR

Numerous national and international organizations have addressed the AR problem using a variety of mechanisms. Most developed countries have national level policies but some of the focus has been at the health system level, where institutions have been created to collect and monitor data, inform stakeholders and change health practices. More recently, there have been measures to stimulate R&D in infectious diseases, although most of these have focused on neglected diseases and bioterrorism rather than AR. This section outlines a selection of these responses to AR within the EU and the United States and very briefly describes their perceived level of success to date.

Surveillance and ABS are two major tools that health systems have developed to reduce antibiotic use. Europe and the United States have taken a number of actions on these fronts, albeit to varying degrees. As resistance typically varies regionally and even between local administrative zones, there is a need to establish both national and local surveillance systems. These aim to achieve a number of goals, including understanding and predicting of AR; detecting new resistance mechanisms; monitoring and understanding the impact of changes in antibiotic prescribing; devising public health guidelines for infection control; identifying outbreaks of resistant pathogens; and educating health-care stakeholders and the public about AR, inter alia (Karlowsky & Sahm 2002; Masterton 2000). Crucially, findings from surveillance help to raise alerts to burgeoning emergencies in which existing lines of antibiotics become impotent against bacteria in our environment.

The parameters and definitions of ABS vary across countries and within the literature. In general, ABS is a continuous effort to optimize the use of antibiotics within health-care institutions in order to improve patient outcomes; achieve cost-effective treatment; and reduce AR, particularly within hospitals (Dellit et al. 2007; MacDougall & Polk 2005). ABS programmes can encompass a number of different interventions, some of which include education and guidelines; formularies and restricted prescribing; review and feedback for providers; information technology to assist in decisions; and antibiotic cycling.[30] Overall, proper ABS entails the selection of an appropriate drug, optimization of the dose and duration and minimization of toxicity and conditions for selection of resistant pathogens (Fishman 2006). Box 5.1 provides a brief summary of the literature on policies to guide antibiotic use.

Box 5.1 *Literature on policies to guide appropriate antibiotic use*

This box provides a brief overview of the literature highlighting the variable effectiveness of interventions to decrease inappropriate and overall antibiotic prescribing. Comprehensive systematic reviews of prescribing interventions point to the limited evidence previously available to decision-makers. The most common interventions target non-financial incentives and are generally categorized as persuasive (i.e. facilitating change in prescribing behaviour) or restrictive (i.e. forced change) initiatives. Gaps in the literature remain.

Simple persuasive interventions

The use of low-cost interventions – such as audit and feedback or printed educational material – shows a small, although often statistically significant, reduction in overall prescribing (Arnold & Straus 2005; Mainous et al. 2000). Educational outreach visits by academic detailers (from government or third-party payer organizations) also demonstrate a small but consistent reduction in prescribing, but the long-term effects are unknown (O'Brien et al. 2007).

Use of best-practice or consensus-driven guidelines can be a successful intervention to improve antibiotic prescribing (Chapman et al. 2004) but guidelines can be difficult to implement at individual clinician level. One option is to use clinical decision support systems (CDSSs) which may reduce hospitalization time and the potential of acquiring a nosocomial infection by reducing medication errors and optimizing drug dosages (Durieux et al. 2008; Kawamoto et al. 2005). The most effective CDSSs are implemented properly; available at the point of decision-making; and provide specific directives and/or advice (Kawamoto et al. 2005). Importantly, CDSSs may not address the root cause of inappropriate antibiotic prescribing as this returns when the intervention is removed (Durieux et al. 2008).

Simple restrictive interventions

In comparison with persuasive interventions, restrictive interventions have demonstrated a more statistically significant reduction in inappropriate antibiotic prescribing (Davey et al. 2005). Successful implementation of interventions that target

---

[30] Antimicrobial cycling entails a scheduled rotation of the antimicrobials used within the inpatient setting and also within specific units of the hospital e.g. ICU. Enthusiasm for this has lessened recently.

formularies to limit the use of certain drugs for specific diagnoses are effective at influencing prescribing behaviour (MacCara et al. 2001). Delayed prescribing has also been shown to be highly effective for certain conditions, e.g. upper respiratory tract infections (Arnold & Straus 2005), although a systematic review by Spurling et al. (2007) outlines its limited capacity.

Complex multifaceted interventions
Comprehensive multifaceted interventions appear to be the most effective mechanism for addressing AR and inappropriate antibiotic use (Arnold & Straus 2005; Dellit et al. 2007). Effective interventions incorporate both financial and non-financial interventions and coordinate multidisciplinary experts (e.g. infectious disease specialists, clinical microbiologists, pharmacists, administration). The programmes may also be combined with rigorous hospital-based infection control programmes to address both prescribing practices and the emergence of nosocomial infection. Dellit et al. (2007) find evidence to support the financial viability of effective multifaceted ABS schemes. They draw on data from recent studies to highlight that such programmes have the ability to reduce antibiotic prescribing by 22% to 36% in the United States. The literature documenting the cost-effectiveness of such interventions is small but growing.

5.1 Examples from Europe

In 1998 the EARSS was founded to coordinate the monitoring of AR in Europe (Metz-Gercek & Mittermayer 2008). Its objectives were to standardize laboratory practices; improve data reliability and validity; and foster the creation of national networks for the collection and testing of samples for AR. EARSS is now the largest and most comprehensive surveillance system in the world, including more than 800 microbiological laboratories that cover over 1300 hospitals in 31 countries (Metz-Gercek & Mittermayer 2008). It collects information on the *S. aureus, S. pneumoniae, Escherichia coli, E. faecium/faecalis, Klebsiella pneumoniae* and *P. aeruginosa* pathogens.

Established in 2001, the ESAC monitors antibiotic use by means of an annual longitudinal database covering 33 countries. Gathering this data is challenging as collection is delineated according to ambulatory, inpatient and nursing home care, each with different methodologies. For instance, countries often have dispense data but no data on actual consumption, also electronic health systems are still not widespread or well-supported in all countries (Metz-Gercek & Mittermayer 2008). However, the ESAC project is actively working to improve data collection and develop quality indicators for antibiotic use.

Several countries have comprehensive pre-existing ABS programmes, including Belgium and Austria (Allerberger et al. 2008). In 2006, with the support of nine Member States,[31] the EC established "ABS International – Implementing antibiotic strategies for appropriate use of antibiotics in hospitals in Member States of the European Union". The two-year EU-financed project implemented ABS tools such as the development of antibiotic lists and quality indicators for antibiotic use; mechanisms to analyse consumption data; and the training of national experts and national ABS trainers.

Table 5.1 highlights the degree to which several northern European countries (Denmark, Finland, the Netherlands, Norway and Sweden) have implemented successful interventions to address AR. Other factors, such as lower bed occupancy rates, cannot be discounted but sustained aggressive policies to combat AR have had a striking impact in two particular countries – Sweden and the Netherlands (Prins et al. 2008; Wertheim et al. 2004). The Swedish Strategic Programme Against Antibiotic Resistance integrates research, policy formation and implementation and engages multiple relevant stakeholders (Molstad et al. 2008). The Programme has access to annual regional data on the antibiotic susceptibility of six bacterial species, whilst the Swedish Reference Group for Antibiotics methodology subcommittee has been effective in standardizing the

Table 5.1 Susceptibility (S)/Resistance (R) results for S. aureus isolates in a selection of European countries, 2007

Country	Number		Total	Percentage	
	S	R	N	S	R
Austria	1364	139	1503	90.8	9.2
Belgium	656	199	855	76.7	23.3
Bulgaria	105	16	121	86.8	13.2
Switzerland	740	104	844	87.7	12.3
Denmark	1304	11	1315	99.2	0.8
Estonia	188	18	206	91.3	8.7
Spain	1224	418	1642	74.5	25.5
Finland	801	13	814	98.4	1.6
France	3154	1096	4250	74.2	25.8
Croatia	234	141	375	62.4	37.6
Luxembourg	83	22	105	79.0	21.0
Malta	50	55	105	47.6	52.4
Netherlands	1449	20	1469	98.6	1.4
Norway	789	1	790	99.9	0.1
Sweden	2151	11	2162	99.5	0.5
Slovenia	387	35	422	91.7	8.3

Source: European Antimicrobial Resistance Surveillance System 2008.

---

31 Austria, Belgium, Czech Republic, Germany, Hungary, Italy, Poland, Slovakia and Slovenia.

microbiological laboratories. Apoteket AB, Sweden's state-owned wholesale pharmaceutical supplier, also provides comprehensive data on outpatient antibiotic sales in Sweden. This highly coordinated effort, which now includes stringent hospital-based infection control policies, represents one of the most effective strategies in the EU (Molstad et al. 2008).

In the Netherlands, the Dutch Working Party on Antibiotic Policy (Stichting Werkgroep Antibioticabeleid) coordinates efforts against AR, including the national surveillance system. Since 2002, the Netherlands has employed restrictive antibiotic prescribing practices and a rigorous search-and-destroy policy in hospitals. Patients admitted to hospital are assessed for potential risk (four risk groups) of MRSA infection that determines which rigorous screening/monitoring, sanitation and isolation protocol will be implemented. The prevalence of MRSA is now below 1% (Nulens et al. 2008; Wertheim et al. 2004).

The Netherlands has also adopted a notable mentorship role within the EU. The 36-month EUREGIO[32] MRSA-net Twente/Münsterland project created a highly integrated regional network for the control, monitoring and epidemiological standardization of infectious disease protocols for MRSA along a section of the Dutch–German border. The scheme incorporated regional and national governments, academic institutions, hospitals, microbiological laboratories, public health offices, professional associations, nursing homes and patient transportation services (Friedrich et al. 2008). The transfer of knowledge and effective practices achieved through this project could serve as a model for other regions characterized by stark dichotomies in prevalence or expertise.

In Europe there is also increasing interest in using financial incentives to change behaviour, such as pay-for-performance schemes (Pirson et al. 2008). The 2008–2009 National Health Service contract for acute services in England incorporated financial penalties for failing to meet nosocomial infection targets and the Department of Health has set a target of reducing *Clostridium difficile* infections by 30% by 2011. Primary care trusts will administer the scheme, levying penalties capped at 2% of income on hospital trusts that do not achieve the yearly target reductions (Walker et al. 2008).

5.2 Examples from the United States

A broad range of surveillance systems collect data on AR in the United States although this information is not available in a single place. Individual states have the final decision on collecting data related to AR and the associated economic and health costs. The CDC has no authority to require states to collect data.

---

[32] Evaluation of Cross Border Activities in the European Union.

Thus far, the American Federal Government has not been heavily involved in studying ABS and, unsurprisingly, the availability and quality of ABS programmes varies widely. However, organizations such as the IDSA have become actively involved in providing guidelines for ABS (Dellit et al. 2007). Echoing the results of previous studies (Lawton et al. 2000), a survey conducted within top academic hospitals in the United States from 2001 to 2003 found that most hospitals had not implemented such programmes. This was largely due to uncertainties surrounding the application of the programmes to their specific institutions as well as financial difficulties in obtaining the resources and trained personnel to run them (Barlam & DiVall 2006).

The reimbursement and accountability structure of treatment expenses in American hospitals may also hinder infectious disease control. Third-party coverage of expenses arising from AR reduces incentives for hospitals to control infections. The US Deficit Reduction Act which became operational in October 2008 responded to this problem by shifting a significant portion of the financial burden of treating nosocomial infections to hospitals. Under the new legislation, Medicare will no longer reimburse the cost of treating nosocomial catheter-associated urinary tract infections, vascular catheter-associated bloodstream infections and surgical site infections associated with certain elective procedures including mediastinitis, some orthopaedic surgeries and bariatric surgery (Graves & McGowan 2008; Lancet Infectious Diseases 2008).

Without any federal strategy to tackle AR in the United States, there is fragmented research on transmission, prevention, clinical therapy and product development. In 1999, Congress established the Interagency Task Force on Antimicrobial Resistance to coordinate federal efforts. However, with little authority and funding, it was unable to implement the Public Health Action Plan to Combat Antimicrobial Resistance before its authorization expired in 2006.

In 2007, Senators Brown and Hatch raised a key proposal to consolidate efforts in the form of the Strategies to Address Antimicrobial Resistance (STAAR) Act (S.2313). This proposed the establishment of the Antimicrobial Resistance Surveillance and Research Network at sites across the country to work in collaboration with the CDC, the NIH and other federal agencies to actively bring together experts in surveillance, prevention and research. Sites were intended as a clinical research network, similar to those that the NIH uses to study other priority disease areas, and would include isolate collection capacity. The STAAR Act proposed enhancing the Task Force's authority to review data, make recommendations and integrate efforts in the Public Health Action Plan. It also proposed establishing an office of antimicrobial resistance in the Department of Health & Human Services to coordinate interagency efforts and act as a central repository for data on the amount of antibiotics used in humans and animals in the United States, including an advisory board to help learn from international experts. The Act did not pass upon first introduction but was reintroduced by Representative Matheson on 13 May 2009 and, at the time of writing, is being considered for inclusion in an upcoming omnibus bill on AR.

Chapter 6
Analysis of opportunities and incentives to stimulate R&D for antibiotics

This section organizes proposed incentives to stimulate antibacterial R&D into four categories: (i) push; (ii) pull; (iii) lego-regulatory; and (iv) hybrid. These incentives may entail changes in the health system, the regulatory infrastructure, or may require government assistance. The section is also punctuated with a number of case-studies that explore some of the current experimental models or practical experience in more depth. The advantages and disadvantages of each proposed incentive are provided, along with evidence regarding practical implementation when available. Applicability to antibiotics and implications for smaller developers are also discussed. The length of discussion regarding each of the individual incentives is largely a function of the amount of relevant literature identified. In a few cases (those serving as a basis for key recommendations) the length of discussion is also a reflection of the incentive's perceived relative merits.

6.1 Push incentives

Push incentives focus on removing barriers to developer entry largely by affecting a developer's marginal cost of funds for investments in R&D. They tend to impact the earlier stages of the development process (Sloan & Hsieh 2006). This section considers examples of push incentives implemented at an institutional level to target structural changes (e.g. opening-up research and stimulating human resources) as well as more fiscal approaches targeting individual companies or developers (e.g. direct funding and tax relief mechanisms).

6.1.1 *Increasing access to research*

Recent years have seen a movement towards increasing access to research. For example, the computer software industry has demonstrated innovative and subsequent commercial success in using more collaborative models. Awareness of their success, combined with a growing recognition of the collaboration-limiting nature of the patent system, has led to a growing interest in the use of open-source models within biomedical sciences.

The open-source principle aims to increase access to research. The breadth of application varies from opening-up scientific databases and compound libraries through to the creation of comprehensive decentralized virtual communities where all potential contributors (from scientists to members of the public) can pursue challenges, review others' contributions, download computerized tools, publish their findings and consult others through on-line fora (Maurer et al 2004; Munos 2006). One fundamental characteristic of these ventures is the use of general or public-domain licensing as the mechanism to manage IP protection. Important examples include the:

- General Public License – requires any follow-on innovators to share any improvements they make;

- Creative Commons Attribution License – permits anyone to use the information for any purpose as long as correct attribution is given and licences (for developing world products) allow commercialization outside of this context;

- Creative Commons Licence – developer waives all rights to his/her work (Maurer et al. 2004).

Munos (2006) argues that similar processes have been positively contributing to medical innovations for a long time, citing the example of crucial idea sharing amongst physicians that establishes novel uses of existing drugs (off-label prescribing). The number of product development partnerships (PDPs) has increased in the past decade, initially inspired by the bioinformatics sector these include an open-source approach as one element of their virtual-pharma model. The Structural Genomics Consortium – SGC (Box 6.1), the Human Genome Project, the Single Nucleotide Polymorphism Consortium and Collaborative Drug Discovery (for TB research) are high-profile examples of such collaborations. More recently, many formalized web-based initiatives have been expanding and gathering momentum in:

- publishing, e.g. the Public Library of Science (PLoS), an open-access peer-reviewed library;

- clinical trials, e.g. WHO International Clinical Trials Registry Platform (ICTRP), European Clinical Trials Database (EudraCT);
- specific diseases, e.g. the cancer Biomedical Informatics Grid (caBIG);
- groups of diseases, e.g. Open Source Drug Discovery (OSDD) covers neglected diseases.

The newest facility is the Initiative for Open Innovation. This has a broader scope as it aims to create a "a comprehensive global cyberinfrastructure that is sector, discipline, jurisdiction and language agnostic" (Initiative for Open Innovation 2009). The intention is to provide a means to explore the boundaries of open innovation to create, test, validate and support new modes of collaborative problem solving made possible through the transparency of its system.

It is widely acknowledged that communication promotes the advancement of science. DeBresson and Amesse (1991) expand this by suggesting that the weak links that characterize open-source approaches lend themselves more to innovation while other more formalized networks tend to reinforce existing orthodoxies. This finding is corroborated by evidence that innovation spikes when diverse minds interact frequently in an unstructured manner (Hollingsworth & Hollingsworth 2000). It has also been argued that open-access approaches overcome some of the market distortions created by the patent system, such as the absence of natural collaboration amongst commonly driven stakeholders (e.g. different pharmaceutical companies, governments, academia etc), which results in less innovation overall (International Expert Group on Biotechnology, Innovation and Intellectual Property 2008). Other more tangible benefits of this approach include the reduction of duplicated research and the possibility for collaborative approaches to exist alongside more traditional competitive models (Munos 2006). It may also lead to rapid accumulation and application of knowledge and faster technology diffusion. For pharmaceuticals specifically, the advantages of this approach are likely to be greatest during the knowledge-based phase of development. This occurs early in the drug development life-cycle, i.e. identification of targets, understanding metabolic networks, designing clinical trials or computerized disease models (Munos 2006).

However, it has also been suggested that the application of open-source approaches is less successful in biomedical research. High costs, high failure rates, tighter regulation and more burdensome IP arrangements make the pharmaceutical industry quite different from the software industry (Munos 2006). The most challenging obstacle is likely to be the proprietary culture that currently exists in pharmaceuticals but even this can be overcome.

Examples from the United States

The Federal Research Public Access Act was introduced to the Senate in May 2006 by Senators John Cornyn and Joe Lieberman and reintroduced by the same sponsors in June 2009. The Act requires manuscripts of journal articles stemming from grants made by US government agencies to be openly available on the Internet within six months of publication.

Application to treatments for priority bacterial diseases

The expansion of open-source approaches to stimulate innovation for antibiotics holds promise. However, few of the requisite tools and knowledge are yet in the public domain. The impact of these approaches may be limited in the short term as they are compounded by a history of a strong proprietary nature in the field, further reinforced by recent high profits. However, the combination of the questioning of the patent system; development of knowledge-sharing technologies; and the changing development landscape more generally suggests that open-source approaches will provide important contributions to product development quite soon.

Application to SMEs

Given that SMEs face lower revenue thresholds and their limited size offers potentially greater gains from working collaboratively, it would appear that open-source approaches to drug discovery have much to offer them.

Box 6.1 *The Structural Genomics Consortium**

The SGC is a PDP funded by 11 public and private entities: Swedish Governmental Agency for Innovation Systems (VINNOVA), Swedish Foundation for Strategic Research, Knut and Alice Wallenberg Foundation, Canadian Institutes of Health Research, Canada Foundation for Innovation, Genome Canada, Ontario Genomics Institute, Ontario Ministry of Research and Innovation, Novartis, Merck, GSK. Total funding amounts to US$ 120 million, of which US$ 20 million comes from the pharmaceutical industry (International Expert Group on Biotechnology, Innovation and Intellectual Property 2008).

The SGC's goal is to determine the three-dimensional structures of proteins related to medicines and place them without restriction in the public domain. It investigates proteins selected by academic and participating industrial researchers and all investigation results are promptly made publicly available on free databases. No one has prior access or rights to data or progress information, not even the funding partners.

* For further details see SGC web site: http://www.sgc.utoronto.ca/sgc-webpages/sgc-toronto.php, accessed 24 May 2010.

6.1.2 Scientific personnel

Anecdotal evidence from interviews with independent scientists and pharmaceutical companies indicates a vital need for more scientific personnel with knowledge in infectious diseases. The lack of experienced scientists stems from a number of causes. At one time it was thought that science had conquered infectious diseases, the leaders of many pharmaceutical companies began their careers when this was a widespread belief (Croghan & Pittman 2004). The resulting long-term decline in R&D for infectious diseases led to an entire generation of researchers experienced in antibiotics being forced to switch research areas and resulted in a lack of personnel with the appropriate scientific experience (Sellers 2003).

In an attempt to counter some of this brain drain, fellowship programmes have been established in the EU and United States. High-profile examples include those offered under the EC's FP7, a people-specific programme that evolved from its predecessor – FP6. FP7 is dedicated entirely to human resources in research, with an overall budget of more than €4.7 billion over seven years (ending in 2013). This represents a 50% average annual increase over FP6. In 2006 nearly €9.478 million was distributed to health through Marie Curie Actions, developed from Marie Curie Fellowships to encompass all stages of a scientist's career path. Training and development receives significant contributions from professional societies such as the European Society of Clinical Microbiology and Infectious Diseases; European Society for Paediatric Infectious Diseases; and IDSA, which offers joint awards with the Education and Research Foundation and the National Foundation for Infectious Diseases. Private foundations also contribute, e.g. the United Kingdom's Medical Research Council (MRC) and the Wellcome Trust (WT) (see Box 6.2).

Postdoctoral fellowships and increased grant funding are two prominent means of attracting newer scientists, with proven success. However, new researchers may not have the depth of knowledge and experience in working with infectious diseases. Therefore, any strategy must aim to recruit both new and experienced researchers. Munoz (2006) proposes that open-source approaches potentially offer a flexible and therefore attractive way of re-engaging more experienced (possibly retired) scientists in coordinating, shepherding or facilitating roles.

6.1.3 Direct funding of research

There is a long history of national level funding of research, especially through public research institutions. For example, the United Kingdom channels its research expenditures through two main routes – the MRC and the National Institute for Health Research. The United States channels funding through

> **Box 6.2** *The Wellcome Trust*
>
> One of the world's largest medical research-oriented charitable foundations and the United Kingdom's largest donor, the WT spends approximately £600 million annually on biomedical research with diversified investment assets of £13.1 billion (Wellcome Trust 2008a). For many years the WT has been an ardent supporter of research addressing AR (see Box 6.6) at all stages of the product development cycle. It funds projects that both advance knowledge and use knowledge – the former through basic science (biomarker discovery, gene identification [Sanger Institute]) and scientific careers (PhDs, post doctorates, fellowships etc); the latter within drug discovery (project and programme funding) (Wellcome Trust 2009a).
>
> For 2008, the WT provided £525 million in funding (27% increase on 2007) in the form of 1131 grants (2999 applications) (Wellcome Trust 2008a). The current five-year strategic planning cycle (2005-2010) provides an annual commitment of £450 million (Wellcome Trust 2009a).* The majority of the WT's funding covers basic science; in 2008 approximately 5% was earmarked for technology transfer (see Box 6.6) (Wellcome Trust 2008a). Within the funding of basic science, the WT places a strong emphasis on supporting scientists and clinicians in the early stages of their careers – in 2008 it provided approximately £58 million in fellowships. There are commitments to increase the budget in order to implement a more systematic approach for monitoring progress and increase the number of international projects (Wellcome Trust 2009).[†]
>
> * Reviewed annually to reflect investment performance.
> [†] Currently approximately 90% of funding is for UK-based projects.

a number of agencies such as NIAID, NIH, Department of Health and Human Services (HHS), CDC and the Biomedical Advanced Research and Development Authority (BARDA). In many countries the not-for-profit sector also plays a pivotal role in directly funding or subsidizing research (see Box 6.2), in some cases as part of PDPs.

Examples from Europe

The FP7 programme runs from 2007 to 2013 and is the EU's main funding mechanism for research. Its focus is on increasing Europe's growth and competitiveness, with four main areas of funding:

1. cooperation – entails cooperative research between nations in 10 thematic areas (one of which is health);
2. ideas – focuses on riskier research and does not define specific research areas;

3. people – supports European researchers through training, career development and mobility; and

4. capacity – aims to improve research capacities within Europe.

FP7 has a €6 billion budget for cooperative health research, corresponding to an annual average of approximately €900 million. In relation to AR, FP7 included a call for research into major infectious diseases that pose a threat to public health. This theme included calls for global collaborative research into preventing AR; research on how specific antibiotic products influence resistance in humans; and research on diagnostic tests for identifying specific pathogens and antibiotic susceptibility to resistance.

One recently announced FP7 project (EMbaRC) is a collaboration between 10 research centres in seven countries with the aim of synchronizing how they preserve and identify samples. The project will also explore alternative approaches for identifying and classifying organisms. The EC has provided funding for three years (€4.2 million) but the consortium will explore ways of gaining private funding beyond this time (Community Research and Development Information Service 2009).

The Innovative Medicines Initiative (IMI), a PDP, is another example of the use of FP7 framework funding and is described in Box 6.3.

Box 6.3 *The Innovative Medicines Initiative (IMI)*

In 2007, the EC and the European Federation of Pharmaceutical Industries and Associations (EFPIA) launched IMI to explore new patient-centric approaches, methods and enabling technologies addressing key bottlenecks of drug development. IMI projects are designed as independent entities bringing together industry and academic experts specifically to tackle safety and efficacy bottlenecks in the drug development process. These precompetitive projects focus on improving the ability to predict the safety and efficacy profile of a development compound in patients. Better predictability would allow candidate compounds with lower probability of success to be discontinued earlier, thereby saving time and creating savings for companies and public funders. Resources could then be concentrated on the more promising compounds.

The IMI comprises a governing board that directs operations and oversees implementation of the Strategic Research Agenda developed jointly by industry and other stakeholders, e.g. academia. At the time of writing the board comprised ten members – five from the European Commission and five from EFPIA, representing the European Community and the research-based pharmaceutical industry in Europe, respectively.*

* Membership of the governing board can be found at: http://imi.europa.eu/news01_en.html, accessed 24 May 2010.

Box 6.3 *contd*

IMI funds precompetitive collaborative projects by way of a multistaged call process. With input from other stakeholders, the EFPIA participants select issues (re predictability of safety and efficacy) on which they would like to collaborate and provide the specific scientific project outline. The IMI administration publishes the selected calls intended for all potential partners from academia, SMEs and other non-EFPIA groups (including public authorities, patient groups, non-EFPIA companies). Interested groups together submit an expression of interest (EOI) to the IMI Joint Undertaking (IMI-JU) for selection by a scientific panel consisting of leading scientists from academia and industry. The original EFPIA participants and the selected group jointly develop the full project proposal for approval by the IMI administration. EU funding is allocated only to academic groups/ SMEs/ patient groups. Participating EFPIA companies match the level of EU funding through in-kind donation of resources (staff, laboratory facilities, materials, clinical research, etc.).

The initiative's budget for 2008–2013 is €2 billion – half from the 28 (current) EFPIA company participants, half from the EC's FP7.

Participation in IMI-funded projects is intended to appeal to SMEs by providing the opportunity to validate their know-how, product prototypes and offerings in collaboration with large pharmaceutical companies. It is argued that this collaboration will help to attract more venture capital. The initiative is also intended to appeal to academics by offering opportunities to work with large companies with better infrastructure capabilities; government; and patient groups. Also, this provides the opportunity to apply their ideas in basic research to a patient-centric drug development process. Finally, IMI is expected to provide large pharmaceutical companies with crucial tools for making the development process more efficient, and thus less costly, and for early involvement with government to harmonize standards for the development process.

It is argued that IMI's potential success derives from its focus on "precompetitive" technology which increases the chances for close collaboration and sharing of knowledge. Also, as an industry-driven initiative, it is expected that the IMI will receive full industry buy-in. However, the research location requirements will entirely preclude participation by EFPIA members with anti-infectives arms based in the United States. In addition, the industry lead may present drawbacks – chosen areas of work may be more likely to derive from pure financial interest rather than reflect the most pressing therapeutic needs.

On IP, IMI's stated mission is to ensure that the learning from projects is widely available on "fair and reasonable terms" (not open source) – initially to project participants and extended to the wider community at the end of a project. The first call process received

> approximately 150 applications; 15 full projects were accepted. At the time of writing the second call for full proposals was approaching closure. Crucially, this call included the topic of "identification and development of rapid point of care diagnostic tests for bacterial diagnosis to facilitate conduct of clinical trials and clinical practice with focus on respiratory tract infections (pneumonia, bronchitis etc.)" (Innovative Medicines Initiative 2009).

Examples from the United States

As part of the HHS, the NIH is the main agency responsible for conducting and supporting medical research in the United States. The main NIH body responsible for infectious diseases (NIAID) conducts and funds basic and applied research in infectious and other diseases. In 2007, NIAID invested US$ 800 million towards the support of basic and translational research in antimicrobials, US$ 200 million[33] of this was put towards resistance (Peters et al. 2008). NIAID-funded projects have included research on potential targets for new anti-infectives; development of efflux pump inhibitors; research on the structure and physiology of biofilms; and reduction of toxicity in antibiotics. For vaccines and rapid diagnostics, NIAID has also funded translational research to help researchers advance from basic research to an approved product. Another interesting development is NIAID's engagement in PDPs, for instance – helping to establish the Lilly Not-For-Profit Partnership for TB Early Phase Drug Discovery in 2007 and collaboration with the Medicines for Malaria Venture.

Funding was a problem until the passage of the 2009 American Recovery and Reinvestment Act which increased the NIH budget by 34% for two years (NIH Record 2009). Between 2004 and 2008, the NIH faced flat budgets, budget cuts or minor budget increases. As reported by some interviewees and the literature, only a fraction of NIH extramural grants receive funding, for instance – Dove (2007) reported that only 18% of NIH extramural grants received funding and the average age of first-time grant winners was over 40.

Concerning incentives for infectious disease R&D, NIAID and BARDA are the main agencies that provide basic research and funding for preclinical and clinical development of treatments. The NIAID is heavily involved in biodefence research, particularly in funding basic research and early stages of clinical development. Most recently it awarded a biotechnology company (Achaogen) funding of up to US$ 26.6 million over five years to develop countermeasures to Gram-negative bacteria such as *Yersinia pestis* (cause of bubonic plague) and *Francisella tularensis* (cause of tularaemia) (Kosikowski 2009).

---

[33] It should be noted that many experts believe this to be less than adequate given the dimensions of the resistance problem.

> **Box 6.4** *Project BioShield*
>
> In July 2004 the United States implemented the Project BioShield Act, giving the HHS authority to expedite research, develop and purchase priority countermeasures for chemical, biological, radiological and nuclear threats from terrorists (US Department of Health and Human Services 2007). In 2004 the government allocated US$ 5.6 billion in funding for a 10-year period (Trull et al. 2007). The HHS agencies involved in BioShield include the:
>
> - NIH, FDA and the Agency for Healthcare Research and Quality (AHRQ) – together manage all R&D-related issues; and
>
> - CDC and the Office of Emergency Preparedness – handle preparedness-related issues.
>
> In December 2006 the Pandemic and All-Hazards Preparedness Act (PAHPA) clarified which drugs, biologics and medical devices were considered national security priorities under Project BioShield (US Department of Health and Human Services 2007). The Act indicates that the BioShield programme can be used to stimulate research or acquire treatments for an infectious disease only if the countermeasure is also a national security countermeasure. PAHPA created the BARDA to facilitate R&D of countermeasures to security threats.

While NIAID helps fund early stage development, BARDA focuses on mid- to late-stage product development. Its portfolio includes projects on broad-spectrum antibiotics,[34] vaccines[35] and RDTs. In 2006 BARDA received a two-year US$ 1.07 billion budget to facilitate R&D of countermeasures; subsequent appropriations have been made on an annual basis (US Department of Health and Human Services 2007). BARDA offers milestone-based payments to companies it partners to take bioterrorism countermeasures further through the development process. If determined essential for the success of the contract, BARDA is authorized to pay up to 50% of the contract amount for milestone achievement. A separate clause from the original BioShield Act also allows BARDA to authorize an advance of up to 10% of the contract but the company must refund this if the product cannot be delivered to the national stockpile programme. The fact that BARDA is funded on an annual basis rather than longer term (as the procurement function of BioShield) creates difficulties for long-term planning. In particular, the US Congress's delay in passing the 2009 budget forced BARDA to operate under the previous year's budget, unable to initiate new projects until a new budget was passed.

---

34 BARDA is concerned with developing antibiotics that can be used to address a range of terrorist threats rather than a one bug one drug solution.

35 Intent is to stockpile vaccines for an emergency so BARDA is most interested in single-dose stable vaccines that do not need to be frozen. Has also encouraged companies to develop methods of administration that are easier in the event of an emergency, for instance nasal administration or patches.

General considerations for future application

Government efforts to fund large-scale R&D projects have a mixed record of success, failures include the Carter administration's synthetic fuel programme and the Clinch River Breeder Reactor (Glennerster & Kremer 2001). It is questionable whether a government is best suited to judging the viability of research programmes given the inevitable information asymmetry between the decision-maker and the researcher —research groups have the incentive to present their research in the most positive light; decision-makers to present funded projects in the best possible light to increase their available budget (Glennerster& Kremer 2001). However, these problems are inherent in other funding mechanisms (e.g. PDPs) and even, to some degree, within private companies.

One of the most significant pitfalls of government-funded research is the connection with politics. For instance, government funding is often set on an annual basis and is thus dependent on the individuals in power, the economic climate and other perpetually changing factors. Provision of longer-term funding (e.g. the nine-year period [2004–2013] apportioned in Project BioShield) is one means of creating more stability for government-funded research. Also, the connection between politics and government funding may result in politicians setting the research agenda – this may have little connection to areas of unmet need or more connection with issues affecting their constituents. However, many of the problems with government funding are more limited with smaller programmes. For antibiotics, targeted small-scale financing could be made available, e.g. for basic research into AR and potential targets (biomarker discovery), gene identification, platform technologies, clinical development and scientific careers (PhDs, postdoctoral research fellowships etc) as discussed in Section 6.1.2.

6.1.4 Translational research

Translational research involves cooperation between basic scientists from academia and clinical scientists in industry for the purpose of carrying research "from bench to bedside."[36] It involves close interaction between investigators of diverse backgrounds in the conception, preclinical testing and clinical evaluation of a diagnostic or therapeutic approach (Parks & Disis 2004). It requires the mastery of molecular biology, genetics and other basic sciences, as well as appropriately trained clinical scientists working in strong laboratories that are equipped with cutting-edge technology and have supportive infrastructure within the institution (Woolf 2008).

---

36 This definition should not be confused with other uses of the term. The other main definition refers to dissemination of new treatments and research knowledge in order that they reach the patients or populations for whom they are intended and are implemented correctly (Woolf 2008).

Translational research success stories include recombinant growth hormone, angioplasty and stenting for coronary artery disease (Martin & Kasper 2000). There are several reasons why translational research may be particularly attractive for antibiotic research. First, academic and public laboratories often provide the fundamental insight to find novel ways of attacking diseases (MacCoss & Baillie 2004) and may be best-suited for the necessary trial and error of target identification given their push funding base. Second, companies are generally best suited for onward development. Their participation can be crucial given that the main challenges in this type of work revolve around biological and technological mysteries, trial recruitment and regulatory concerns (Woolf 2008). For example, companies are generally better placed, with access to large compound libraries and screening facilities that allow high-throughput screening to identify chemicals that inhibit a given target. Despite the operational challenges posed by academic/industry collaboration, most experts agree that translational research approaches hold the key to overcoming AR.

Examples from Europe

In Europe, translational research forms a major part of the EC's budget for health-related research. With a budget of €6.1 million, FP7 (2007–2013) is placing much focus on the translation of basic discoveries into clinical applications, specifically in the areas of cancer and of cardiovascular, infectious, mental and neurological diseases, such as those linked with ageing (e.g. Alzheimer disease; Parkinson disease). The EU expects that these projects will result in the development of new drugs and treatments within a shorter time frame (European Commission 2009).

Examples from the United States

In the United States, the NIH has prioritized translational research by forming dedicated centres within its institutes and by launching the Clinical and Translational Science Award (CTSA) programme in 2006 (Woolf 2008). By 2007, 24 CTSA-funded academic centres had been established and other universities were transforming in order to compete for further CTSA grants (Woolf 2008). It is expected that the NIH will fund 60 translational research centres with an annual budget of US$ 500 million by 2012 (National Institutes of Health 2007). The programme announcements for the Small Business Innovation Research (SBIR) grants and Small Business Technology Transfer (STTR) grants offered through NIH are of particular interest to potential antibiotic developers.[37]

---

37 SBIRs require the principal investigator to be an employee of the company; STTRs require the principal investigator to be an academic in an academic research institute that subcontracts a portion of the work to the company (http://grants.nih.gov/grants/guide/pa-files/PA-10-051.html, accessed 26 April 2010).

6.1.5 *Tax incentives*

Tax incentives for R&D typically take three forms: (i) tax credits; (ii) tax allowances; and (iii) tax deferrals, of which the first is increasingly and overwhelmingly predominant. All tax incentives increase the NPV of prospective research projects (Organisation for Economic Co-operation and Development 2002) but they can be applied in different ways – usually to a developer's current (personnel and material) expenditures or to a company's capital (equipment and facilities) expenditures.

Tax credits and allowances are similar in that they apply to current expenditures, reduce the after tax cost of R&D and limit a company's annual claim. However, there are two important distinctions. First, credits are a specified deduction (percentage) against final tax liability whereas allowances enable companies to deduct more from their taxable income than they actually spend on R&D. Second, credits are independent of the corporate income tax rate. Frequently, tax credits and allowances are designed to include a deferral characteristic, greatly increasing their appeal to SMEs. Tax allowances and credits also have a temporal element —allowances can be used to offset future tax and credits can be carried forward to offset tax in future years. The level of tax credit and allowances varies between countries (allowances range from 13.5% in Belgium to 150% in the United Kingdom) but all allow companies to deduct up to this percentage of qualifying income expenditure on R&D activities when calculating their profit for tax purposes in the year they are incurred (Her Majesty's Revenue and Customs 2006).

For capital expenditures, some countries allow an immediate and full write-off against a business's taxable profits (Canada, Denmark, Ireland, Spain, United Kingdom). Other countries require taxable profits (or a proportion) to be depreciated over their economic life. In the United Kingdom, companies declare the cost of capital instead of depreciation (not taxable) in the commercial accounts (Her Majesty's Revenue and Customs 2009). Thus tax designs enable tax payments to be deferred and made more or less appealing to SMEs. However, it is also possible for tax incentives to be bought, sold or invested (Nathan & Goldberg 2005).

There is considerable variation within the designs of the three forms of tax incentive. Some may be more accurately classified as a pull incentive, for example tax credits for marketing expenses which function as an award for reaching the market. Some tax credits can be difficult to distinguish from direct funding or subsidies (see previous section), especially where SMEs receive a refund for the excess tax credit even when their tax bill is initially too small to benefit. This is the case for the Orphan Drug Act (ODA) 50% tax credit which functions effectively as a research subsidy for many SMEs. Tax credits can be directed not only at the specific gap of concern but also at basic research, assets or applied R&D. In particular, they can target companies that are likely to produce the greatest social return for the lost government tax revenue. They are often designed with small companies in mind and frequently target collaborative research such as PDPs (Organisation for Economic Co-operation and Development 2009). As the design is also dependent on the structure and national tax framework in which it applies, there is much variation and little comparison across and between OECD and EU countries (Organisation for Economic Co-operation and Development 2009). For example, Sweden and Finland demonstrate high private R&D expenditures in the absence of substantial direct and indirect funding. This is accounted for largely by structural considerations such as their focus on highly skilled, human capital-intense production; their business tax rates (28% and 29%, respectively) are amongst the lowest in the OECD area (Organisation for Economic Co-operation and Development 2009).

Examples from Europe

In 2008, the French Government undertook a major reform of its tax system to maintain and promote R&D and to make France an attractive country for innovation, thereby addressing the brain drain and absence of competitiveness (Swanick & Le Claire 2008). The French Finance Act 2008 includes a reduced rate of corporation tax arising from income resulting from IP. Basic and applied research activities are also eligible for preferential tax treatment:

- depreciation of assets dedicated to R&D projects (including patents acquired);
- costs of employees with the appropriate technical skills (including social charges) dedicated to R&D projects;
- operating expenses dedicated to R&D, assessed at 75% of the former amount;
- subcontracted research activities (even within the EU);
- certain type of expenses related to compliance with regulatory standards.

Examples from the United States

In addition to the ODA, in 2007 Senator Charles Schumer introduced S.2351 into the Senate and Representative Edolphus Towns introduced HR 4200 into the House of Representatives to create a 50% R&D tax credit for companies developing treatments for qualified infectious diseases. The tax credit was non-deferrable and therefore a company could not retain the tax credit until it became profitable. Eligible products would have included drugs and biologics, vaccines and diagnostic tests. The broad criteria for which products would qualify would have included areas like HIV/AIDS. However, the bill never came up for debate and thus was never passed.

General considerations for future application

In addition to the advantage of reducing the effective costs of R&D investments, tax incentives have the benefit that the industry remains in control of R&D while profits continue to be largely market-driven. This suggests that tax incentives result in fewer market distortions than more direct government funding and will incur fewer transaction costs. Frequently, concerns are raised regarding the efficiency of these incentives and the difficulty of linking changes in R&D activity to fiscal measures but it is now widely acknowledged that tax incentives can increase private expenditure to a level equal to, or just below, the lost tax revenue (negative price elasticity) (Organisation for Economic Co-operation and Development 2009; Yin 2008). Tax incentives have been particularly important for encouraging basic research in the context of neglected diseases and vaccines.

Tax incentives also face several criticisms. These particularly concern their effect on government expenditure and innovation as tax credits for R&D expenditure can increase government expenditures substantially. Between April 2000 and April 2006 around 22 000 claims for R&D tax credits (for all eligible sectors) in the United Kingdom cost the Treasury almost £1.8 billion (Her Majesty's Revenue and Customs 2006). One proposal to relieve this government expenditure is for developers to provide marginal cost pricing in return for substantial tax relief (Lybecker & Freeman 2007). For public purchasing of pharmaceuticals this would mitigate concerns that governments pay twice for elements of innovation. Another criticism is that despite large government expense tax incentives do not guarantee development of an innovative product. Governments could overcome this by providing tax credits for marketing expenses or combining push-based tax incentives with pull mechanisms (Tickell 2005; Yin 2008). In the context of antibiotics the latter are more favourable to governments as reductions in the costs of post-launch activities, such as sales and marketing, will run counter to resistance-control efforts. The additional costs incurred in preventing companies from employing creative accounting to maximize their claims (Kremer & Glennerster 2004) may negate the transaction cost savings. Additionally, tax incentives tend to be less transparent than more direct funding mechanisms and favour near-term rather than longer-term (more exploratory) projects and investments. Finally, EU competition laws and World Trade Organization protectionism rules need to be considered when designing tax incentives.

Application to antibiotics

If tax incentives are to be expanded to promote R&D for antibiotics they must target the earlier R&D phases as links to marketing or sales would counter conservation efforts. The French case presents some examples of how tax incentives could be designed and targeted to antibiotic development, for example, a tax incentive on platform technology patents or more tax relief for specialist anti-infective personnel.

Application to SMEs

Tax incentives generally favour companies with taxable profits and therefore lack appeal for smaller developers and startups. However, tax incentives are increasingly being designed specifically for SMEs and some provide more generous relief to SMEs than to larger companies (Organisation for Economic Co-operation and Development 2009). For example, in some cases the credit can be deferred to a later time and are particularly appealing if the deferral can hang over many years (e.g. 10 years in Canada). Tax incentives on capital expenditures have proven to become more appealing to SMEs, with both 100% write-downs and accelerated depreciation schemes increasing their appeal. Some argue that tax incentives aimed at SMEs are unlikely to have a significant effect on aggregate investment spending but may encourage innovative expenditures at the margin; others consider that these schemes have lower uptake among SMEs and that they are less likely than larger companies to take full advantage (Organisation for Economic Co-operation and Development 2009). However, SMEs might find this option more useful if the tax incentive could be sold on the open market (transferrable to developers with immediate tax liabilities). As yet there is no precedent for this type of transaction.

6.1.6 PDPs

PDPs are voluntary collaborations between state and non-state organizations to drive the development of drugs that ordinarily might not make it to market (Moran 2005; Moran et al. 2005; Widdus 2005).[38] Participants in PDPs can include the pharmaceutical or biotechnology industry, government, non-profit organizations, academia and other public organizations. Some debate surrounds the definition and parameters of these partnerships (Brown 2006) but it is beyond the scope of this report.

The classic PDP model is a partnership between a publicly funded organization and a private pharmaceutical company, with both contributing resources

---

38 PDPs that focus on improving access to medicines and that deal with global coordination and financing mechanisms are also prominent. Given the focus of this report on innovation, only PDPs that deal with the development of drugs and vaccines are considered.

(Moran et al. 2005). The private pharmaceutical company provides industry expertise and the public organization obtains the majority of funding for the project. Funding is provided principally via grants from philanthropic organizations, such as the Bill and Melinda Gates Foundation, the Rockefeller Foundation and the WT. Contributions from pharmaceutical companies have not been as significant as anticipated but there are notable exceptions – for instance, by 2007 the Global Fund had received US$ 150 million from the Bill and Melinda Gates Foundation and US$ 2 million from the industry (Buse & Harmer 2007). Government funding has also been less than expected. As of April 2005 governments were responsible for less than 20% of total funding for PDPs (Moran et al. 2005). Importantly, the majority of funding for PDPs comes from the Bill and Melinda Gates Foundation and there are concerns about the sustainability of many if this funding source were to end (Buse & Harmer 2007).

Depending on researchers' definitions, estimates of the number of existing PDPs range from 23 to 100 (Buse & Harmer 2007). One estimate of PDP activities suggests a total spending of at least US$ 500 million thus far (Herrling 2009). Within the health arena, PDPs' primary focus has been on neglected diseases (e.g. malaria, leishmaniasis) with efforts to produce vaccines, microbicides and diagnostics (Widdus 2005). The Malaria Vaccine Initiative and the International AIDS Vaccine Initiative are two prominent examples. Although most PDPs are less than 10 years old, this approach to stimulating innovation already has examples of success. Between 1975 and 1999, a number of pharmaceutical companies were exiting the field of neglected diseases and only 13 new drugs were being developed for neglected diseases during this period. As of September 2005, nearly three quarters of all neglected disease R&D (47 projects) were being conducted by PDPs working with small and multinational pharmaceutical companies (Moran et al. 2005).

Box 6.5 *Examples of promising drugs developed through PDPs*

Artemether. In 1989 Chinese researchers presented their results on artemisinin derivatives at the CHEMAL special meeting in Beijing (Special Programme for Research and Training in Tropical Diseases 2007). CHEMAL was the steering committee that funded research on malaria chemotherapy for the Special Programme for Research and Training in Tropical Diseases (TDR). As the artemisinin derivatives were not protected by patent, the product was not attractive to the pharmaceutical industry. CHEMAL therefore undertook initial R&D studies of artemether. The organization then entered into partnerships with the Kunming Pharmaceutical Factory and the pharmaceutical company Rhone-Poulenc Rorer (now Sanofi-aventis) to develop the injectable

> **Box 6.5** *contd*
>
> artemether for severe malaria. Arthemether obtained marketing authorization in France in 1996 and elsewhere thereafter.
>
> **Artemotil.** Injectable artemisinin derivative for the treatment of severe malaria (Special Programme for Research and Training in Tropical Diseases 2007). Developed by TDR in collaboration with a Dutch company (Artecef) and the Walter Reed Army Institute of Research. Received marketing authorization in 2000.
>
> **Miltefosine** (Impavido). Antiprotozoal drug originally tested for treatment of cutaneous-cancer patients. Research in the late 1980s indicated that the drug could be a potential treatment for leishmaniasis (black fever) (Croft & Engel 2006). TDR moved the molecule through the initial stages of testing and then formed a partnership with the Indian government and a German developer (Zentaris) to develop the drug. Miltefosine is currently available in a number of countries (Pham & Bartlett 2008) and is under investigation as a potential treatment for HIV infections (Dorlo et al. 2008).
>
> **Moxifloxacin** (Avalox or Avalex). Synthetic fluoroquinolone developed by Bayer. Prior to its approval for treatment of TB, moxifloxacin was available for treatment of other conditions such as upper respiratory infections and skin and skin-structure infections. In 2005 Bayer and the Global Alliance for TB Drug Development (GATB) entered into a partnership to test and develop the drug for treatment of TB (Smart 2005). Bayer donated moxifloxacin for use within the clinical trials and covered the cost of regulatory filings; GATB coordinated and funded the clinical trials with additional funding from the CDC, the FDA Orphan Products Development Center, the European and Developing Countries Clinical Trials Partnership and the British MRC. Avalox is currently awaiting regulatory approval for TB treatment.
>
> **Paromomycin.** Farmitalia donated the holding license of paromomycin to the WHO in the 1990s. Originally developed for oral use against gut pathogens, in this case the antibiotic was being tested as an injectable to treat visceral leishmaniasis (Croft 2005). Farmitalia believed the drug was unlikely to be profitable due to the high cost of clinical trials and the relative poverty of those affected by the disease. (Mandelbaum-Schmid 2004). WHO began running Phase I and II trials; the Institute for OneWorld Health (iOWH) completed the clinical trials. The drug achieved market authorization.

PDPs can be appealing to industry as they provide a direct reduction in the costs and risks of innovation. They exploit the comparative advantage of all participants and allow the developer to choose the timing and level of partnership with the public organizations. Specifically, the developer can focus on the less costly discovery phase of new chemical entities and partner with a PDP during the more expensive drug development and/or clinical trial stages (Moran 2005). The public sector then bears most of the risk, offsetting much of the developer's opportunity costs (Buse & Walt 2000). The developer must agree to take a reduction in eventual profits under this model. It has been suggested that, even if the financial and logistical challenges of development cause a developer to abandon further R&D for a product, a PDP may work with another company or organization to complete the process (Moran 2005). Paromomycin (see Boxes 6.5 and 6.7) is a successful example of one PDP taking over a product license from another and bringing the product through development.

Box 6.6 *Wellcome Trust: Technology Transfer division*

In 2008, the WT's Technology Transfer division spent a total of £44.7 million, £30.2 million of which was spent on grants provided through its three programmes: (i) seeding drug discovery (compound discovery and/or lead optimization); (ii) translational awards; and (iii) strategic translation awards (distinguishable by WT's much larger involvement). The Technology Transfer division comprises less than 5% of total WT funding (see Box 6.2). It covers all therapeutic areas in a variety of fields. The division's activities vary from shared risk endeavours (see Box 6.2) to its core activities which more closely resemble a PDP.

The division is a recent development but six (non-drug) products have been successfully launched since its inception in 2003 (Bianco 2009 [personal communication]). Additionally, antibiotic-related support for technology transfer has totalled £75 million for 39 projects (Bianco 2009 [personal communication]). Key examples of the WT's translational support for AR are detailed below.

- **Achaogen, Inc.** (Wellcome Trust 2009a). In May 2008, received £4.1 million award for three years to develop novel broad-spectrum aminoglycosides with superior efficacy and improved safety as therapies to treat MDR Gram-negative bacterial infections (e.g. *Enterobacteriaceae*) and MRSA. Company obtained US$ 27 million follow-on funding from NIAID.

- **Novacta Biosystems Limited** (Wellcome Trust 2005) In 2004, received £3.9 million award for two years to discover and develop a type B lantibiotic (lanthionine-containing antibiotics), including analogues of mersacidin and development of a new treatment for *C. difficile* infection.

- **Prolysis Limited*** (Wellcome Trust 2008b) In October 2006, awarded £3.5 million for less than 3 years. Research involved progressing a novel antibacterial chemical

* Acquired by Biota Holdings 12 November 2009.

> **Box 6.6** *contd*
>
> series that specifically inhibits Staphylococcal cell division through a chemical optimization programme, preclinical development and into Phase 1 clinical trials. Also received a LINK grant in applied genomics from the Biotechnology and Biological Sciences Research Council and the Department for Business, Innovation and Skills (formerly Department of Trade and Industry).
>
> - **GSK Infectious Diseases Center of Excellence for Drug Discovery (ID CEDD)** (Wellcome Trust 2007) In April 2007, awarded £4 million for three years to help support a new class of Gram-negative antibacterials to combat drug-resistant infections that commonly cause hospital-acquired pneumonia and septic shock. This is GSK's eighth centre of excellence and will act as an independent business entity. WT stepped in when an in-licensing drive resulted in a greater number of projects than GSK was able to support and that were not seen as sufficiently lucrative for the level of resource required. WT will receive a financial consideration for any commercial product resulting from the collaboration with GSK. However, since the initial grant, follow-on funding and procurements have been secured:
>
>   – *September 2007*: Defense Threat Reduction Agency provide US$ 41 million for five years to develop antibacterial compounds for Gram-negative biothreat agents (GlaxoSmithKline 2007).
>
>   – *June 2008*: Mpex Pharmaceuticals provided GSK with access to their novel efflux pump inhibitors, shown preclinically to overcome efflux-based resistance to multiple classes of antibiotics in both in-vitro and in-vivo studies. GSK will pay Mpex US$ 8.5 million upfront, US$ 6.5 million in equity financing and US$ 200–250 million for each product candidate. Additionally, Mpex will receive tiered royalties, dependent on sales achieved (GlaxoSmithKline 2008).

One key lesson learnt from existing PDPs is that functioning management is essential for multiple partners as each has its own agenda, strengths and weaknesses. Buse and Harmer (2007) indicate that the quality of management can differ vastly between PDPs but most could improve their practices in certain key areas.[39] These include their governance structures (particularly laying out partners' roles and responsibilities; performance monitoring; overseeing corporate partner selection; managing conflicts of interest) and provision of transparent decision-making processes (Buse & Harmer 2007). Also, failure to prioritize performance monitoring produces little accountability not only in the respective partners but also in the PDP itself. Transparency is also thought to be an issue amongst many of the PDPs, especially concerning their choice of research areas.

---

[39] This report does not discuss all of the lessons in Buse & Harmer (2007) as their paper covers all PDPs, not just those related to R&D.

The literature and interviewees raise a common theme – the problematic procedures governing partner selection. In a review of 18 partnerships, Buse (2003) found that only 4 practised any screening of partners. The rationale seemed to be that the very act of corporate participation was a sufficient predictor of good corporate behaviour. Moreover, a number of stakeholders have expressed concern about the process for vetting developers' applications for involvement in a PDP. In particular, the pharmaceutical applicant knows far more about the product's likelihood of success and may be prone to over-emphasize its potential. Different partners offer different expertise, inputs, levels of funding and levels of competence, requiring long and costly due diligence to determine which is the safest partner. This has been proposed as a significant barrier to collaboration (Moran et al. 2005).

Box 6.7 *Institute of OneWorld Health (iOWH)*

With a staff of approximately 30 experienced pharmaceutical scientists, the iOWH aims to challenge the assumption that pharmaceutical R&D is too expensive to create new medicines exclusively for the developing world. Focused on four therapeutic areas of great unmet medical need, it follows a largely standard PDP model combining open-source approaches in the early stages with outsourcing in the latter stages (Munos 2006). However, iOWH maintains a flexible approach in order to adapt to the specific requirements of the therapeutic area and demands of the partners.

The iOWH's work on visceral leishmaniasis and malaria involves existing compounds – the former has resulted in a new formulation and its first drug approval; the latter has resulted in an innovative manufacturing strategy. For visceral leishmaniasis, the iOWH signed a collective licensing agreement with TDR to develop an injectable formulation after it was unable to find a sponsor for a large-scale trial. Now included on the WHO Essential Medicines List, paramyosin IV was given orphan drug status by the FDA in 2005 and is currently manufactured in India and made available at cost. The iOWH work on malaria treatment has resulted in a new low-cost technology platform to assist with artemisinin scale-up and supply issues. The innovative enabling knowledge was licensed royalty-free from academia to a biotechnology company that optimized the strain, purified and developed the scalable process. Sanofi-aventis eventually became involved to assist with the industrial manufacturing process, each stage coordinated and facilitated by iOWH.

The iOWH has also been successful in gaining access to Roche's compound libraries for diarrhoeal diseases. A biotechnology company has now been recruited to perform high-throughput screening of more than 780 000 molecules to select up to 40 new antisecretor drug leads which will undergo preclinical studies at the International Centre for Diarrhoeal Disease Research, Bangladesh. Also, a grant from the Bill and Melinda

> **Box 6.7** contd
>
> Gates Foundation is funding an exploration of drug candidates against soil-transmitted helminth infections. To date, two products are in the early phases of development – one post-screening, the other nearing the end of preclinical studies.

Larger, or umbrella, PDPs have the ability simultaneously to adopt numerous projects dealing with the same health condition. Generally, pharmaceutical companies do not concentrate resources on single indications in order to avoid creating competing products. However, it has been suggested that diminished concern for profit allows greater focus on single indications, thereby reaping economies of scale concerning knowledge and ideas across projects (Croft 2005). The MMV provides a successful example from the neglected disease arena, building up a portfolio of 10 preclinical and clinical and 11 discovery stage projects within the first 5 years (Croft 2005). It also succeeded in taking novel synthetic peroxides from basic research to clinical trials in only four years.

Application to treatments for priority bacterial diseases

For antibiotics, PDPs offer clear benefit in their potential for reducing AR – the relegation of profit weakens marketing pressures and in turn can allow health systems to restrict the prescribing of products more easily. However, they also face the key challenge of negotiating an acceptable return for the private sector partner. As has been seen with PDPs for neglected diseases, it can be difficult to attain the necessary balance between improving public health and allowing developers to maximize profit (Aiello et al. 2006; Buse & Walt 2000). Partnership arrangements for drugs developed for both developing and developed country markets are particularly difficult to negotiate (Pecoul 2009 [personal communication]), especially for IP protection and pricing (Tickell 2005). One proposed solution is to separate the various stages of antibiotic development and licensing (Tickell 2005). Specifically, a not-for-profit foundation could be created for development stages up through Phase II trials and products could then be licensed to commercial companies for completion and sale in the industrialized market. Sales in the developing world would remain on a not-for-profit basis, as in the Coartem case mentioned below.

Application to SMEs

PDPs are likely to appeal to SMEs because early stage funding can be accessed. Also, SMEs that have scientific expertise but lack the necessary regulatory and marketing expertise can benefit from the contributions of a partner within the PDP at these stages of development. Thus, PDPs can provide SMEs with the necessary funding, technical support and help with market entry (Moran 2005; Moran et al. 2005).

6.2 Pull incentives

Pull incentives lure R&D investments in a desired direction by offering financial reward upon completion of technological advances. They gained favour in the 1950s and 1960s with proponents arguing that demand not only drives the rate and direction of innovation but also crucially directs companies in rectifying inefficiencies (Nemet 2009). This section explores prizes in several forms, AMCs and patent buyouts.

6.2.1 *Monetary prizes*

Prize systems featured strongly throughout the 19th and 20th centuries as the predominant mechanism to stimulate innovative solutions to society's challenges, especially in the aeronautical and space industries. As early as 1802 the British Parliament awarded Edward Jenner a prize[40] of £10 000 and (five years later) a further £20 000 for the discovery and development of the first vaccine – against smallpox (Barquet & Domingo 1997). The 1990s saw renewed interest in using prizes as a mechanism to stimulate innovation in the life sciences. During a World Business Council for Sustainable Development meeting in 2001, a global discussion was initiated regarding possible new business models for drug development (Love 2007). This was the premise of the Medical Innovation Prize Fund Act (HR 417), a United States congressional bill introduced by Representative Bernard Sanders (Love & Hubbard 2007) in 2005. This bill proposed country-wide implementation of direct rewards for developers, based on a drug's incremental therapeutic benefit to consumers, through a Medical Innovation Prize Fund comprising 0.5% of the United States GDP. At the same time the WHO was being lobbied to consider proposals for a new global Medical Research and Development Treaty (Dentico & Ford 2005), including the suggestion to develop a global fund (as a way of funding a prize system) in which every country should share the costs of drug development. To date, no large fund has been created to support a prize proposal on the scale of these discussions but a number of prizes have been announced in recent years. These include the 1994 Rockefeller Foundation prize for sexually transmitted disease diagnostics; the 1996 Critical Assessment of Techniques for Protein Structure Prediction prize; and the 2006 X PRIZE Foundation prizes for genomics (the latter is also offering a prize for a TB diagnostic – see Box 6.8). These larger prize schemes complement the smaller (<US$ 1 million)

---
40 It can be argued that this reward was not a prize – it was offered ex post as a token of Parliament's appreciation for Jenner's work.

> **Box 6.8** *Example of a prize for a diagnostic test, X PRIZE Foundation*
>
> X PRIZE is a financial award given to the first team to achieve a specific goal set by the foundation.* In 2008, the X PRIZE Foundation received a planning grant from the Bill and Melinda Gates Foundation to apply the prize concept to the development of an effective point-of-care TB diagnostic targeted for use in the developing world.
>
> Whilst still in the design phase, provisional features of the prize include those detailed below.
>
> - Prize fund of US$ 20–30 million will be accumulated from philanthropic donors. No formal metric was used to determine this value, although the literature was consulted and interviews performed to establish approximate development costs. These were then risk adjusted.
>
> - Prize will be awarded within a time frame of five to seven years.
>
> - Prize fund will likely be split amongst multiple winners determined by ranking teams according to their final performance against weighted predetermined criteria, at the discretion of an independent panel of stakeholders representing a range of expertise including clinicians, patients, public health administrators, entrepreneurs and scientists. Additional (bonus) prizes are also under consideration for achievement of other specifications such as applicability in HIV patients and in drug susceptibility testing.
>
> - Any IP arising from the prize will remain with the winner as, at the time of writing, no specific licensing terms were likely to be specified.
>
> - Incorporates requirement for "enforced" collaboration, an additional and interesting design feature that separates it from previous prizes. Introduced partly in acknowledgement that an individualistic, non-competitive approach is unlikely to succeed, partly to help teams overcome potential practical barriers (regulatory hurdles, access to specimen banks, manufacturing expertise, etc). Foundation will provide expert advice to guide teams through the process and will pay for certain important development elements (laboratory evaluations, clinical studies) in return for participation at a number of summits aimed at information-sharing and fostering collaboration.
>
> Assuming that the necessary sponsorship can be secured, the remaining major challenges are likely to be determining a product specification that balances what is achievable with what is sufficiently useful (innovative); and developer certainty (in terms of fixing the prize fund, product specification, competition terms) with necessary flexibility – a downfall of the 1994 Rockefeller Foundation Prize for an STD diagnostic (Krohmal 2007). These will ensure that the prize is targeted effectively and adopted successfully by the market.
>
> * The 2004 Ansari X PRIZE was granted for development in commercial lunar travel.

prizes offered by InnoCentive, a web-based registry for scientific innovation prizes founded by Eli Lilly in 2001. Eighty prizes have been awarded to date.

Monetary prizes may or may not allow a manufacturer to retain its patent and can take a number of different forms – elective systems such as the optional reward scheme, milestone monetary prizes and best entry tournaments, amongst others. Each of these incentives is discussed below.

Monetary prize – winner foregoes patent

As an alternative to exclusive patent rights, governments could reward innovation with large monetary prizes linked to the impact of the innovation[41] (Hollis 2005). This would be a compulsory scheme in which successful companies would agree to forego patent rights to their products.[42] The rationale behind monetary prizes that require the award-winning developer to forego patent rights lies in the potential to reduce the deadweight welfare losses associated with monopoly pricing (Davis 2004) that arise from the patent system. Love and Hubbard (2007) estimate that consumers must spend US$ 8–9 in order to stimulate US$ 1 of R&D; whilst the private sector's contribution to R&D was less than 9% (around US$ 51 billion) of global pharmaceutical sales in 2005.

In addition to reducing deadweight welfare losses associated with the patent system, several additional advantages arise from using monetary prizes to decouple reward and innovation. Prizes may be particularly useful in areas that provide a social benefit but are not financially attractive for companies (Love & Hubbard 2007) and because they reward researchers who have produced successful products (i.e. prizes do not subsidize unsuccessful research). Prizes allow the donor to determine the value of the research incentive without granting companies monopoly power over pricing (Shavell & van Ypersele 2001).

Prize systems pose challenges in timing; how to reward follow-on innovators; and potential duplication of efforts. The Sanders bill addresses this issue by suggesting that prize payments for a new product reflect the incremental value of the improvements and the degree to which the new product has built on or benefited from the innovation of the original product – the original innovator continues to receive payments even if their market share falls to zero (Love & Hubbard 2007). The timing of payoffs is another challenge as it is difficult to calculate the long-term benefits of a newly introduced drug. Some suggest staggering prize payouts over time in order to counter this uncertainty (Love & Hubbard 2007).

---

[41] For instance, there have been proposals for awards to be made according to the improvement in quality-adjusted life years (QALYs).
[42] Another possibility is a voluntary scheme that allows the winning company to choose between a monetary prize and a patent. This is discussed below as the optional reward system.

> **Box 6.9** *Ex-ante award calculation*
>
> Incentives in which the magnitude of rewards is estimated ex ante (e.g. monetary prizes, AMCs) pose significant challenges due to the difficulty of determining the size of reward necessary to attract investment without overpaying. In choosing the appropriate level of reward, the donor effectively chooses the social value of the innovation and thus replaces the market. The deadweight welfare loss under a patent system can only be mitigated fully if the value is calculated optimally but this is difficult when it may only become apparent ex post (Davis 2004). One argument asserts that a monetary prize must be larger than a subsidy, as competing companies still bear the risk of failure under this incentive (Laxminarayan et al. 2007). Assuming that the monetary prize would apply only to treatments for priority bacterial diseases, the reward would still need to compete with drugs that have higher NPVs. In this case the outlay for the reward would be larger than the outlay required for a system such as funding for basic and some clinical research. Kremer (1998) has argued that the value should be the private value multiplied by a fixed mark-up set at roughly the difference between the social and the private value of the invention. Other mechanisms have been proposed for determining social value in the absence of the market mechanism. These include Kremer's (1998) auction system to determine the private value and Hopenhayn's mandatory buyout approach (Hopenhayn et al. 2006). The latter recognizes the value of incremental or follow-on innovation through a system in which the innovator pays a prearranged buyout amount to the owner of the prior state-of-the-art innovation.
>
> Hubbard, Love and Hollis propose that a fund's value is fixed to enable budget predictability (Love & Hubbard 2007). Most proposals also suggest that the judging of the winner and distribution of the prize funds should be proportional to the relative innovation or benefits. However, the metric (usually QALYs) for assessing this also presents some challenges in practice. Also, a fixed prize will cause extensive pressure to ensure that the method for valuing the inventions is fair and efficient. It has been suggested that a prize of US$ 3 billion should be awarded to the first effective treatment for a high-priority pathogen (Outterson 2008) but the discussion has not been taken further.

The pull mechanism inherent in prizes may offer a number of important advantages for antibiotic R&D but of course this is dependent on appropriate calculation of any prize (see Box 6.9 for discussion). Also, separation of sales from the recouping of R&D costs helps to preclude overmarketing and subsequent overconsumption of the final product.

Generally, existing large pharmaceutical companies do not include plans to forego patent rights within their business models but smaller companies may be more likely to adopt this less orthodox approach. However, monetary prizes will be attractive to SMEs only if they already benefit from early stage funding in the form of venture capital or other forms of push funding. Certain business models will make prizes more attractive to some SMEs than to others. For example, those pursuing a strategy to bring one product to market (rather than develop a further portfolio of drugs) will be particularly interested. Given the lower revenue requirements of smaller companies, it should also be noted that smaller awards could be used.

Monetary prize – winner keeps patent

In practice it can be difficult to create a fund sufficient to purchase patent rights from a manufacturer, particularly for governments faced with annual budgets. Another form of monetary prize offers a smaller reward to the first company to market but allows the company to retain patent rights. To combat resistance, the prize could require the company to comply with marketing restrictions, as suggested by IDSA and Outterson (Outterson, 2008 p. 190).

Again, this design has the advantage of being able to advance innovation if the prize amount is calculated appropriately. The main disadvantage is that consumers not only subsidize the monetary prize[43] but also are forced to pay monopoly prices for the drug (often through state purchase) unless lower prices are negotiated as an explicit precondition.

Optional reward system

Shavell and van Ypersele (2001) suggest an optional reward system in which a developer is free to choose between a monetary reward and a patent. This would give the developer more time to assess the value of the product within a more up-to-date economic and competitive environment and to choose the reward accordingly. Thus, the optional reward system reduces the amount of risk faced by the developer by passing it to the funder.

Abramowicz (2003) suggests that a developer who believes the government is offering more than the true value of the product will choose prizes over patents. It could also be argued that a developer may be willing to take a lower payout under the optional reward system if the utility associated with the certainty of payout is perceived to outweigh the utility associated with a higher but more uncertain payout. Furthermore, due to asymmetry of information, the developer may know that a new drug will have a shorter than expected length of effectiveness and therefore the government reward will be more attractive. This is particularly relevant to the uncertainty surrounding the growth of AR and presents a major drawback for the optional rewards proposal. Patents and

---

[43] A system could be devised whereby a company that receives a monetary prize reimburses the government for some or all assistance received in researching and developing the product. However, the prize would likely need to be even larger as there are already insufficient incentives for companies to develop antibiotics despite government funding of basic research.

prizes do not occur in isolation therefore Davis (2004) suggests the need for further research to determine how the two interact.

Milestone prizes

This incentive scheme rewards researchers for reaching certain milestones within the product development process, for instance – rewards for completing Phase I and Phase II trials. This provides similar advantages to other pull mechanisms except it represents a lower risk to developers as they can earn rewards incrementally. Smaller companies may be more attracted to this scheme as they receive earlier reimbursement of development costs, helping to cover inputs and potentially making it easier to attract venture capitalists to fund later stages of development.

Milestone prizes have the disadvantage that the funding body rewards both successful and unsuccessful research. For example, a product that completes Phase I and receives an award for reaching that milestone may fail during Phase II trials. However, as a significant proportion of molecules fail during Phase I, this particular weakness can be eliminated by setting the first milestone for successful Phase I trials. Also, a large milestone payment after Phase II would help SMEs to find the additional funds to conduct Phase III trials, the most expensive stage of clinical trials.

Best-entry tournament

Related to monetary prizes, in a best-entry research tournament a sponsor provides a reward to the developer who has made the most progress in research by a specified date (Kremer & Glennerster 2004). This system has been used to select architects for construction projects but has not yet been applied to drug development. This model relies on a pull mechanism and single reward to promote competition but may attract risk-averse developers as it does not specify the required development stage to be achieved. Of course, the ability to create competition will depend largely on the number of developers with promising molecules in sight as well as the level of collusion amongst them.

The main advantage of this incentive design lies in its ability to attract developers who believe they have a chance of winning – those with existing molecules that have been set aside. Whilst these molecules may be useful for developing follow-on products it may be that they are less likely to develop into promising novel products, this needs to be investigated further. A major disadvantage of this proposal is that donors commit to paying the reward even if overall progress is not significant and the product never makes it to market.

6.2.2 AMCs

In an AMC[44] a third party or parties (donors), typically a government or international agency, agrees to subsidize the purchase of a pharmaceutical product at a pre-agreed price and volume (Kremer et al. 2005; Nathan & Goldberg 2005; Outterson et al. 2007). Among a number of variations, the two most common AMCs are the winner-take-all and the multiple-winner approaches.

Largely based on the model proposed by Kremer, the AMC concept was endorsed initially by the British Government in 2004 as a means of promoting R&D for a malaria vaccine. The G8 added its support in 2005 (Berndt et al. 2005a) but the proposal did not become a reality until 2007 when five countries (Canada, Italy, Norway, the Russian Federation, United Kingdom) and the Bill & Melinda Gates Foundation pledged US$ 1.5 billion to GAVI to fund an AMC for vaccines to target pneumococcal pneumonia (Braine 2008). This AMC is currently a pilot programme, aiming to stimulate late stage development and manufacturing of suitable vaccines at affordable prices. A price of US$ 3.50 has been committed for low-income countries (it is available for over US$ 70 per dose in industrialized countries). GAVI will spend US$ 1.3 billion through 2015, implementing countries will also provide a small co-payment (GAVI Alliance 2009). A number of nongovernmental organizations (NGOs) (von Schoen-Angerer 2008; Oxfam International 2008) have criticized this specific model as a poor use of donor funds. This is not only because of the existence of developed world demand (a natural market to spur investment) but also because two candidate vaccines were already nearing regulatory approval when the AMC was announced in 2005. Rather than stimulate development of a vaccine that would not have been developed this AMC served more as a procurement contract to encourage companies to meet demand in poor countries at subsidized prices (Oxfam International 2008). In terms of additional pharmaceutical profits, the costs associated with this have been estimated at around US$ 600 million (von Schoen-Angerer 2008).

AMCs – winner-take-all approach

By specifying the volume (number of doses) to be purchased and their price, an AMC has the key advantage of reducing a developer's risk and potentially increasing the size of the market. Consistent with most pull mechanisms, AMCs reward successful outputs with predetermined characteristics rather than inputs into research that may not succeed (Webber & Kremer 2001). In this way AMCs explicitly link payment to (initial) product quality (Barder 2005). Additionally, the developer is free to pursue whichever R&D approach

---

[44] Also known as an advance purchase commitment (APC).

or mechanism appears to maximize the chance of success. Finally, it has been suggested that AMCs combine the incentives of patents and monetary prizes but eliminate the price distortions associated with patents because the profit-maximizing developer does not set the final price (Glennerster & Kremer 2001; Kremer 1998).

Clauses and provisions within the contract prevent an AMC from remaining unfilled indefinitely by allowing the sponsor to exit if the product is not delivered within a specified time (sunset clause) or if changes to the disease environment negate the need for the product (*force majeure* clause). Ultimate authority lies with the independent regulatory body in order to prevent abuse by either the third party payer or the pharmaceutical company (Barder 2005). Proposals now make AMCs legally enforceable by contract law thereby providing the credibility necessary to influence investment behaviour (Barder 2005) and to remove any uncertainty over commitment, for all parties (especially developers). In addition to the price guarantee, co-payment and volume commitments are legal commitments, binding from the outset and overseen by an independent body, such as an adjudication committee (Barder 2005).

Despite these systems, there are still concerns regarding the public funder's ability to fulfil its commitments. This is especially a concern in the developing world where infrastructural weaknesses impact ability to procure and deliver in practice. In all contexts the political cycle causes further uncertainty as it is rarely longer (<5 years) than the proposed duration of the commitment (10–15 years). Reneging by some countries on commitments to purchase flu vaccines in recent years will likely exacerbate these concerns. These issues of credibility have prompted calls for private foundations to act as sponsors (Barder 2005) and for further mechanisms to provide assurance, such as combining future purchase commitments with enhanced purchases of existing and frequently underused products (Webber & Kremer 2001). The latter has been demonstrated successfully by GAVI in cooperation with the Bill and Melinda Gates Foundation.[45]

As yet there is no solution to the free-rider issue that arises when other markets benefit from products developed under an AMC but this may be mitigated by the higher prices paid by parties outside of the contract or contracted parties. It is possible that a global fund, such as that proposed to counter free-riding of the products of prize funds (Dentico & Ford 2005), could be applied to AMCs. For parties within the contract, the most common proposal has been a two-tiered pricing structure (Barder 2005) that enables more rapid recovery

---

[45] GAVI's strategy for new and underused vaccines reached an estimated additional 213 million children between 2000 and 2008, primarily with vaccines for hepatitis B, *Haemophilus influenzae B* (Hib) and yellow fever. Support took the form of five-year grants with the expectation that countries would increase their national contribution, leading to eventual financial sustainability. This immunization programme is widely perceived as a successful model for effective purchase of vaccines (Webber & Kremer 2001).

of their investment and with greater certainty. A high (guaranteed) price is paid for the first treatments and combined with an additional commitment to supply further treatments at a lower (base) price close to the marginal cost of production. Barder states that this transfers a proportion of the risk from the companies to the sponsors, since the NPV of revenues to the company is much more stable than it would be under a single price charged over a longer period. However, Barder (2005) does acknowledge that it will not be easy to persuade purchasers (funders in developing countries) to make a finite commitment to pay the risk-adjusted costs of R&D and acknowledge that this is a cost-effective use of scarce resources.

Support for AMCs has recently emerged amongst key stakeholders within governments and the pharmaceutical industry. Concerns over political feasibility have abated since the British government and the G8 advocated in their favour. Further exploration into the practicalities of implementation has also helped garner support for their use. For example, an analysis of requirements for implementing the malaria AMC concluded that no additional legislative approval was deemed necessary before entering a legally binding commitment (Barder 2005). The simplicity of AMCs has garnered strong political support (at the time of writing) and several countries have committed funds but no new product has yet been produced through an AMC and thus no country has actually distributed payments for product development. For example, the Department for International Development in the United Kingdom has indicated that any AMC expenditure would not be recorded in the national accounts until the government is actually buying vaccines. In addition to government support for AMCs, industry is supporting their use. This is assumed to be due to their voluntary nature and the prospect of industry retaining control over IP (Light 2009). Notwithstanding the growing support of government and industry and the administrative feasibility it is, as yet, unclear whether this will be eroded by public resistance to the prospect of large amounts of public finance being directed to what is seen as a highly lucrative industry.

There is some question that the competition created by AMCs will stifle, rather than foster, collaboration; duplicate funding; and crowd-out other incentives (Light 2009). Their current use in conjunction with other initiatives (e.g. push incentives also supporting development of malaria and pneumoccocal vaccines) will inform this debate and determine if AMCs may serve as a complementary tool. As with other pull mechanisms, there are difficulties in determining the appropriate contract terms and level of reward that brings the right product to market, providing sufficient developer incentives without overpaying. The executive committee faces the challenge to accurately determine the appropriate contract terms and price and volume commitment ex ante – before knowing the costs of production, advances in science and regulatory changes. Even manufacturers find this difficult and thus it is challenging to assess whether an AMC is worthwhile.

An AMC may be considered a variation of a monetary prize (although more complex) because the product must receive approval from the regulatory agency before the purchase agreement can be fulfilled. This means that AMCs do not entirely eliminate the developer's risk because only successful products are rewarded (Berndt & Hurvitz 2005; Berndt et al. 2007). One alternative is the multiple-winner approach discussed earlier but, due to the impossibility of anticipating all contingencies and writing them into the product specification, Barder (2005) suggests that contracts should not specify a minimum threshold quantity. If a superior product becomes available and also qualifies for the price guarantee, recipient countries should be able to choose the products they want to use. This more closely mimics an actual market and ensures subsequent developers are rewarded, proportional to the product value determined by the market. However, it also removes some of the market certainty that draws developers. Application of an AMC in a developed market may enable better demand forecasting, which can alleviate some of this problem. Pricing structure and the terms that dictate how a developer may exploit monopoly protection will also impact developer reward and hence risk.

Application to treatments for priority bacterial diseases
Like monetary prizes, an AMC is a one-time payment that does not provide an ongoing stimulus for R&D and therefore does not address the continual need for novel products to combat resistance. This could be combated by putting out calls for research to receive AMCs every few years but this is an expensive proposition. Also, the potentially high cost of an AMC would require the reward to be conditional on developing truly novel products. In the case of multiple winners, the products would also have to display distinct properties (namely MoA). Another relevant question for antibiotics and AMCs concerns the determination of the purchase volume given changes in the epidemiological environment. One option would be for a government to commit to purchasing a specified amount – any surplus would simply be stockpiled (see Box 6.10).

Application to SMEs
Existing AMCs seem to have targeted predominantly large pharmaceutical companies (Finkelstein 2004). It has been suggested that the modelling undertaken thus far has largely assumed price levels for blockbuster rather than relatively successful products (Light 2009). They have also not included design features that would increase their appeal for SMEs, e.g. milestone payments (Light 2009). Despite the targeting of large companies, numerous academics (Barder 2005; Finkelstein 2004; Moran et al. 2005) and these large companies

> **Box 6.10** *Stockpiling*
>
> Historically, antibiotic stockpiling at both the national and the supranational level has been minimal, managed at the level of each facility and largely uncoordinated at high institutional levels (i.e. regional, national, supranational). However, these trends are set to change in response to the recent bioterror and pandemic threats (Tegnell et al. 2002). In Europe this will likely take place within the programme of cooperation on preparedness and response to biological and chemical agent attacks (BICHAT).
>
> A product's acceptance for a national or European stockpile presents a potentially lucrative opportunity for developers. However, in order to qualify it is likely that antibiotics will have to be formulated for simple consumption to ensure that they can be disseminated widely to the public in an emergency. Indeed, anecdotal evidence from the United States suggests that antibiotics in their originally marketed parenteral formulations are generally not considered for stockpiling. This may have substantial cost implications for developers and must be taken into account in calculating incentive rewards aimed at producing products for stockpiling.

have suggested that AMCs may be most relevant "in areas where most needs can be met through adaptive research [incremental innovation]" (International Federation of Pharmaceutical Manufacturers and Associations 2005). This runs counter to the Center for Global Development's (CGD) assertion that AMCs will serve as a "long, deep pull back to basic research" that might lead to the development of truly novel products (Barder 2005).

Again, without some form of venture capital or early stage push funding, smaller companies are unlikely to be able to benefit from AMCs. Designs to attract smaller companies would need to shift forward some of the reward in order to meet their need for early stage funding.

AMCs – multiple-winner approach

The multiple-winner approach arose as an attempt to mitigate developer risk arising from the winner-take-all approach, in which subsequent developers face the risk of receiving no reward or return on their investment. This design could also mitigate purchaser unease that a winner-take-all design would oblige them to reward only the first developer, even if subsequent drugs were superior. Other advantages of opening the guaranteed market to multiple products would be to stimulate greater competition and, potentially, downward price pressure. Additionally, this could contribute to a wider distribution by increasing the continuity of supply (Berndt et al. 2007).

Under the multiple-winner approach, more than one company can receive a proportion of the AMC. Some authors suggest that the first several products meeting the specification through independent means, even if not necessarily superior, would be eligible for the price guarantee. This would be conditional on an improvement on existing products – for example for certain target populations or conditions (Berndt et al. 2007). Variations would be to reward all those achieving the minimum specification or on the basis of clinical superiority, the latter has been discussed in the context of prize funds (see Section 6.2.1).

This approach has several inherent disadvantages. Both the smaller overall reward and the increased risk (if payouts are not predetermined for each developer) would diminish the strength of the incentive and possible lead to the development and purchase of cross-resistant drugs. Additionally, manufacturers that feel under-rewarded could discontinue R&D. Multiple winners also adds administrative complexity and is likely to dilute the reputation gains that may add appeal for developers.

6.2.3 *Patent buyout*

A patent buyout takes place when a fund is used to purchase the IP of a new product and secure it in the public domain. Buyouts can be used as components of prize mechanisms or AMCs or as simple product purchases by a public body. By compensating the developer for the cost of R&D (including opportunity cost) in a one-off payment, buyouts help maintain control over eventual product prices and thereby can improve patient access (for example through segmentation of markets by income). Also, as the patent no longer belongs to the developer, the new patent owner (i.e. the public body) may license others to improve upon the existing product for commercial purposes during the patent life. However, the possibilities for follow-on innovation will be limited if such licences are not granted. As with other pull mechanisms, the main disadvantage of buyouts relates to the calculation of the optimal buyout price.

Kesselheim and Outterson (2010) suggest that the patent buyout model would be particularly interesting if the antibiotic were to be first-in-class (not conferring cross-resistance at the time of the buyout). Given that effective alternatives may initially limit demand for the newly developed product they argue that society could be better off if some drugs were procured and held for future needs in what they call a strategic antibiotic reserve (analogous to a strategic petroleum reserve).

6.3 Lego-regulatory incentives

Lego-regulatory mechanisms are intended to lure drug development using enlarged rewards. Those considered here are similar to pull incentives although they use the market itself to determine reward size. Some of these incentives lure development by extending early effective patent life by lowering the regulatory bar to achieve approval earlier. Indeed, given the risky nature of the drug discovery and development process and the significant expense involved, one option to stimulate R&D is to improve the regulatory process for developers willing to take on the challenge. A number of stakeholders in the antibiotic field argue that regulatory processes are prohibitive and need streamlining to foster innovation (Finch & Hunter 2006). Changes could involve accelerating the development process by adopting less onerous requirements, speeding market authorization and reduced liability measures. Other lego-regulatory mechanisms lure development through higher drug prices achieved by way of late patent-term extensions or pricing and reimbursement policy reforms. This section will explore some of these proposals.

6.3.1 *Clinical trials*

Clinical trial requirements

Most clinical trials for antibiotics involve the comparison of the test drug against an active control, generally another antibiotic that the regulatory agency has approved for that indication. Noninferiority trials have been undertaken in most cases but these have several inherent weaknesses – no internal demonstration of assay sensitivity; no single conservative analysis approach; lack of protection from bias by blinding; and difficulty in specifying the noninferiority margin (Snapinn 2000). The latter is a margin represented by a delta value and used to determine whether there is a clinically acceptable difference between the test drug and the active control (Murphy & Albrecht 2001). The size of the delta has created much controversy within the pharmaceutical arena and led to numerous changes in regulation over time.

Under a sliding-scale approach, the acceptable delta value is contingent upon the anticipated number of patients that could be evaluated for that condition and the expected cure rates (Power 2006). In the past, requirements for most antibiotics included a delta value of 15%. The FDA's major concern with the sliding-scale approach was a fear of bio-creep – slightly inferior products could be approved sequentially over time given that drugs with lower efficacy rates could use wider deltas. This could result in approved products that were merely equivalent to a placebo (Murphy & Albrecht 2001). However, stricter approval requirements had the unintentional effect of substantially increasing costs for pharmaceutical companies. In particular, decreasing the delta from 15% to 10% obliged pharmaceutical companies to more than double the number of patients enrolled in clinical trials. Consequently, the new statistical parameters doubled the costs of running clinical trials, inflated the overall expense of developing a new antibiotic and thus eliminated incentives to invest in R&D (Power 2006; Shlaes & Moellering 2002).

Under the FDA and EMA statistical guidelines it has been estimated that the NPV for a novel Gram-positive antibacterial would reduce from 100 to 35 (Power 2006). This change in the delta value is credited with causing Bristol-Myers Squibb and Eli Lilly to withdraw from antibiotic research programmes and with delaying the development of tigecycline (Power 2006). Faced with this industry response, the FDA dropped the across the board 10% delta requirement and moved to a case-based approach in which the indication, projected efficacy and comparators are taken into account (Power 2006). The EMA (2004) *Note for guidance* states that the choice of delta should be carefully considered for each individual trial and requires applicants to justify their choice, taking account of the anticipated efficacy of the reference treatment in the indication under study. However, EMA states that in many instances the delta is likely to be 10%.

Superiority trials are undertaken to show that a new drug is indeed better than those on the market or, at the very least, better than a placebo. They do not share the weaknesses of the noninferiority trials (Snapinn 2000) and normally require fewer patients, which can lower costs. Yet superiority trials may be more difficult to conduct and can only be undertaken for mild to moderate (generally self-resolving) infections when they involve the use of a placebo arm.[46] There is significant debate about their acceptability, particularly the ethics of not providing treatment for the control group (Spellberg et al. 2008b; Tillotson & Echols 2008).[47] For antibiotics specifically, some argue that superiority trials do not take account of the fact that an antibiotic that currently fails to demonstrate superiority to the standard therapy may become an effective therapy when resistance develops to the standard antibiotic (Projan 2003). Consequently, superiority trials for antibiotics may not factor in the importance of projected efficacy. Despite the debate, the FDA has started calling for clinical trials with superiority design for certain indications, specifically acute bacterial sinusitis, otitis media and the exacerbation of chronic bronchitis (Spellberg 2008b). Recently it has also issued guidance on community-acquired pneumonia (CAP) and on the appropriateness of superiority trials. The main impetus for this regulatory shift appears to be concern over whether the antibiotic is better than placebo (no treatment) for mild infections,[48] particularly given the possibility that treating mild infections with antibiotics may accelerate resistance. EMA still requires noninferiority trials with a licensed control for the approval of

---

46 An active arm is used in trials for severe infection.
47 It is important to note that the debate does not centre around the use of superiority trials for mild infections but rather around the need for superiority trials for some strains of infections like CAP.
48 Some patients may improve spontaneously, regardless of whether or not they have taken an antibiotic.

new antibiotics. However, for infections like otitis media and other mild to moderate (generally self-resolving) infections the current guidance prescribes a superiority trial (against placebo) as "desirable". Following a recent report by the EMA/CHMP[49] (Committee for Medicinal Products for Human Use) a reconsideration of the strict adherence to noninferiority trials with a defined delta for evidence of efficacy is recommended. The issue is currently under consideration.

It is argued that the drug approval process has been further complicated as the FDA accepts fewer adverse side effects from antibiotics than from other classes of therapeutic agent (Chopra et al. 2008). Rubin (2004) explains that the increase in required Phase III testing followed the withdrawal of the antibiotic Raxar and the restrictions placed on Trovan in 1999, despite the fact that they were less dangerous than the average new drug. Rubin (2004) considers that the FDA's additional testing for antibiotics is not economically rational with respect to improving patient welfare, suggesting that a more cost-effective alternative would be to approve the drug in the normal manner and allocate additional resources for Phase IV analysis.

Pharmaceutical companies may hesitate to initiate new clinical trials for antibiotics because the guidelines in this therapeutic area remain unclear. The IDSA responded to such uncertainty by pushing heavily for clinical trial guidance from the FDA, with recommendations to: "accelerate the publication of updated guidelines for antibiotic clinical trials to provide needed clarity, and revisit existing guidelines as appropriate to ensure their relevance" (Infectious Diseases Society of America 2004). The FDA has now published clinical trial guidelines (Spellberg et al. 2008a) but clinical trial guidance for antibiotics has not been issued since autumn 2006. The FDA has held a number of workshops and issued guidance on conditions including bacterial sinusitis, acute bacterial otitis and CAP but, at the time of writing, the industry is reporting significant frustration with the clarity, consistency and timing of guidance. Without a very clear picture of regulatory requirements ahead of and during trials (often lasting beyond 10 years), it is unlikely that developers will be compelled to engage.

The lag in publishing guidance for indications is likely due to insufficient resources devoted to the area. In the case of the FDA it has been exacerbated by the severe lack of personnel in recent years (following controversy over the safety of an accepted drug). The EMA and FDA may require greater funding and more staff to expand guidance sufficiently.

---

[49] Report can be found at: http://www.emea.europa.eu/pdfs/human/itf/12731807en.pdf, accessed 26 April 2010.

Tools for proving safety and efficacy

The traditional tools used to assess product safety and efficacy (e.g. animal models, in vitro screening) have not changed in many years and are known to be imperfect predictors of responses in humans. Scientists are therefore looking for better methods for predicting the effect of drugs. Pharmacometric analyses refers to the increasingly sophisticated ability to model an agent's pharmacokinetic (PK) or pharmacodynamic (PD) properties and their effect on disease progression (Bhattaram et al. 2005). Provisional trial data are inputted into a model to determine optimal dosing based on risk-benefit assessment and then extrapolated to assess the safety and efficacy findings for the wider patient population. This in silico or computer-based technology is argued to have revolutionized the product development process in, for example, the automotive and aeronautical industries that are now developed and tested largely using computer-based systems (WHO Commission on Intellectual Property Rights 2006).

So far, discussion around pharmacometrics' expanding role in regulatory applications has largely focused around situations or circumstances in which demonstration of safety and efficacy within populations can be problematic, those concerning: (i) special populations, e.g. children; (ii) rare pathogens or those with reduced susceptibility; (iii) specific types of infection. A recent FDA study (Bhattaram 2005) looking at approvals over a four-year period across three therapeutic areas indicated that phamacometric data were used when reviewing a new drug application (NDA) in 17% of cases (42 out of 244). These data were retrospectively deemed pivotal in 54% of cases and supportive in 46%. Of the 14 reviews that were pivotal to approval-related decisions, 5 identified the need for additional trials and 6 reduced the burden of conducting additional trials.

The FDA notes that some commentators believe the extensive use of such technologies could reduce drug development costs by 50% and generally favours the concept of model-based drug development, using pharmacostatistical methods (WHO Commission on Intellectual Property Rights 2006). One American trial quantified potential savings as "3 years of drug development time and 1 clinical trial" (Bhattaram 2005), when seeking early regulatory support. It was also suggested that "the time and money needed to perform the pharmacometric analysis is negligible compared with the costs of unsuccessful trials" (Bhattaram 2005). In Europe this prospective estimation of safety and efficacy has recently gained wider acknowledgement from regulatory agencies given a mounting body of supporting evidence (European Agency for the Evaluation of Medicinal Products 2000). The EMA maintains a broad stance that PK/PD analysis is recommended where appropriate and acknowledges its role in potentially reducing the number of Phase I/II studies necessary. However, it currently issues no definitive guidance on when PK/PD approaches may be used to supplant formal clinical investigation, proceeding on a case-by-case basis and currently does not support their use in significantly reducing the scope and content of Phase III programmes (European Agency for the Evaluation of Medicinal Products 2000). However, revised guidelines were being developed at the time of writing.

Application to treatments for priority bacterial diseases

On the surface, clinical trials for antibiotics appear to be less complex than for other conditions as most patients with bacterial infections typically recover within a few days or weeks of receiving treatment, thereby providing clear therapeutic endpoints. Research on animal models is also generally easier for antibiotics as the animals can easily be infected with the pathogens for study. Nonetheless, it is not clear whether clinical trials for antibiotics cost more or less than clinical trials for other conditions. Some suggest that the total cost of these trials is US$ 500–800 million (Norrby et al. 2005), similar to the US$ 400–800 million (DiMasi et al. 2003) DiMasi estimate for drugs generally. Other literature suggests that the cost of clinical trials is particularly high for hospital-based infections, at around US$ 50 000 per patient (Sellers 2003). Phase III costs alone have been estimated to run to US$ 500 million (Sellers 2003) and for antibiotics can be 60% higher than the average of all drug classes (Rubin 2004).

Whilst the exact cost is unknown, one certainty is that if developers seek indications of severe infection then trials must include a significant number of subjects with resistant pathogens. In comparison with products in many other clinical areas, one broad-spectrum antibiotic can target multiple diseases, e.g. *S. aureus*, pneumonia, skin and soft tissue infection, etc. (Infectious Diseases Society of America 2004). Multi-indication trials were permitted in the past but now pharmaceutical companies must run clinical trials for each indication for which they intend to market their product. This significantly increases the cost and difficulty of these trials as patient recruitment occurs prior to the nature of the pathogen being revealed and it is impossible to predict when resistance will occur. This problem is further compounded by the difficulty in identifying the pathogen quickly due to a lack of advanced point-of-care diagnostics as well as the requirement that clinical trials be performed on antibiotic-naive patients (Rice 2006). In the IDSA report (Infectious Diseases Society of America 2004), the authors illustrate the patient recruitment problem by describing one company's difficulty in trying to develop an antibiotic to treat VRE. Using patient entry criteria developed in conjunction with the FDA, the company was able to enrol only three patients over two years of the study. During a second study, the company was able to enrol only 45 patients over 18 months, despite the fact that annually there are at least 26 000 hospital-acquired cases of VRE in the United States (Infectious Diseases Society of America 2004).

Some experts contend that the characteristics of bacteria and antibiotics particularly lend themselves to PK/PD modelling. For example the ease with which pathogens can be isolated and the relative ease with which potency, potential doses and schedules (most likely to slow the development of resistance) can be determined potentially facilitate a greater dependence on these tools relative to other therapeutic areas (Drusano 2004). However, others believe that their use in helping to understand antibacterial activity is not sufficient to predict patient response to treatment (European Agency for the Evaluation of Medicinal Products 2000). Overall, current evidence appears to lean towards the suggestion that the quantity and robustness of data provided by these models are currently insufficient to support expansion of their application, especially in replacing human trials. However, the determination of appropriateness is far beyond the scope of this report. The inclusion of these models in this report should simply be taken as a reflection of the extensive amount of interest in this area. Serious investigation of these tools within the context of lightening the regulatory burden is currently taking place elsewhere.

6.3.2 *IP mechanisms*

IP protects products from competition for a given period in order for developers to recoup high R&D costs and make a profit if prices/reimbursement are sufficiently high. This section explores incentives that use altered IP protection arrangements to promote the development of antibiotics.

Patent pools

A patent pool is a coordinating mechanism that enables the collective acquisition and management of IP for use by third parties for a fee. Patent holders from the public or private sector may contribute patents to the pool. Subsequently, a developer wanting to use the patent to develop a new product can seek a licence from the pool against the payment of royalties to produce the medicines. This reduces the transaction costs and barriers to market entry resulting from IP protection. The pool design, specifically the geographical area of licence coverage, will determine the level of competition. The wider the area, the larger the demand and the more producers may be expected to compete. This would drive down prices. Conversely, as the patent holders retain the right to license the patents outside of the patent pool – the smaller the pool, the lower the demand. This results in fewer competitors and beneficiaries to the scheme.

Historically, there is experience with patent pools in the fields of agriculture, electronics and information technology. Within health-care they have largely been discussed when IP barriers are the cause of access or scale-up problems, e.g. for responses to the SARS outbreak in the developed world; newer HIV medicines in the developing world. For the latter, in July 2008 UNITAID[50] began to use a tax on airline tickets to fund a pool aiming to scale-up access to newer antiretroviral medicines for HIV treatment in developing countries and to encourage the development of adapted formulations (UNITAID 2009). Initiated by James Love and completed by UNITAID, a cost-benefit analysis of the pool estimated that (for developing countries) only a 1% impact on generic competition would be required for it to pay for itself. This excluded other benefits such as increased competition, development of better manufacturing processes or new fixed dose combinations (Love 2008). A broader proposal for an Essential Medical Inventions Licensing Agency is still under review.

In March 2009, GSK announced the launch of a patent pool to address neglected tropical diseases (NTDs)[51] (GlaxoSmithKline 2009b). While in its infancy and not currently including other institutions or organizations, GSK has made available the IP of approximately 80 patent families. The company has declared the patents that it is actively pursuing and is accepting applications for licences in areas and indications that are not being pursued. If an application is successful, GSK has committed to providing licences for the development of medicines for the treatment of NTDs in low-income countries on favourable terms, albeit with geographical and therapeutic area restrictions.[52] It has also indicated willingness to consider, on a case-by-case basis, licensing pooled IP for use outside low-income countries under two arrangements: (i) third party allowed to sell into a low-income country on a royalty basis; or (ii) GSK licensed (via one-off fee or royalties) to sell the products directly to developed countries (GlaxoSmithKline 2009a).[53]

In 2005, WHO convened a panel to examine the feasibility of a patent pool to ensure rapid access to vaccines or medicines in case of a SARS outbreak. Initial support – including that of the relevant patent holders – seemed favourable and the patents are currently under review by two American law firms. However, it remains unclear whether this proposal will come to fruition.

Within patent pools, efficiency gains are made through the collective management structure that centralizes, simplifies and streamlines the administrative, legal and bureaucratic processes of obtaining and managing licences from a multitude of patent holders. This is true for both simple and,

---
50 For further details on this organization see: http://www.unitaid.eu/, accessed 24 May 2010.
51 Sixteen diseases that WHO classifies as NTDs.
52 Details of these restrictions were unavailable at the time of writing.
53 Alnylam is the first company to add its patents to the patent filings GSK provided to populate the pool (GlaxoSmithKline 2009a).

especially, blocking patents (patents frequently belonging to a patent cluster or thicket). The use of patent clustering as an anticompetitive tool was highlighted by the EU's recent competition enquiry into the pharmaceutical industry. The possibility of a one-stop-shop rather than multiple individual agreements reduces costs and market entry barriers to potential new developers or manufacturers ('t Hoen 2009). Further cost-savings may be achieved through the reduction of litigation costs for patent infringements. Also, perhaps more importantly, pools increase access to IP as developers and manufacturers no longer need to wait out the patent term. This can allow faster downstream innovation, technology transfer and scale-up as and when necessary ('t Hoen 2009).

Application to treatments for priority bacterial diseases

Patent pools have largely been discussed in the context of ensuring rapid access to existing technology and enabling incremental progress through follow-on technology rather than their ability to stimulate brand new innovation. In the antibiotic market, where follow-on generations of products are unlikely to provide a long-term solution to the problem of resistance, it can be argued that such an arrangement may not bring the necessary innovation to produce truly novel products. The applicability of a patent pool for antibiotics may also be limited if royalties are not perceived to be sufficient compensation for relinquishing IP rights, especially if the patented technology has any chance of contributing to the development of a novel product.

Application to SMEs

Theoretically, any developer could benefit from patent pool arrangements if they are well-placed to carry forward subsequent development of a product. Generally, however, smaller companies stand to gain more from such arrangements as the traditionally costs associated with obtaining access to existing IP are reduced. However, this does not negate the obvious advantage of larger companies – they have the capital necessary to explore many molecules through extensive trial and error exercises.

Extended IP protection

The argument behind extended IP protection is the fact that obtaining market authorization usually involves a long process that reduces the effective life of a patent. Proponents suggest that a company may not obtain sufficient profits from selling its product during the effective patent life to justify the costs of R&D, particularly in the case of products with high R&D costs and/or lower revenue potential. Extended IP protection is thus argued to be a necessary requirement to increase revenues to a level sufficient to assure the recouping of R&D costs and acceptable levels of profit.

Examples from Europe

Within Europe drugs can qualify for increased IP protection under three programmes: (i) supplementary protection certificates (SPCs); (ii) paediatric drug legislation; and (iii) orphan drug legislation (see Section 6.4.1).

Regulation regarding SPCs came into existence across the EU in 1993[54] (de Pastors 1995). An SPC allows the manufacturer to gain additional protection for time lost in regulatory reviews. As a separate right from the patent it comes into effect only once the patent expires and provides protection for a specific active ingredient that has received marketing authorization. In the case of numerous patents on a product, patent holders must select one basic patent and file an application in each Member State issuing the patent and from which an SPC is sought (French 2005). The duration of protection is calculated from the time between patent filing and market authorization. This figure is then reduced by five years and subject to a maximum of five years; total market exclusivity usually cannot exceed 15 years.[55] No more than one SPC may be granted per patent holder but two different patent holders may receive SPCs for the same product as long as applications are filed before the first SPC is granted. More than one SPC can be granted on a basic patent if the products have a different active ingredient and separate marketing authorization. SPC protection extends to the particular use of the product that was the subject of the marketing authorization as well as to any other use of the product authorized before the expiry of the basic patent, even if authorizations were secured by third parties (French 2005).

The further protection provided by SPCs has been found to significantly increase sales revenues from high-selling drugs. For example, French (2005) points out that 80% of Prozac sales in Europe over the last 10 years of effective patent protection were achieved in the five years covered by the SPC. In 2007 the EU enacted paediatric drug legislation requiring companies applying for marketing approval of a new drug to produce a paediatric investigation plan (PIP). This includes information on the timing and proposed means of testing the quality, safety and efficacy of the product in a paediatric population (Kölch et al. 2007). Some components of a PIP can be deferrable and manufacturers can obtain exemptions in certain situations. However, there are incentives to comply – the SPC for newly approved products can be extended by six months if the company files a PIP; orphan drugs potentially gain an additional two years. Drugs exclusively for paediatric use or (all-age) paediatric formulations launched before the legislation came into effect can also receive the Paediatric Use Marketing Authorisation (PUMA) which grants up to 10 years of data exclusivity. These drugs must not already have patent protection or be covered by an SPC.

---
54 Regulation did not come into force until 1994 in Austria, Finland, Norway and Sweden.
55 Can be extended to a maximum of 15.5 years for products demonstrating the paediatric provisions.

Examples from the United States
In line with some of the programmes for extended IP protection available in Europe, antibiotics can qualify for increased IP protection under four programmes: (i) Hatch-Waxman Act; (ii) FDA Administration Modernization Act; (iii) QI Program Supplemental Funding Act; and (iv) the ODA.

The 1984 Drug Price Competition and Patent Term Restoration Act, commonly known as the Hatch-Waxman Act, specified that certain drugs could qualify for patent term extensions equal to half the time spent in clinical testing plus all the time spent in the marketing application process (Congressional Budget Office 1998). The extension may not exceed five years and patent protection cannot exceed 14 years after approval of the product. Importantly, as the Hatch-Waxman Act explicitly excluded antibiotics from extended IP protection, the 1997 FDA Modernization Act (FDAMA) extended the patent extension provisions to antibiotic products not submitted in an application prior to 1997. Most recently, the United States Congress enacted the QI Program Supplemental Funding Act in 2008, providing three years of market exclusivity for the approval of a new indication for an already approved older antibacterial drug and five years of market exclusivity for the approval of a previously unapproved older antibacterial drug (Boucher et al. 2009).

Enacted as part of the 1997 FDAMA, the Pediatric Exclusivity Provision[56] grants six months of additional market exclusivity to manufacturers that successfully perform studies in children as specified by the FDA (Li et al. 2007). A number of antibiotic products have benefited from this exclusivity provision, including ciprofloxacin and ertapenem.

General considerations for future application
Extended IP protection allows companies to charge higher prices for drugs over a longer period (where there is free pricing) and restrict generic competition. Health systems and/or patients pay higher prices, diverting resources from other priorities and posing potential barriers to access. Generic companies also lose as they must forego profits that could be made by entering the market at the time of the normally scheduled patent expiry. Not surprisingly, under orphan drug legislation (see Section 6.4.1 for more detail), many drugs for rare and neglected disorders have been very lucrative. For instance, five of the top ten best-selling biotechnology drugs worldwide in 2001 were originally approved as orphan drugs (Maeder 2003) and the first generation of AIDS treatment was a profitable orphan drug (Rohde 2000).

However, it is also suggested that extended IP protection is an inefficient mechanism for stimulating R&D. Outterson et al. (2007) calculate that

---
56 Provision applies to drug and biological products approved under Section 505 with patent life remaining on listed patents or for which exclusivity remains under the Drug Price Competition and Patent Term Restoration Act (Pub. L. 98-417) or the ODA (Pub. L. 97-414).

approximately 17.5% of revenue from extended IP protection would be funnelled back into R&D, yielding approximately US$ 910 million in additional R&D globally per year. A significantly larger proportion of the returns from extended IP protection, approximately US$ 4.29 billion per year, would be spent on other corporate expenses and profits. Moreover, even if a binding commitment compelled firms benefiting from this scheme to channel the profits into R&D for infectious diseases, it is suggested that this would lead to the production of only one new antibiotic drug per year (Outterson et al. 2007). Currently, no such commitment exists within orphan drug and paediatric legislation in either the EU or the United States.

Application to treatments for priority bacterial diseases
Much of the discussion on extending IP protection for antibiotics surrounds their ability to inhibit the emergence of resistance. This is explored in some detail in Boxes 6.11 and 6.12. It is unclear whether the social loss associated with monopoly pricing is outweighed by the gains from reduced consumption. Additionally, some argue that the social cost of extended IP protection fails to counter the benefits that new antibiotics create through treating MDR bacteria (Spellberg 2008a). Kades (2005) also claims that the benefit of a longer useful life outweighs the cost. However, Outterson et al. (2007) argue that extended protection could postpone the development of new drugs, thereby accelerating the resistance problem, as a developer has no incentive to develop a follow-on drug until the patent is nearing expiration.[57]

Application to SMEs
Extended IP protection is certainly attractive to developers who can afford to support basic and clinical research but this is unlikely to apply to many SMEs. Again, without some early funding SMEs are unlikely to gain much benefit from purely pull mechanisms such as extensions to IP protection.

Extensions of data exclusivity

Data exclusivity was introduced in Europe in 1987 to compensate for insufficient product patent protection in some countries (European Generic Medicines Association 2007). During this time generic competitors are prevented from applying for market authorization based on the clinical evidence of the originator product. It is an expression of trade secrets (undisclosed information) and hence distinct from the patent system.[58]

As part of the new EU pharmaceutical legislation aimed at harmonizing processes across Member States, data exclusivity was extended in 2004.

---

57 As discussed above, later generation antibiotics offer a number of advantages (Power 2006).
58 Market exclusivity determines when a generic equivalent can be placed on the market; patents determine when a regulatory agency can begin to review applications from generic competitors. Both are calculated from the point at which the initiator product was authorized. The difference usually extends market exclusivity 1-3 years beyond the data exclusivity period whilst registration and marketing occurs.

Fig. 6.1 *8+2(+1) arrangements in the EU*

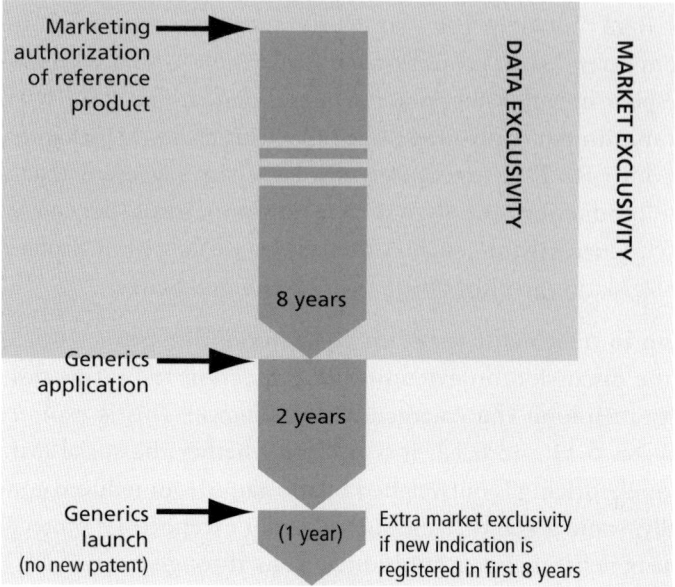

Source: Adapted from European Generic Medicines Association 2007.

The 8+2(+1) model was adopted (see Fig. 6.1) for application to all new chemical entities. The new model allows for eight years of data exclusivity from the date of initial authorization in the Community, plus two years of market exclusivity and an additional year (+1) for a new indication (European Generic Medicines Association 2007). However, the 8+2(+1) model applies only to new applications for originators filed after 2005. Many products remain on the market subject to the previous data protection rules which allow Member States the choice between six and ten years. Since 1997, the equivalent period in the United States is five years for a new chemical entity (NCE) application or three years of data exclusivity for a non-NCE.

Theoretically the market incentive of data exclusivity is less restrictive than patents as it does not legally restrict other competitors from generating their own registration data. In reality, the time and expense that generic companies expend generating pharmaceutical registration data and compiling submission dossiers means that data exclusivity provisions act as a significant market barrier. For most drugs, the period of data exclusivity appears shorter than the market exclusivity offered under patent protection. However, this may not always be the case, e.g. if the development period of a drug is particularly long; if drugs do not benefit from full patent protection; or for biosimilars (generic versions of biological products). An IMS Health (2001) report suggests that "very few high-selling drugs gain further marketing monopoly from data exclusivity

Box 6.11 *Using IP mechanisms to inhibit development of resistance*

Many argue that the main benefit of extended IP protection is a potential reduction in AR (Horowitz & Moehring 2004). Extended IP protection is criticized for restricting generic competition but this may actually be a benefit against antibacterial resistance.* Specifically, generic competition lowers prices, which can accelerate consumption and resistance. It is argued that, by stretching out the duration of IP protection, the government is essentially delaying the growth in resistance that may occur when IP protection is exhausted.

Conversely, it is argued that the extension of IP protection would increase the growth rate of resistance by deterring the production of follow-on products and inhibiting (postponing investment) innovation (Outterson et al. 2007). Outterson et al. also argue that longer patent periods are financially inefficient given that so little of the increased revenue will be used to fund further antibiotic R&D.

The current patent system could be contributing to the growth of resistance. It is argued that resistance might accelerate a few years before the exhaustion of IP protection as companies have an incentive to maximize sales before the arrival of generic competition, otherwise known as patent holder waste (Laxminarayan et al. 2007; Outterson et al. 2007). The authors cite Linezolid as an example of patent holder waste – the manufacturer was issued with an FDA warning letter for overzealous marketing of the antibiotic. Spellberg (2008b) suggests that patent holder waste is not an issue by arguing that pharmaceutical companies typically front-load the marketing of a drug soon after market authorization. Additional literature also refutes the patent holder waste theory as brand advertising has been found to start declining two years before patent expiry (Caves et al. 1991).

Tragedy of the commons may emerge if several patents within the same antibiotic class are held by different companies (Horowitz & Moehring 2004; Outterson et al. (2007).

Individual companies cannot control the antibiotic sales of their competitors and therefore all companies aggressively market their own drug and accelerate the development of resistance. With a small number of patent holders of cross-resistant drugs, companies could privately coordinate to regulate total sales (similar to the Organization of the Petroleum Exporting Countries. However, this would require changes to current collusion and anticompetition laws that bar companies from coordinating in this manner (Outterson 2005). Proposed solutions include broad patents for drugs with resistance-related characteristics groups (Outterson 2005), sometimes called functional resistance groups (FRGs) (Laxminarayan 2002) (see Box 6.12).

* Evidence of this assertion is lacking and there is a clear need for research on the relationship between generic competition and antimicrobial resistance.

provisions … only those without SPCs or those taking an exceptionally long time to complete the process gained significantly". Conversely, generic companies perceive data exclusivity as an extension or additional layer of monopoly protection that keeps their products off the market across the board (European Generic Medicines Association 2001).

Application to treatments for priority bacterial diseases

Given that the duration of data exclusivity allows for an unchallenged period on the market, even for products protected by weak patents (e.g. patents granted on the basis of formulation), these mechanisms can substantially postpone competitors' entry. Data exclusivity extensions to antibiotics raise similar issues as patent term extensions.

Box 6.12 *Broadening IP protection*

A variation of patent extension incentives is to apply patents over whole resistance groups in order to reduce resistance arising from competition between individual drugs (Laxminarayan 2002; Laxminarayan et al. 2007; Outterson 2005 & 2008). In the FRG proposal (Laxminayaryan 2007), an antibiotic belongs to a particular FRG if the use of that antibiotic causes resistance to other antibiotics in the FRG but not resistance to antibiotics in other FRGs. This system has the advantage of incentivizing patent owners of FRGs to manage the marketing and use of their drugs in order to slow the development of resistance (Laxminarayan & Brown 2001; Pray 2008), effectively internalizing the cost of resistance. The theory is that broad patents will stop companies from competing for the same pool of effectiveness within an FRG while incentivizing companies without patents for FRGs to develop new antibiotics outside of the patented classes (Laxminarayan & Brown 2001). This system would raise drug prices and increase social costs but it is argued that the benefits of conserving antibiotic effectiveness may outweigh the social costs of oligopolostic power (Laxminarayan et al. 2002).

This proposal has a number of practical challenges. First, significant research would be needed to understand how to divide, amalgamate and compensate developers within this type of system as multiple patents and off-patent products already exist within FRGs. Second, FRGs would also need to be defined using some sort of dynamic classification as resistance develops across groups. Third, possibly the biggest challenge (see Section 6.3) is the requirement not only for a relaxation of antitrust laws to allow companies to collude in this way but also consideration of a *sui generis* right. The latter may be necessary given that many classes of antibiotics contain off-patent drugs or drugs patented to different companies. Finally, developers would have no incentive to research drugs in other FRGs for which patents already exist (Laxminarayan et al. 2007). This may hinder the development of follow-on antibiotics that can help slow resistance in the short-term.

Wildcard patent extensions

Wildcard patent extensions enable a company that successfully develops a new antibiotic either to transfer a patent extension to another drug in its portfolio that is approaching patent expiry or to sell it to another company with such a product (fully transferable). Suggested patent extension times range from six months to two years in the United States (Sonderholm 2009; Spellberg et al. 2008b); up to five years in the EU (Moran et al. 2005; Towse & Kettler 2005); or proportional to therapeutic benefit. The main advantage of this scheme is that it presents a significant reward for large companies with lucrative products to protect or for small companies that could sell on the extensions.

Much debate surrounds the overall cost calculation of wildcard patent extensions. Spellberg (2008b) stresses the need for the cost estimate to take account of the present cost of MDR infections and argues that no more than a handful of drugs will be eligible for a patent extension at any one time due to the difficulty of developing priority antibiotics. Spellberg et al. (2007) suggest that wildcard patent extensions could well be cost-effective as they can mitigate the present cost of drug resistance (through faster development times). They estimate that wildcard patent extension would cost US$ 7.7 billion over the first two years and US$ 3.9 billion over the next 18 years, rendering the incentive cost neutral in 10 years. On the other hand, Outterson et al. (2007) estimate that the global cost of granting just ten two-year wildcard patent extensions is likely to exceed US$ 40 billion – more than US$ 4 billion per new antibiotic, net of tax credits, grants and orphan drug benefits. They argue that the cost could double if the incentive allowed the stacking of extensions on a given drug. Sonderholm (2009) argues that the cost could be much lower if extensions were limited to six months, reducing the stated estimates by 75%. The magnitude of these respective estimates should be compared with the estimates of total development costs per new drug (see Section 4.4).

Another major criticism of wildcard extensions is that they transfer the cost of developing a new drug for one disease to patients with another, raising concerns about equity and transparency (Kremer & Glennerster 2004; Outterson et al. 2007). The ethical implications of this cost-shifting between unrelated patient groups and concerns over the resulting bad publicity are the main reason why they have not recently been campaigned for by the EFPIA and the Pharmaceutical Research and Manufacturers of America (PhRMA). Sonderholm (2009) challenges this argument by suggesting that the burden is borne not by other patient groups but rather by all those who have insurance (or contribute to a national health system). This implies some greater fairness in shifting the cost to all contributors. In private insurance systems (or work-defined social insurance systems), aside from the many thousands of individuals who are not covered by insurance and would bear the full cost, it should not be assumed that risk is shared sufficiently to achieve this assumed level of fairness across a population. Kapczynski (2009) mentions that wildcard patent extensions would tie rewards not to the NPV of the antibiotics market but rather to the NPV of the market for heart disease, heartburn or asthma, or whatever blockbuster market to which it is applied. In effect, this breaks the link between the price signal and the incentive (Kapczynski 2009). Also, importantly, the race created by the incentive could result in other developers investing enormous sums with an overall value entirely disproportionate to the value of bringing an antibiotic to market just days or months sooner (Kapczynski 2009).

The anticompetitive nature of the scheme further hinders its applicability as wildcard patent extensions delay generic entry in a particularly inequitable manner. Generic companies awaiting patent expiry would suddenly be blocked and forced to wait longer before entering the market in which the patent extension is applied. If this became common it would create the risk of generally disincentivizing generic companies from investing in the demonstration bioequivalence until the brand-name patent has expired, i.e. when there is certainty that the patent cannot be extended. This would lead to slow entry of generics into any market in which wildcard patent extensions might be applied – the most lucrative markets and those that need more competition, not less. The additional time lag also provides further time for the patent owner not only to develop follow-on products to capture market share but also to spin off friendly generics to nullify any exclusivity granted to their first competitors.

Currently no wildcard schemes are in operation for pharmaceuticals in either the EU or the United States. The most recently proposed scheme was the Biodefense and Pandemic Vaccine and Drug Development Act of 2005, also known as BioShield II, which was intended to stimulate countermeasures to biological weapons. In this case the exclusivity provision attracted such vehement opposition from the generics industry that it was removed before the Act was signed into law.[59]

Application to treatments for priority bacterial diseases

Spellberg and colleagues (2007) estimated the costs of the wildcard patent extension compared to the savings derived from a new antibiotic drug to treat multidrug-resistant *P. aeruginosa*. The authors found that a wildcard patent extension applied to one new antibiotic would cost US$ 7.7 billion over the first two years and US$ 3.9 billion over the following 18 years. The most conservative estimates indicate that, even if the new antibiotic reduced the annual cost of *P. aeruginosa* infections by only 50%, the wildcard

---

59 See Laxminarayan (2002) for further details. An initial block on sales of wildcards led to the eventual quashing of even the non-tradable wildcard extension proposal.

patent extension would be cost neutral by 10 years after the approval of the new antibiotic and save society US$ 4.6 billion by 20 years after approval. They conclude that the patent extension is an economically viable incentive for antibiotic R&D and will result in cost savings to society over time if applied appropriately.

To contain the social costs, Spellberg and colleagues (2007) argue that the wildcard extension could include a profit compromise that caps the profit that the benefiting company can earn. Alternatively, IDSA proposed a stipulation that 10–20% of the profits gained from the patent extension on the lucrative drug be targeted toward R&D for antibiotics (Infectious Diseases Society of America 2004). These proposals deserve attention but the risks of overcompensation, inequity and significant market distortion would likely prevail.

Application to SMEs
SMEs will have little to gain from this scheme unless it includes a provision that allows a developer to sell its wildcard patent extension (fully transferable). Those most attracted to the scheme would be developers with lucrative drugs approaching patent expiration (Nathan & Goldberg 2005). Furthermore, a large developer with no interest in antibiotic R&D might purchase a small developer dedicated to developing antibiotics just to procure a wildcard patent extension for a lucrative drug in its portfolio (Nathan & Goldberg 2005).

A patent extension that was transferable across companies would be more attractive to SMEs as it could be sold on to companies with blockbuster drugs. However, the incentive could significantly distort the eventual market to which it is applied. Thus there is a trade-off between luring SMEs to the scheme and minimizing the distortionary nature of the wildcard.

6.3.3 *Expedited regulatory review*

Fast-track programmes, priority review and vouchers that make these benefits transferable, are incentive mechanisms that reduce the length of regulatory review to advance the recouping of investments and increase first mover advantages. Under fast-track approval, the regulator helps eligible drugs to receive marketing approval more quickly through close guidance. Priority review can be performed separately or as part of the fast track and reduces the time taken for drug registration. Vouchers for fast-track or priority review make the privilege transferable to other products and to other developers (Moran 2005; Ridley et al. 2006). Additionally, if the award of one voucher proves insufficient to stimulate innovation then the regulatory body may award multiple vouchers simultaneously to boost the strength of the incentive (Ridley et al. 2006).

Examples from Europe

The EMA accelerated review procedures aim to provide a regulatory decision within 150 days of submission. In addition, there are two other procedures: (i) conditional approval (functionally equivalent to the FDA's accelerated approvals), introduced in 2006; and (ii) approval for exceptional circumstances, introduced in 2004.

Table 6.1 Differences between EMA accelerated review mechanisms

Conditional marketing authorization	Marketing authorization under exceptional circumstances
Demonstrate positive benefit-risk balance, based on scientific data, pending confirmation	Comprehensive data cannot be provided (specific reasons foreseen in the legislation)
Authorization valid for one year, on a renewable basis	Annual reassessment procedure reviews risk-benefit balance
Once pending studies are provided, can become a standard marketing authorization	Normally does not lead to the completion of a full dossier to become a standard marketing authorization

EMA has more limited experience with accelerated approval procedures than the FDA – only 7 conditional approvals and 17 exceptional circumstance approvals since each programme's inception (see Table 6.2) (European Medicines Agency 2009a).

Table 6.2 Products with conditional and exceptional circumstance EMA approvals to date

	Outcome year				
Opinion	2004	2005	2006	2007	2008
Normal	26 (89.7)	20 (87)	33 (84.6)	38 (82.6)	42 (91.3)
Exceptional	3 (10.3)[a]	3 (13)[b]	3 (6.7)[c]	5 (10.8)[d]	3 (6.5)[g]
Conditional	NA	NA	3 (7.6)[e]	3 (6.5)[f]	1 (2.2)[h]
Total positive	29 (100%)	23 (100%)	39 (100%)	46 (100%)	46 (100%)

Source: European Medicines Agency 2009a

[a] EC 2004: Orfadin, Prialt, Velcade
[b] EC 2005: Aptivus, Naglazyme, Revatio
[c] EC 2006: A Tryn, Elaprase, Evoltra
[d] EC 2007: Atriance, Daronix, Focetria, Increlex, Yondelis
[e] CA 2006: Diacomit, Prezista, Sutent
[f] CA 2007: Isentress, Vectibix, Tyverb
[g] EC 2008: Celvapan, Ceplene, Pandemrix
[h] CA 2008: Intelence
* EC: Exceptional circumstances CA: Conditional approval

A conditional approval may be granted for medicines that satisfy an unmet medical need (i.e. for which no treatment is readily available) and when the

CHMP believes that the data suggest that the product benefits outweigh the risks but are incomplete. The company must fulfil obligations to conduct further studies. Unlike the FDA system, EMA conditional approval is renewed annually until all obligations have been fulfilled. Two drugs received conditional approvals in 2008; one of these (Tyverb) received confirmation of the 2007 positive opinion (which had reservations regarding safety) but has yet to receive full approval.

EMA exceptional circumstances approval is normally granted when the applicant is unable to provide comprehensive data on the efficacy and safety of the medicine for specified reasons. This is usually due to the rarity of the condition, limited scientific knowledge in the area concerned or ethical considerations concerning the collection of such data. As for conditional approvals, the applicant is required subsequently to demonstrate the safety of the product and apply for approval on a yearly basis. In 2009, EMA granted exceptional circumstances approval to three products, two of which (Pandemrix, Celvaplan) were approved by consensus for prophylaxis of influenza under pandemic situations (European Medicines Agency 2009a).

Both the FDA and the EMA programmes retain the option to take a drug off the market if clinical benefit or subsequent trials are not completed. The EC maintains the additional option of imposing financial penalties if post-marketing studies are not delivered as agreed.

Examples from the United States

An FDA fast-track mechanism has been in place since 1993. Evidence from these programmes indicates that they are successful in reducing overall drug development time by up to three years – a two to two and a half year cut in clinical development plus a one year cut in regulatory review time (Moran 2005). Recently the FDA has extended the scheme to cover non-life-threatening diseases.[60]

The FDA priority review mechanism has been in place since 1992, aiming to cut the average review time from ten months to six months (Berndt et al. 2005b). In 2007 as part of the FDA Amendments Act, the FDA implemented a priority review scheme for neglected diseases (Waltz 2008). This legislation affects some infectious diseases occurring primarily in developing countries in which there is significant unmet need, for instance – TB, dengue fever and cholera. Coartem was the first drug to receive a priority review voucher. This antimalarial drug was developed by Novartis and has been available outside of the United States for several years.

---

60 It has been suggested that these extensions may dilute the effectiveness of this system unless resources are similarly scaled-up.

General considerations for future application

Some argue that the provision of priority review compromises the safety of regulatory review (Kesselheim 2009). Olson (2008) examined how review speed, user fees and other factors affect the counts of adverse reactions amongst new drugs. She found that drugs receiving faster reviews had higher counts of serious drug reactions after approval, including those resulting in hospitalization and death, than drugs receiving slower reviews. Other studies do not support the contention that accelerated review compromises safety (Ridley et al. 2006; Tufts Center for the Study of Drug Development 2005). However, regardless of the actual safety risks, the safety issue may still arise as an argument within the political arena.

Some suggest that improving the current system of post-marketing surveillance could provide more evidence on the safety questions and alleviate safety concerns (Ridley et al. 2006). Others propose that increasing staffing and relying less on deadlines could result in the same degree of review efficiency without increasing the risk. Design considerations include payment of a supplemental fee, passed along to the developer to cover the additional resources needed to speed up review and prevent review compromise of other waiting products (as in the current FDA model).

Conversely, others have suggested that this process results in a net public health gain. Philipson et al. (2005) found that faster approval of drugs between 1979 and 2002 offered consumers a net gain of 180 000 to 310 000 life years, compared with only 56 000 life years lost as a result of fast-track approval and lower safety. The authors also found that fast-track approval and regulation increased the return on investment by US$ 11–13 billion (Philipson et al. 2005).

When not transferrable to other drugs, accelerated regulatory review processes provide faster access to the desired innovative drugs without delaying access to cheaper generic drugs. However, this design may be of limited financial value to the developer unless other mechanisms are in place to achieve a high price for the product upon entry.

When accelerated privilege is transferrable to other products it will likely be applied to a blockbuster drug. This makes the voucher a potentially strong incentive with appeal to both small and large companies. However, the voucher incentive imposes distortions in the market to which it is ultimately applied by causing other companies to discontinue development of their drugs in that class (Moran 2005). It is also argued that a lack of transparency is created by selling the voucher to developers with blockbuster products (Kesselheim 2009). The voucher incentive is intended to reward innovation (omitting drugs with only incremental benefits) but this has been undermined by the lack of restriction on a voucher's eventual application. For example, Novartis was awarded a voucher[61] with an estimated worth of more than US$ 100 million for a drug that had been available in other markets for over ten years (prior to voucher issuance), thereby mitigating the focus on innovation (Anderson 2009).

Application to treatments for priority bacterial diseases

In principle, antibiotics for serious infection already qualify for expedited regulatory assessment in both the United States and Europe if they fulfil certain criteria common to all applications for accelerated assessment. The persisting lack of new antibiotics being produced (European Medicines Agency and the European Centre for Disease Prevention and Control 2009) suggests that these incentives offer insufficient benefits to attract the necessary R&D. The possibility of using vouchers is relatively new (and yet to be adopted in Europe) and clearly would increase the strength of the incentive.

Application to SMEs

Accelerated review mechanisms provide a chance of (albeit faster) payoff in the future and therefore are likely to be less attractive to SMEs which typically face an immediate need for cash to fund R&D. A smaller company could try to use the future possibility of a voucher as a bargaining chip with a venture capital firm or a large pharmaceutical company seeking to purchase a company's drug pipeline (Waltz 2008) but it is unclear whether this would be a sufficient attraction.

6.3.4 *Pricing and reimbursement*

Pricing and reimbursement present an important opportunity to influence the antibiotics market. Optimal reimbursement and pricing policies aim to depress economic rents to avert exploitation of the purchaser and to offer sufficient reward for innovation to ensure future investments in research. In Europe pharmaceutical prices are regulated in several ways, through direct means – reference pricing, formulary pricing, capping or item-by-item price negotiation – and indirectly, through rate-of-return regulation (McGuire et al. 2004). However chosen, levels of reimbursement for products are a result of negotiation between the developer and the purchaser who respectively act as monopolist (the developer with the innovative product) and monopsonist (the purchaser, often a regulatory body) (McGuire et al. 2004).

---

61 On 8 April 2009, the FDA announced that it had awarded Novartis a one-time priority review voucher (PRV) to use towards a future new drug application. The PRV was awarded to Coartem (artemether and lumefantrine) – a malaria treatment.

In theory, if pharmaceutical developers achieve increasing returns of scale and scope such that average cost decreases with increasing levels of output (and thus average cost exceeds marginal cost of production), incentives to promote R&D allow some monopoly profit to be retained by the developer by offering a price that is higher than average cost (McGuire et al. 2004). However, the regulator's inability to observe R&D costs makes the process of finding the appropriate price difficult in practice.

Box 6.13 *Health technology assessments (HTAs)*

Member States are increasingly using HTAs to support reimbursement and pricing decisions (Sorenson et al. 2008). HTAs estimate the relative costs and benefits of a technology by evaluating the production, synthesis and/or systematic review of a range of scientific and non-scientific evidence (Sorenson et al. 2008). Providing health-care decision-makers with crucial evidence from the micro-, meso- and macro-levels, they are often seen as the bridge between evidence and policy-making (Battista & Hodge 1999). Generally, HTAs use a multidisciplinary framework to answer four main questions (UK National Health Service 2003).

1. Is the technology effective?
2. For whom does the technology work?
3. What are the costs entailed in its use?
4. How does the technology compare with currently available treatment alternatives?

The roles of HTA agencies vary between Member States. In countries such as the Netherlands and Denmark they serve an advisory role, making recommendations on pricing and reimbursement to the national or regional government, ministerial department or self-governing body (Zentner et al. 2005). HTA agencies in France, Finland, Sweden and the United Kingdom take a regulatory role and report to health ministries. They are responsible for listing and pricing drugs (Zentner et al. 2005), sometimes in conjunction with other agencies.

Generally, the drug in question is evaluated against a specified standard of performance or other drugs (Sorenson et al. 2008). The choice of comparator is clearly vital to understanding the relative costs and benefits of the product in question. Agencies often use two different selection procedures (Zentner et al. 2005) and some require more (Sorenson et al. 2008). In Sweden assessments of new drugs usually include comparators from routine practice, non-medical intervention and "do nothing"(Sorenson et al. 2008). For inclusion in the positive list a drug is compared with all drugs in the therapeutic group – within the same second or fourth level of the WHO ATC classification (Sorenson et al. 2008). In the Netherlands drugs are compared against standard (routine daily practice) or common therapy (Sorenson et al. 2008). In France, drugs are considered in the same therapeutic group, the most frequently prescribed, the least expensive and the most recently listed in the positive list for reimbursement (Sorenson et al. 2008). For most bacterial infections the comparators will include generic

> antibiotics so any new antibiotic must prove to be cost effective when compared with much less expensive drugs (depending on how the indication or disease category is defined). This helps place a downward pressure on prices for any potential new drug in a therapeutic area and can contribute to a disconnect between the price the public payer pays for the product and the therapeutic benefit achieved from that particular product (including the public benefit of slower growth of resistance in the case of novel products).

Kesselheim and Outterson (2010) and others have proposed a system of reimbursement for antimicrobials based on their social value.[62] The system would entail modelling the health impact of new antibiotics and then negotiating with manufacturers to encourage them to price according to the results. For instance, a new antibiotic that reduced the number of inpatient stays could be priced higher to account for savings to the system (see Box 6.14).

It may be possible to limit pricing reform to better reflect therapeutic value in the medium term or while a more holistic social-value based system is under development. The (fulfilled) promise of higher prices would in itself lure developers to antibiotics. Also, in contrast to patent-term extensions, reimbursement incentives would allow developers to recoup R&D costs at an earlier stage and reduce their amount of risk.

Reimbursement and pricing reform should be explored further with respect to the particular financing arrangements in each European Member State. However, their success in luring developers to invest in R&D for antibiotics is likely to be much greater within a standardized European system that could credibly offer a given price (or level of priority) for a product with stipulated characteristics on a large scale.

Application to antibiotics

Antibiotics for severe infection are life-saving products and therefore would stand to attain high prices under a reimbursement system basing prices on therapeutic or social value. Indeed, they would likely be amongst the most rewarded. In addition, unlike patent-term extensions, reimbursement-based incentives have the ability to influence other stakeholders such as doctors and patients. It is argued that the higher prices attainable in a value-based reimbursement system could reduce the prescription and consumption of antibiotics to more appropriate levels, thereby helping to conserve them for future use (Outterson 2009). Also, as the ACE Programme proposal suggests (see Box 6.14), reimbursement incentives could be used to reward infection control measures and ABS too.

---

62 Authorities in countries such as the United Kingdom have considered similar proposals (for all pharmaceuticals, not just antimicrobials) to price drugs according to societal value.

Box 6.14 *ACE Programme proposal (Kesselheim & Outterson 2010)*

The debate surrounding AR is complicated by the dynamic interaction between the two pillars of control – conservation of existing antibiotics and production of new antibiotics. The former shrinking the market to stimulate the latter. Experts argue that an optimal incentive structure would need to do both, thereby aligning incentives more closely with public health goals. The ACE Programme proposal is a cluster of integrated solutions to address systematically the AR issue and consider these dynamic complexities with the key objective of creating and maintaining better markets for continual antibiotic effectiveness. At its core lie three proposals which require no changes to the existing drug approval and IP protection systems.

1. **Rewards for new antibiotics** based on meeting public health and conservation goals through tying market exclusivity provisions to the continuing effectiveness of the drug. It is argued this would internalize the negative externalities of consumption although it would also provide a relatively modest incentive on its own. In practice, the regulatory agency would set targets, e.g. requiring morbidity from the agent to remain below a set percentage.

2. **Antibiotic reimbursement mechanisms** based on value-based purchasing, to support usage patterns more aligned with their intrinsic value and thus rational development of new drugs. In practice, companies would price their drugs freely, based on the health impact of their new product, and reimburse ABS and infection control activities similarly.

3. **Limited waivers of antitrust law** to enable coordination of market activities where cross-resistance may result. Specifically, the authors propose that for identified drug-bug pairings (where cross-resistance is a problem) the regulatory agency would coordinate with the antitrust agencies to issue certificates or waivers authorizing limited joint coordination of conservation activities that would not result in prosecution. Competition agencies in the United States and the EU have indicated provisional openness to such a suggestion.

Pre-empting challenges to their proposal, the authors emphasize the following: the pharmaceutical industry is an appropriate (the most powerful and upstream) target to make responsible for the utilization of its agents; an expensive effective antibiotic is preferable to one that is cheap but ineffective; the federal health board created as part of the American Recovery and Reinvestment Act 2009 will make health impact modelling possible; collusion and gaming are limited by waiver specificity. Additionally, supplementary cash prizes are proposed if incentives are ineffective. Lastly, a patent buyout is suggested as an alternative to the reimbursement mechanism.

> **Box 6.15** *Health impact fund (HIF)*
>
> Hollis and Pogge (2008) propose establishing an HIF to reward developers retrospectively based on the actual health benefits brought about by their products in the previous year. In exchange, developers would agree to sell their products at near cost. HIF would use market forces to establish the relative size of the reward. For example, if all registered products were estimated to have saved 20 million QALYs, a product that had saved 2 million of these would receive 10% of the money in the fund. The HIF would have no involvement in funding research but would simply issue rewards for fully developed products according to their assessed impact (Hollis & Pogge 2008). Thus, the HIF could act as a pull mechanism to lure development of new products that are not reimbursed adequately given their relative therapeutic value. It would also remove the incentive to create therapeutically equivalent me-too products that provide little additional benefit. The HIF programme would be optional, likely attracting only the developers of products that have the ability to save lives or significantly reduce morbidity. As an optional scheme, the HIF would provide a self-adjusting system to set reward size: if payments are too high, more products will be registered with the HIF (individual product payments will then fall as the funds will be spread over more products) and vice versa (Hollis & Pogge 2008).
>
> *Application to treatments for priority bacterial diseases*
> Under an HIF programme, novel antibiotics would not be rationed on the basis of price. In many ways this is crucial to improving access, especially in poorer countries. However, some would argue that the removal of the price limitation could lead to overuse of the novel product, especially as it would be seen as the best product on the market (having established high therapeutic value). If technical (and biological) barriers to producing novel antibiotics are sufficiently low, high volume sales of a new product lead to a greater number of new products entering the market. If the barriers are high, there will be no or few competitors and the use of a highly precious resource could be over-facilitated. Stringent guidelines and prescription controls are necessary. On a practical level, the emergence of resistance and the relative therapeutic benefit of newer and older products would need to be tracked very regularly. Comparative trials and monitoring would have to become routine.

Application to SMEs

As with other pull incentives, this proposal would not provide the crucial early stage funding that many SMEs need to survive. However, the assurance that higher prices will eventually be paid for a fully developed product is likely to increase SMEs' chances of attracting venture capital to fund early stages of development.

6.3.5 *Liability protection*

Pharmaceutical industry representatives previously interviewed by the IDSA were found to consider liability limitations a strong incentive to develop new antibiotics (Infectious Diseases Society of America 2004). This type of liability protection has been applied to childhood vaccines in the United States under the Vaccine Injury Compensation Program (VICP), ratified by Congress in 1986. Funded by an excise tax imposed on vaccine doses, the VICP is intended to protect medical doctors and vaccine manufacturers from liability in cases of injury caused by vaccines. The law was enacted to address the vaccine supply shortages that resulted from the exodus of manufacturers following numerous court cases in the 1970s and early 1980s.

The IDSA recommends that liability limitations be extended to antibiotics that treat targeted pathogens. Others have recommended limited liability for areas of high unmet need including pandemics and paediatric indications (Thompson et al. 2004). The BioShield II (S. 975) legislation ratified in December 2005 was partly a response to the failure to ensure sufficient liability protection for industry within BioShield I (S. 666) (Mayer 2007). Part of BioShield II was passed in the form of the Public Readiness and Emergency Preparedness Act (PREP). This liability protections and no-fault compensation scheme was an attempt to internalize the positive externalities associated with the development of possible bioterrorism and pandemic countermeasures and to address the market's lopsided risk-benefit ratio for developing biodefence medicines (Mayer 2007). The primary effects of the legislation hinge on liability protections for drug companies (effectively shifting them to federal government) under provisions intended to remove financial risk barriers for any new vaccines that need to be rushed to market in case of an emergency. Mayer's (2007) concerns around the legislation in BioShield II include inadequate compensation for affected individuals; insufficient deterrence of negligent tortfeasors; and the impact of precedent setting on normal medicinal product liability.

In Europe, the developer normally bears liability as soon as any type of market authorization is granted; under Conditional and Exceptional Circumstances Approval the developer bears full liability. However, certain provisions within the EU Regulation can be used if a Member State chooses to allow distribution of a product prior to authorization (e.g. during an epidemic). For example, for the H1N1 pandemic, the antiviral Relenza (zanamivir) with a Rotocap/Rotohaler inhalation device (instead of the authorized diskhaler) was distributed using Article 5(2) of Regulation (EC) No 83/2001 as production of the traditional device could not meet the increased demand (European Medicines Agency 2009b). This legislation allows for temporary distribution of unauthorized products with full Member State liability. The distribution of

Tamiflu for paediatrics was permitted using Article 5(3) of Regulation (EC) No 726/2004 which allows distribution based on the scientific opinion of the EMA (European Medicines Agency 2009c). Liability was therefore assumed by the Member State but the developer has since provided the necessary evidence to receive full market authorization and hence now bears full liability.

Application to treatments for priority bacterial diseases

If liability limitations were to be reserved for only the more severe and previously untreatable indications, their application to antibiotics could potentially be justified. Indeed, there would be less opposition if the product were a last resort treatment. However, given the public outcry in recent years regarding safety concerns with products authorized and subsequently removed from the market, it should be expected that proposals on liability limitations will face potentially significant public, and hence political, opposition.

6.3.6 Antitrust laws

As mentioned briefly in the context of extending IP protection, one firm's inability to control the sales of antibiotics by other companies creates a tragedy of the commons (Horowitz & Moehring 2004; Outterson et al. 2007). This results in aggressive marketing of the drug and thereby accelerates the development and spread of resistance (including cross-resistance). In response to this problem, there is a proposal to relax antitrust laws (Outterson 2005) in order to allow a company to sell the rights to its product to another pharmaceutical company with a competing antibiotic, thereby creating monopolies over groups of similar products. This would allow patents to cover resistance-related groups rather than individual drugs (see Boxes 6.11 and 6.12) and incentivize developers to manage sales and consumption patterns in order to control resistance (Laxminarayan & Brown 2001; Pray 2008).

6.3.7 Sui generis *rights*

Laxminarayan et al. (2007) propose using a sui generis right to deal with off-patent products under an FRG scheme (see Boxes 6.11 and 6.12). The authors explain that these rights have already been proposed and occasionally adopted to protect semiconductor designs, databases and biodiversity. Like a patent, a *sui generis* right over an off-patent antibiotic would allow only the holder to produce the covered antibiotic. They argue that this should be perpetual and assign the rights to all off-patent antibiotics from a given antibiotic FRG to the same developer or individual, although different groups of off-patent antibiotics could be assigned to different developers or individuals. While the ability to market products in perpetuity would draw much interest from developers, there could be significant implications for the wider patent system.

6.4 Combined push–pull incentive models

There is growing acknowledgement that neither push nor pull mechanisms alone are sufficient to stimulate innovation. This section explores existing orphan drug legislation and the Call Options for Antibiotics model – COA.

6.4.1 *Orphan drug designation*

The EMA's Committee for Orphan Medicinal Products defines an orphan product as a significantly beneficial product that prevents, treats or diagnoses a life-threatening or chronically debilitating disease afflicting a maximum of 5 in 10 000 people. As of April 2000 drugs eligible for orphan drug designation are entitled to 10-year market exclusivity and other incentives such as access to the EMA's centralized approval procedure, fee reductions for regulatory procedures and free scientific advice (Heemstra et al. 2008). While not explicitly stated in the legislation, its application provides orphan drugs with added protection – when market exclusivity expires for one indication it remains valid for the other orphan indications. This provides an incentive to explore new indications. Also, while not standardized, orphan drugs also receive tax incentives from the Member State level.[63] The outline of EU and United States legislation is included in Table 6.3 (Rinaldi 2005).

In theory, antibiotics can qualify for orphan status under the current legislation and products with antibiotic properties have already received orphan designation and market approval. However, in order to qualify as an orphan product, developers must prove that the the product is intended for a prognosis or expression of the disease that is different from the general condition. This is generally not easy but, given orphan legislation's success in creating new markets, the possibility of altering current legislation to better suit antibiotics or of creating a new orphan-like incentive should be considered. It would likely be more expedient to build on the core of existing legislation but the eligibility criteria that lie at its base are not set out in a manner designed for acute short-term conditions. It may be better to draft new antibiotic-specific legislation that crucially would allow incorporation of all the lessons learnt from using the existing legislation over the past decade (e.g. on pricing, access, salami-slicing indications, off-label prescribing).

---

63 Lessons from the United States suggest that the market exclusivity component of this type of legislation is the primary attraction for the pharmaceutical industry (Kremer & Glennerster 2004).

Table 6.3 *Comparison of United States and EU orphan drug legislation and processes*

	United States	EU
Administrative body	FDA/OOPD	EMA/COMP
Legislation	ODA (1983); Orphan Drug Regulation (1993)	Regulation (CE) No. 141/2000 (2000)
Eligibility criteria	7.5 per 10 000	5 per 10 000
Incentives		
Market exclusivity	7 yrs	10*yrs
Data exclusivity	5 yrs (NCE); 3 yrs (non-NCE)	10 (+1) yrs NCEs
Funding	Grants for clinical research (pharma and academia eligible)	Framework programmes for research plus national measures
Tax credits	50% of clinical costs	Managed by Member States
Protocol assistance	Yes	Yes
Accelerated review	Yes	Yes
Reconsideration?	No	Yes (every 6 years)
No. of designated orphan drugs (as of April 2005)	1449	269
No. of orphan drug marketing authorizations (as of April 2005)	269	20
2004 market value	US$ 27 billion≠	0.7–1% national medicine budgets (predicted to reach 6–8% of total budgets by 2010)**

* Can be reduced to 6 years if at the end of the 5th year the criteria outlined in article 3 (i.e. product is sufficiently profitable to no longer justify exclusivity) are no longer met.

Source: adapted from Rinaldi 2005 and European Parliament 1999; Stolk et al., 2006; Orphanet (www.orpha.net); EU Community Register of Orphan Medicinal Products (http://ec.europa.eu/health/documents/community-register/html/index_en.htm); US Office of Orphan Products Development (www.fda.gov/orphan)

≠ Visiongain report (PR9.net 2004) ** ALCIMED report (de Varax et al. 2008)

6.4.2 Call options for antibiotics model

Brogan & Mossialos (2006) recently proposed a novel approach for stimulating vaccine development which they term the Call Options for Vaccines (COV) method. This section aims to demonstrate that this method also has the potential to stimulate antibiotic development (as the principles of market limitations apply equally to antibiotics), proposing a new incentive mechanism that combines the COV and AMC approaches discussed above – the Call Options for Antibiotics model. The aim is to demonstrate that a discounted future price in exchange for an initial investment could offer a proper incentive to make neglected antibiotic research attractive and profitable.

COV

Brogan and Mossialos's (2006) COV model proposes a new incentive mechanism that combines both push and pull methods, based loosely on the principles of call options in equity markets. A typical call option allows an investor to purchase the right to buy a share of stock at a later date for a fixed price – paying a premium now for the potential to profit later. However, payment of the premium involves some risk as the profit is not guaranteed. The seller of the call option also undertakes some risk since any potential profit will come at the seller's expense. However, it is quite probable that an initial investment in exchange for a discounted future price could give the proper balance for both parties.

The common thread between antibiotic and neglected vaccine development is that those affected make up a disproportionate share of the world's poor. Therefore, often there is limited funding with which to pay high prices for drugs or vaccines that may ease the burden of disease. From a corporate standpoint, the decision to invest in projects depends on assuring a positive return on that investment; the valuation of such projects depends on three main factors: cash, timing and risk (Luehrman 1997). The greatest challenge is to persuade companies to invest in a market with low returns. Conventional thinking suggests that if it is possible to increase returns, at the very least giving the project a positive NPV that meets a predetermined threshold, then profit-maximizing companies will always invest.

Applying the COV model to antibiotic development

In the COV model, a potential purchaser buys a right (during development) to purchase a specified amount of the drug at a later date for a specified price. If the drug never makes it to market, the purchaser pays only a premium equal to the cost of the initial option contract. The potential purchaser could be allowed to examine all of the data on the product in question and make an independent assessment of its potential. Ideally, this would be an international NGO or charitable foundation with adequate funding to make several investment decisions and create a credible investment commitment, such as The Global Fund or GAVI. A purchaser who considers the drug a good investment will pay an agreed amount (methodology for determining this will be discussed below) in exchange for the contractual right to buy a certain number of doses at a reduced price if the drug makes it to market. If the drug encounters problems during clinical trials and does not receive marketing approval, the development company retains the initial investment and the purchaser has neither an obligation to buy nor any benefit from investment. However, any contract negotiated will need provisions ensuring access and ownership of all products developed from the initial funded line of research. If one avenue proves promising, only to spawn a successful antibiotic from a related mechanism, the purchaser has an equal right to the new antibiotic as it derives from the IP of the funded research. Likewise, the contract could call for financial penalties if a company acquires an option but wants to stop development. This mechanism is explained further with the aid of examples given below.

Applying the COV model to antibiotics – an example

Use of the COV model to purchase an antibiotic can be illustrated in a hypothetical case that closely follows the example given above. A drug company (Pharma1) develops AbX, a new antibiotic that could have remarkable efficacy against a particular pathogen afflicting a developing country. Based on a traditional NPV analysis the target population may not represent a market share of enough significance to make further testing and development profitable. However, an NGO or interested health ministry may help stimulate further R&D through the COV model. In this scenario, the NGO would pay a small upfront fee for every single dose of drug they might buy in the future, at a fraction of what the actual dose will cost. In turn, they will be assured the right to purchase the drug (if it reaches the market) at a significantly reduced price. For example, the purchaser buys an option for each dose needed – perhaps $0.10 per dose for 10 million doses. Therefore, at the outset, Pharma1 receives $1 million in exchange for 10 million options to buy a dose of AbX at $5 per dose in the future. In several years, AbX might make it to market at a market price of $10 per dose, the cost for any individual or health ministry wishing to purchase. The exception is the purchaser of the options who then exercises the right to purchase 10 million doses of AbX at $5 per dose. These doses may then be sold to health ministries at the market price of $10 per dose, gaining a net profit of approximately $49 million[64] ($50 million difference between market value and strike price, minus the initial cost of the outlay). An NGO with no interest in gaining profits from the sale might distribute the drugs at no cost or reduced rates, according to the need of its constituents. The exact details of this would vary with the mission and aims of each organization. Of course, if AbX never makes it to market, the option cannot be exercised and the initial investment of $1 million will never be recovered.

Developing the COA model

As can been seen from the example above, much of the viability of the COV model depends on the balance between the risk of the investment, cost of the initial option, market price of the final drug and the strike price (negotiated

---

[64] A more accurate assessment of the net profit would take account of the interest lost on the $1 million initial investment over the years, thus the actual profit margin would be slightly less than $49 million.

price of the drug for option holders at redemption time). High option prices or excessive risks make an investment unattractive to most investors; low option prices erode the profitability of the project for a pharmaceutical firm and hinder the ability to continue development. Similar problems are encountered in pricing options in the financial world in which mathematical models are employed to determine the likelihood that a stock will reach its strike price (the COV equivalent is the drug making it to market). However, these valuation methodologies assume a volatility with a normal distribution. This is clearly not the case within drug development since the cost at any given time is clearly dependent on the stage of development. The probability of failure in any given stage is also not normally distributed. Hence, a binomial evaluation of options gives a more accurate representation of the modelling of options for drug development. This makes sense intuitively – development at any given stage will either succeed or fail and each outcome can be independently modelled for each stage.

Further work in developing an appropriate binomial option pricing model with applicability to antibiotics has commenced and a detailed explanation will soon be published. However, this work seeks to combine the principles of the COV model with the AMC thereby introducing three new variables to the binomial options pricing model – Q; N and AMC. Q is a parameter measuring the efficacy and novelty of the drug in comparison to its peer group and will range in value from 0 to 1. N is the number of drugs currently available in the same therapeutic class. AMC will be equal to the predetermined dollar amount appropriate to stimulate research for that particular class of drugs. For instance, $3 billion was the AMC amount deemed necessary to stimulate vaccine development. The above variable would be related to the project payoff by the following equation:

$$M = \frac{AMC \times Q}{N}$$

With the development of this new model (the COA) the concept of the AMC could play an integral role in determining the socially acceptable payout for development of a new drug in conjunction with the framework of the original COV model. By increasing the payout for drugs in novel classes with high efficacy and few peers, the COA mechanism actively encourages novel drug development and targets financial rewards to that innovation.

Optimal phase of investment

The COA model depends critically on accurate characterization of the probability of success at any given stage of development. Payne et al. (2007) succinctly summarize data from the Centre for Medicines Research on drug development probabilities per stage, as well as length in years. The exact probability for any given stage will vary depending on the pharmaceutical class but nevertheless the numbers displayed in Table 6.4 are instructive.

Table 6.4 Length of time and estimated success per development phase

Phase description	Length (years)*	Probability of success*	Cost per phase (US$ millions)	Investment cost (US$ millions)
High throughput sequencing to lead	2	0.0702	148.15	1000.00
Lead to development candidate	5	0.5	370.37	851.85
DC to Phase I start	1	0.75	74.07	481.48
Phase I to Phase II start	2	0.25	148.15	407.41
Phase II to Phase III start	2	0.5	148.15	259.26
Phase III to file	0.5	0.67	37.04	111.11
File to launch	1	0.75	74.07	74.07

* Data from Payne et al 2007.

The authors' calculations in the last two columns assume a total development cost of $1 billion, in line with previous estimates of drug development. Assuming that the cost is spread evenly over the various stages, depending on their length of time (a gross over-simplification but useful for the purpose of illustration), then the cost per phase can be calculated. The investment cost at any given phase can then be calculated by summing the costs per phase over the remaining phases.

A mathematical model of the COA has been developed and will be presented in forthcoming work; an explanation is beyond the scope of this text. The data given above can be used to calculate a very rough estimate of the aggregate price of all call options for a drug at any stage of development (see Fig. 6.2).

As shown in Fig. 6.2, the optimal investment phase will be determined by a particular purchaser's appetite for risk and available funds. At the very least, it is instructive to consider the two extreme possibilities: (i) early stage investment of development candidates, or (ii) investment at the filing phase. Investment in the earliest stages carries a significant amount of risk – any single project has a very small chance of making it to market and consequently a call option's purchase price at this stage is correspondingly cheap. If a project does succeed, substantial savings will accrue to the holder of the call option when it is redeemed for a discounted drug. Investment at this stage could be useful for an organization wishing to fund a number of competing projects or significantly different tracks of research to solve a given problem. Investment in a wide spectrum of projects could be obtained for a relatively small amount of

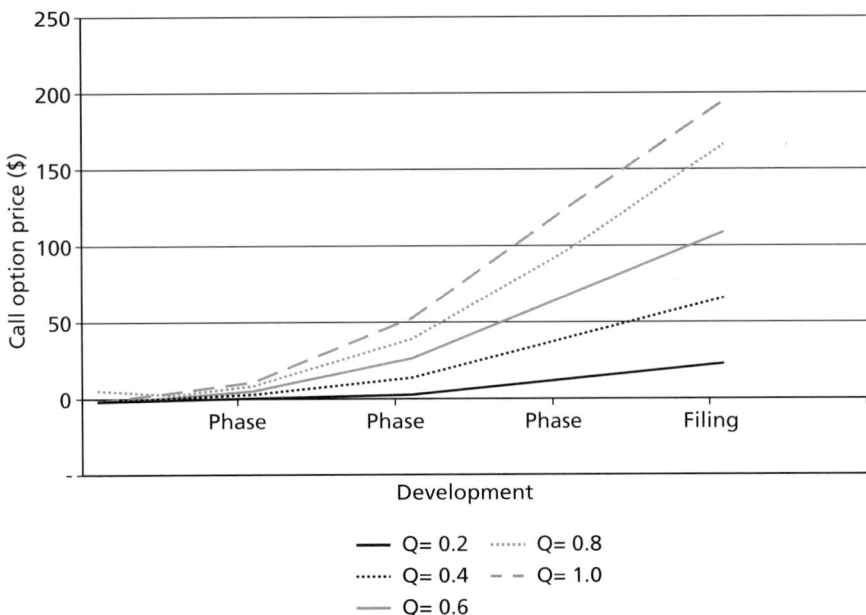

Fig. 6.2 Call option price (US$ millions) as a function of development stage and Q*

* Q is a parameter measuring the efficacy and novelty of the drug when compared with its peer group, with a value ranging from 0 to 1. 1 is an ideal representing a new drug with super efficacy addressing an as yet unmet need. This could be determined by an independent advisory board. Drugs that are isomers of existing products would receive a correspondingly low Q, closer to 0.

money. Conversely, investment in the later stages of development carries far less risk. Investment at the time of filing for drug approval carries little to no risk and consequently the cost of the call option is correspondingly higher. A call option purchased at this stage offers minimal savings but also minimum risk. The risk and return can be customized to each purchaser depending on their appetite and objectives.

The two extremes described are useful examples but are unlikely to be the phases at which most interested parties invest. The selection of candidate drugs for development is a struggle for many pharmaceutical companies and difficult at best. Similarly, purchase of an option at the final stages of development holds little value for purchasers. It is more likely that interested parties will purchase options in Phase I or Phase II, after the mechanism and benefits of the drug have become clear and there are preliminary data on efficacy. Investment at this point also allows substantial savings at further stages of development, with a moderate amount of risk. In this way the model could also help to revive projects that have been abandoned due to lack of access to capital. Projects could be restarted at any stage with the appropriate mix of risk and payment to make them viable once again.

Areas to address

Evaluation of proposed new drugs will be of critical importance if the system is to work efficiently. A multidisciplinary evaluation group is required as it is possible that promising drugs might be conceived by companies ill-equipped to carry through their development. This must be taken into account when making the decision to invest. A committee of financiers, economists and scientists would be necessary to determine if an options contract provides good value for money and worthwhile investment. This drug evaluation group could be an extension of the purchasing organization and any evaluation should include not only a review of the drug and its potential prospects, but also an examination of the viability of the company and its infrastructure. A company would need to ensure full disclosure of all test results (from both animal models and regulatory trials) in a manner similar to that required for licensing approval. Reluctance to disclose such proprietary information should be overcome by the desire to obtain preliminary funding – confidentiality would be essential.

The obvious rationale for scrutinizing potential option purchases is that bad investment decisions could quickly incur large financial losses with no real benefits. This is similar to one of the critiques of push mechanisms – that project managers might prove incapable of deciding on the most promising research plan. This could be rectified by forming an independent body to assess which ideas to fund. Assessment would rely heavily on full disclosure of all relevant documents, which may not be achievable. There is also the possibility that the total cost of development is increased by the additional regulatory trials mandated for marketing approval and may deter some companies from engaging in a contract with a predetermined price. This can be addressed in a number of ways. First, by setting aside a special emergency fund (paid by the purchaser) which can be accessed only in specific cases where additional government trials are required. Second, by building the probability and cost of this scenario into the model – this may slightly increase the premium for the call option. Third, by forming alliances between companies with specific synergistic advantages. This would increase an option's value to the purchaser since it would increase the likelihood of development by adding experience and capital investment during a critical period. Danzon et al. (2003) have shown that alliances tend to be more successful in drug development than solo firms.

Another possible criticism is that the number of projects would be limited and in turn this might reduce the number of potential antibiotics in development. However, it could be argued that exactly the opposite would occur. Companies contractually obligated to sell their first antibiotic at a lower price might also work intensively on more effective antibiotics in parallel, hoping that public pressure would compel purchasers to buy the better antibiotic at full price.

There would still be an incentive to make a good faith effort to bring the original to market as failure would be seen as a breach of contract and likely impact future investment. Similarly, if the IP developed during initial R&D on one project stimulated further drugs or new revenues, option holders on the original project would receive dividends from the new revenue stream. These dividends would be a function of the number of options and the stage at which they were purchased. The exact terms of any agreement could be negotiated at the purchase of the original option. It is imperative that purchasers of options share the fruit of any research produced by the project in which they invest. The key is to maintain a financial incentive for the developer, with a high cost for the release of proprietary information.

Finally, some may argue that larger firms may be more effective at gaming the system. By securing funding for their compounds, rather than those of smaller biotech startups, those most in need of early infusion of capital would be least likely to receive it. This critique elicits two responses. First, the purpose of this mechanism is to correct a market failure and make certain projects more attractive, not sufficiently to capitalize any and all comers. Second, if certain NGOs have an aim to facilitate development of drugs by smaller companies then a two-tiered system of investing could be introduced – one high risk and one low risk (making sufficient adjustments to the upfront options price in return for even more substantial savings at the time of drug approval). In this way, the mechanism can be tailored to fit the particular objectives of the options purchaser.

A way forward

As mentioned previously, the CGD AMC and the COV model have been proposed as independent mechanisms to stimulate vaccine development. Both also hold promise in stimulating antibiotic development and combination of the two may offer the best mechanism to date for stimulating neglected drug development. Further work on their integration is forthcoming. The CGD model helps to define the appropriate market to stimulate development; the COA develops this by allowing the market to function at different points in a drug's life-cycle, not just at the time of marketing. The COA effectively transfers the AMC-proposed subsidy to companies at earlier stages, with appropriate discounts for the time value of money as well as the risk assumed. The underlying tenets of the need for a subsidy are the same, the two mechanisms simply advocate this subsidy at different stages in the product life-cycle.

Chapter 7
Conclusions

7.1 Rationale for intervention in the antibiotics market

Currently, there are too few novel antibacterial agents under development to meet the growing challenge of MDR (European Medicines Agency and the European Centre for Disease Prevention and Control 2009). In 2004, only 1.6% of drugs in development amongst the 15 largest pharmaceutical companies were antibiotics (Spellberg et al. 2004) and overall the industry pipeline has few late-stage candidates for antibiotics that can effectively combat the emergence and spread of drug-resistant bacterial strains (Pray 2008). Without urgent action to spur investment in discovering new products, health facilities will be increasingly unable to treat bacterial infections effectively. Already an estimated 175 000 people die each year from incurable hospital-acquired infections within the EU alone (European Academies Science Advisory Council 2007) and eventually this trend will begin to negate the advances achieved in broader medical care. For example, it may become impossible to perform advanced surgical procedures and cancer chemotherapy in the absence of effective antibiotics (ReAct – Action on Antibiotic Resistance 2007). Faced with this potential health crisis, current incentives to promote R&D in antibiotics are clearly insufficient (Cars et al. 2008). A European strategy to address this lack of new antibiotics – based on the best available evidence – is urgently needed (European Medicines Agency and the European Centre for Disease Prevention and Control 2009).

There are numerous reasons behind the lack of investment in new antibiotics. First, the existence of generic antibiotics on the market that are (to varying degrees) still effective in treating the large majority of infections faced by health services. Second, European public health authorities' emphasis on conserving existing antibiotics intended for severe infection by using generics as first-line therapy wherever possible. This sends a message to industry that effective new antibiotics (when developed) will be dispensed infrequently and kept as last resort treatments even if there are high rates of resistance to widely used antibiotics. Third, the limited duration and fully curative nature (i.e. not mitigating symptoms in chronic disease) of antibiotic regimes decrease expected returns on investment and (in countries where direct company-to-physician marketing is possible) may lead to higher marketing costs to keep products salient in the minds of potential prescribers. Therefore, antibiotics do not appear profitable relative to other therapeutic areas. One estimate suggests an NPV of 100 for antibiotics, compared with 300 for an anticancer drug, 720 for a neurological drug and 1150 for a musculoskeletal drug (Projan 2003). Fourth, an antibiotic that develops resistance rapidly has a shorter clinical lifespan and so it is argued that a developer who invests billions of dollars and takes over a decade to develop a new antibiotic may not reap the full benefits of these efforts (Power 2006). So, in theory, the NPV for an antibiotic falls when resistance to a drug develops and spreads amongst the general population (Power 2006). Fifth, with the lack of appropriate assessment within pricing and reimbursement agencies, the prioritization and corresponding price paid by public purchasers does not reflect antibiotics' relative effectiveness in reducing morbidity and mortality. For example, much higher prices are paid for some drugs (e.g cancer or CNS-related) that offer only a few months of additional life (Outterson 2005).

In addition to the lack of relative profitability in the antibiotics market, inherent market failures further deter R&D in this therapeutic area – the existence of externalities is the key failure.[65] Antibiotics have a positive or public health externality – appropriate antibiotic usage helps treat infections that otherwise could spread to the community (Rubin 2004; Saver 2008) and therefore the general public benefits when an individual consumes appropriately prescribed antibiotic therapy. According to economic theory, an antibiotic developer will not produce enough antibiotics since their firm does not obtain all of the benefits. Indeed, discovery and development of new antibiotics has slowed dramatically over the past 25 years. Another key externality surrounds inappropriate antibiotic usage and ensuing resistance. Developers (usually) choose to mass-market their product to increase sales. Individual companies cannot control the sales of other companies and therefore all may aggressively market their own antibiotic, resulting in over prescription and leading to greater rates of resistance. In turn, resistance extinguishes demand for the product. Private companies may not have an incentive to take account of how their antibiotic sales affect future antibiotic effectiveness through the potential for cross-resistance across different antibiotics produced by various companies in the market (Laxminarayan 2002). Consequently, the market price of antibiotics

---

[65] An externality exists when an individual's behaviour has positive or negative effects on another person who is not directly involved in the transaction.

does not adequately reflect the true social cost of AR and too many antibiotics may be being sold to achieve a socially optimal level of consumption. The positive public health and negative AR externalities associated with antibiotic consumption represent market failures given that developers, patients, physicians and other consumers of antibiotics neither directly reap the full benefits of antibiotic consumption nor incur the full costs of resistance. It is for these reasons that many experts recommend that policies that aim to curb the rapid spread of AR push developers to internalize the costs of resistance as well as reap the full benefits of antibiotic drug R&D.

The discovery of new antibiotic agents offers significant potential savings as better treatment of bacterial infection would lead to fewer and shorter hospitalizations and lower costs associated with lost productivity due to disability or death. Smith et al. (2005) suggest that AR causes GDP to fall by between 0.4% and 1.6% (roughly equivalent to a yearly loss of £5–21 billion) in the United Kingdom. United Kingdom household income, government tax revenues and total national savings are estimated to fall by up to 0.3%, 0.35% and 2%, respectively (Smith et al. 2005). In the EU, the cost associated with MRSA infections alone has been calculated to be €117 million in 2001 (European Parliament 2005).

7.2 Preserving the effective life of existing and new antibiotics

Currently, the high growth of resistance stems in part from overprescription of antibiotics. There is a naive acceptance that infections encountered in hospital and especially in community practice are most effectively managed on the basis of clinical assessment (Finch 2007). Cultures currently require 36–48 hours to provide results (Boissinot & Bergeron 2002) so few infections are microbiologically confirmed sufficiently quickly to guide treatment decisions (Finch 2007). This presumptive treatment of patients means that viral infections are often misdiagnosed as bacterial, leading to inappropriately prescribed antibiotics. Risk aversion on the part of physicians (compounded by a mounting tendency for litigation in some countries) and ensuing overprescription of antibiotics will continue to amplify the growth of resistance until doctors have more sophisticated and effective diagnostics that are quick and easy to use at the point of care.

Such technologies could range from the simple to the complex. Finch (2007) suggests that a simple RDT that indicates whether bacterial infection is present or absent would have value; more sophisticated tests that indicate pathogen species, resistance markers and virulence factors would also have a role.

Rapid progress in recent years suggests that numerous technical barriers to the development of these technologies have been overcome. Also, several patents on key platform technologies have expired recently. This has led many researchers to suggest that the major barriers to the technological improvement of RDTs have been removed. The key bottleneck preventing large-scale marketing of these vital technologies therefore does not seem to arise (at least not solely) from supply.

From the demand side, all immediate signals indicate a potentially large diagnostics market, especially if RDTs were to be developed for use at the primary care level. Unlike the antibiotics market the evidence suggests that there are no inherent market failures within the diagnostics market. Rather the key bottlenecks lie elsewhere. Under policies supporting presumptive diagnosis, a developer of an antibiotic that has a good chance of being prescribed is unlikely to be compelled to produce a formal diagnostic device that would potentially limit prescription of the antibiotic. The current absence of large pharmaceutical companies in the diagnostics market could suggest a perceived disincentive to co-develop drugs and diagnostics, but this needs to be explored further. Conversely, use of the diagnostic in systems which properly incentivize formal diagnosis could increase the chance of prescribing a given antibiotic. In addition, the rate of development could also be affected by diagnostic developers' concerns about the uptake and diffusion of a developed RDT, given previously expressed budget priorities (Noderman 2009 [personal communication]).

Specific recommendations for promoting R&D for RDTs lie outside the scope of this report but it should be emphasized that both supply and demand side measures should be assessed to better understand and support the development of RDTs to guide antibiotic treatment. From the supply side, inputs could take the form of targeted support for basic research and increasing access to enabling technologies –from an economic perspective there is little justification for incentives comprising large financial subsidy. From the demand side, this requires a major review of incentives within the health system structure; financing and reimbursement arrangements; the legal framework (including liability issues); and clinical guidelines. The addressing of systems issues appears to hold the most promise for tackling AR (through more targeted and informed prescribing) and for signalling to the industry that there is a large and lucrative demand for good RDTs for bacterial infections. Tools to help guide policy change should include long-term cost-effectiveness analyses that compare the economic costs and benefits of presumptive treatment with procurement of advanced RDTs – given varying levels of pathogen resistance; varying diagnostic sensitivity and specificity; and varying price levels.[66] Such exercises would help

---

66 Similar analyses have been carried out for malaria – taking account of varying levels of absolute and growth rates of pathogen resistance; of diagnostic accuracy; of treatment and diagnostic price levels, as well as a long-term perspective (Shillcutt 2008).

to determine the maximum price at which the public purchaser could consider the procurement of the diagnostic to be cost effective.

Beyond the development and use of diagnostics, conservation of antibiotics will also require a realignment of incentive structures within health services in primary care services and hospitals and within overall financing structures in order to ensure that physicians are not perversely driven to overprescribe antibiotics. Policies relating to performance measurement and spending should take a longer-term perspective in weighing the risks and benefits of overuse. For example, financing structures are a key means by which consumers and prescribers can be influenced and compelled to reduce the use of antibiotics.

Performance targets are another means to influence prescribing practices. The CMS example (see Box 3.1) highlights the importance of using a holistic approach to design benchmarks to drive performance. If the time interval for achieving a benchmark excludes the possibility of performing diagnostic exams, physicians will have no incentive to carry out appropriate procedures. Also, with decentralized budgeting, there is a greater chance that formal diagnosis will not take place if the prescriber's budget must cover the cost of the diagnostic but not the cost of treating the ensuing worsened infection. ABS must also be made a priority within incentive structures. Successful programmes require support from hospital leadership, including significant initial financial investments (Zaoutis 2009).

Finally, patients should be made far more aware of the risks associated with inappropriate antibiotic use, specifically the increased susceptibility to future infections. Given better information, patients may consume fewer antibiotics. In sum, it is crucial that policy-makers design *coordinated* policies that encourage physicians to meet quality care standards while exercising discretion; promote the development and use of diagnostic tools to determine the most appropriate treatment; and improve patient awareness surrounding antibiotic consumption.

7.3 Key concepts in incentive design

The potential for an impending health crisis caused by the lack of new antibiotics; inherent externalities in the market; and the likely cost savings from improving treatment provide ethical and economic justification for a public body to intervene in the market. However, the chances of success will largely be determined by the design of the incentive.

The approach to designing incentives to promote R&D in antibiotics is fundamentally dependent on whether we believe that the number of antibiotics that can be discovered is finite or infinite. If it is finite and, as some experts argue, all the low-hanging fruit have already been picked then the maximum amount of funding must be directed towards conservation and discrete investments in developing new products, consecutively and one at a time. Ideally this process would be driven at a global level to ensure coordination amongst countries. However, if the number is infinite then overcoming obstacles in antibiotic development is merely a matter of investment and alignment of incentives. In this case the priority is to reignite R&D (alongside coordinated conservation initiatives) and spread efforts amongst numerous promising products. This report cannot answer this fundamental question but the incentives presented can help inform decision-making predicated on either of these crucial assumptions. However, the key recommendations do hinge upon the latter assumption, therefore the overall antibiotics market should be kick-started (alongside robust conservation efforts) with some expectation of decreasing marginal returns to development investment. Indeed, interviews undertaken for this book suggest that numerous targets for antibiotic development have been discovered but are currently shelved. New incentives are needed to spark new interest in exploring these molecules, including their potential to create narrow-spectrum products for use against MDR Gram-negative pathogens.

There is no obvious lego-geographical level at which any intervention should be undertaken. The international growth of resistance suggests that this is a global problem that requires a common strategy (Rosdahl & Pedersen 1998). Also, society as a whole stands to benefit from new antibiotics therefore the ideal incentive would be constructed at the global level. This was suggested under the auspices of the global Medical Research and Development Treaty in 2002 – determining minimum levels of support for R&D with an outside body setting the contribution rate for each country and ensuring that these contribution requirements are met (Love 2007). A global mechanism would overcome or mitigate political sensitivity associated with the requirement for governments to set aside large sums of funding. It would also help to improve developers' confidence in the viability of financial commitments. Unfortunately, creation of a global approach is politically dependent and so is unlikely to provide solutions to the urgent innovation needs. However, global approaches to public health deserve far more attention and should be supported now in order to be implemented and functioning properly in years to come.

In the absence of a global mechanism to promote R&D in antibiotics, the EU could partner with agencies in the United States. Such a collaboration could increase the size of the potential investment and capitalize on both the size of the American pharmaceutical market and the American experience with establishing R&D incentives for priority pharmaceuticals. The announcement of the formation of a transatlantic taskforce on antimicrobial resistance (Council of the European Union 2009) indicates some movement in this direction. However, given the urgency for developing new antibiotics, the EU should not hesitate to move independently in applying its own incentives in the short term.

Timing will possibly have the biggest influence on an incentive's chance of success. Push incentives focus on removing barriers to developer entry largely by affecting the cost of investments in R&D. They tend to impact the earlier stages of the development process (Sloan & Hsieh 2006) and include any subsidy made to a developer in the early stages of drug discovery or development, such as grants or early tax breaks. Push incentives may come from both public and private sources such as venture capitalists or large philanthropic donors. In providing early funding, push mechanism are particularly useful for attracting SMEs that often operate with very limited available money (Biotechnology Industry Organization 2009).[67] However, they are also fraught with difficulties. For example, developers paid through push mechanisms often lack the motivation to progress into the more applied phases of production. Indeed, push incentives pose the risk of spending on activities that may not ultimately lead to the development of new products. There is also the danger that the eventual overpayment produced by push incentives will have a dampening effect on entrepreneurialism (Del Brenna 2009 [personal communication]). Push incentives also pose agency problems as researchers are compelled to show their work in the best light possible and may not accurately reflect the merits of investment. Consequently, the funder bears most of the risk of product development funded through push mechanisms.

In contrast, pull mechanisms involve the promise of financial reward only *after* a technology has been developed. Examples include simple monetary prizes; the promise of tax credits to match eventual product sales; or specified AMCs. Pull incentives offer financial reward upon completion of technological advances in order to lure R&D investments in a desired direction and, as profits increase with decreasing development costs, they better align internal incentives to rectify inefficiencies. Also, pull mechanisms provide a reward only upon full product development and authorization thereby incentivizing researchers to self-select the most promising products and bypass many of the principal-agent problems of push mechanisms. However, dependence on the promise of rewards (as opposed to a fully earmarked existing sum) leaves pull mechanisms at the mercy of changing political and economic (and associated budgetary) tides. It has also been suggested that pull mechanisms may corrode existing non-financial incentives to collaborate and slow the overall search for

---

[67] In the United States, BIO currently estimates that 120 companies (30% of all publicly traded biotech companies) are currently in this situation.

solutions. Finally, as pull mechanisms reap financial rewards only following product development, the financial risk involved in all stages of R&D falls on the developer.

Lego-regulatory mechanisms are similar to pull incentives – using enlarged rewards to lure drug development. However, by using higher prices or extended effective IP protection these mechanisms do not require artificial extra-market determination of reward size. This helps maintain the link between reward and product use (and arguably quality) that can be broken by one-off pull incentive awards. This attribute is crucial for antibiotic development given the difficulty of predicting the growth of resistance and hence the duration of product efficacy. By not requiring large lump sums, lego-regulatory mechanisms do not suffer from the lack of credibility than can be associated with rewards promised by funding bodies subject to political or budgetary volatility. However, all the lego-regulatory mechanisms considered here (except pricing and reimbursement reforms) pose the risk of impeding competition, to varying degrees.

The basic elements of push, pull and lego-regulatory mechanisms can be combined to create hybrid mechanisms. These may help to overcome many of the problems of uniquely push or pull incentives, covering (at least partially)

Table 7.1 *Merits of push and pull mechanisms*

Push mechanisms (early research subsidies)	
Advantages	**Disadvantages**
Require smaller financial outlays	Risk of funding unsuccessful research
Remove barriers to entry	Agency problems
Attract SMEs	Risk borne almost entirely by funder
Useful for encouraging discrete steps in R&D	Risk of dampening entrepreneurial momentum
Pull mechanisms (outcome-based extra-market-determined rewards)	
Reward only successful research	Risk is borne entirely by developer
Minimize developer inefficiencies	Attract only developers with significant funding
More likely to encourage final product development	Promise of large reward may lack credibility due to political and budgeting changes over the duration of product development
Lego-regulatory mechanisms (outcome-based market-determined rewards)	
Reward only successful research	Risk borne entirely by developer
Maintain some link between product use and reward size	Attract only developers with significant funding
Minimize developer inefficiencies	May impede competition
More likely to encourage final product development	

the developer's early R&D costs while also providing the profit lure to complete full product development. In comparing the ability of push, pull and hybrid mechanisms to stimulate the development of effective treatments, Hsu and Schwartz (2003) concluded that a hybrid mechanism was the most viable. Indeed the merits of hybrid approaches are increasingly widely accepted as they may provide crucial impetus to overcome developer reticence at the different (perhaps key) stages of product development – early stage push funding provides the increased financial space to explore early discovery ideas without needing to understand their potential; the larger pull element entices developers to undertake the latter phases of development, including expensive Phase III trials. It is important to balance the respective incentive forces within a hybrid incentive (push to pull) as developers have been understood to respond more to profit incentives at the later stages of the research process (Finkelstein 2004). Incentive packages that combine push and pull mechanisms can be as effective as hybrid mechanisms as both spread risk between the funder and the developer. This balance is especially important for antibiotics as the development of an entirely new product (with a novel MoA) presents a significant technical challenge – and thus a high level of risk in going forward with development.

Incentives that use pull mechanisms in the form of specified rewards (e.g. monetary prizes, patent buyout with Strategic Antibiotic Reserve, AMCs) present a good opportunity for public health authorities to communicate their therapeutic priorities and the price they are willing to pay for products that respond to those priorities. However, the critical challenge of these incentives lies in the required ex ante estimation of the optimal financial reward. The reward should be large enough to attract researchers with the necessary skill set while avoiding overpayment that wastes scarce public or donated resources. This difficult balance is crucial to the success of the incentive and must take account of a number of considerations, especially if the resistance profile is not well-understood at the time the estimation is made. The size of the reward needs to compete with drugs that have higher NPVs (Webber & Kremer 2001) and most proposals also suggest that the judging of the winner and distribution of the prize funds be proportional to the relative innovation or benefits. However, the metric (usually QALYs) for assessing the latter also presents some challenges in practice. For antibiotics specifically, one proposal suggests that an award of US$ 3 billion should be granted to the first effective treatment for a high-priority pathogen (Outterson 2008).

The use of any non-market reward for promoting R&D has an inherent risk of overpaying for the innovation, thereby producing social loss. For this reason it is important not to overemphasize the lack of potential profitability in the antibiotics market. There is a profit to be made from sales in developed countries and, with growing rates of resistance to current treatments, likely legitimate sales of new products will increase even with conservation measures in place. For example, it has been suggested that the temporal increase in the incidence of infections such as MRSA within hospitals and the emergence of CA-MRSA indicate that a market for new treatments does exist and is likely to increase over time with resistance to existing products (Aiello et al. 2006).

Overall, the anti-infectives market is estimated to be worth US$ 79 billion per year, the third largest pharmaceutical market globally after the CNS and cardiovascular markets (IMS LifeCycle™ 2008). The antibiotics market itself is currently estimated to generate sales of US$ 37 billion per year but this position is unlikely to be maintained given significantly slower growth relative to other therapeutic areas. Also, contrary to the theory that the NPV for an antibiotic falls substantially with resistance, some experts suggest that the fall in sales due to resistance occurs only after patent expiry. This would suggest that resistance fails to affect significantly the most lucrative life of the patent. In addition, the developer of a new antibiotic may stand to reap reputational (public relations) rewards from claiming contributions to life-saving products (Aiello et al. 2006; Pompliano 2009 [personal communication]). These advantages are clearly not sufficient to drive the desired level of R&D independently but they should be examined to some degree when calculating an appropriate award. However, when quantifying these gains it should not be assumed that they will be equal to those reaped from research in neglected diseases. Another difficulty in calculating a reward ex ante lies in the political palatability of paying out large sums, given competing priorities within the public sector. Indeed incentives that bypass the overt calculation of reward (e.g. IP extensions) may receive less opposition as the high cost of drug development is hidden.

Some experts suggest that the key strategy for the promotion of drug discovery will be the development of focused cooperation between academic institutions and SMEs (Chopra et al. 2008). Indeed, smaller companies are already starting to fill the gaps left by the larger companies that have pulled out of antibiotics. It has been suggested that SMEs require substantially lower annual sales to recoup investments – perhaps US$ 100–200 million compared with US$ 500–800 million for large companies (Monnet 2005). There is now a precedent for a relatively small company to acquire promising molecules and carry them through development and to market.[68]

---

68 Cubist Pharmaceuticals' development of daptomycin (Cubicin®). Based in the United States, this single-product-driven company purchased the initial molecule from Eli Lilly. It should be noted that daptomycin had undergone some Phase II testing before this purchase. Manufacturing is outsourced to another small company.

7.4 Conclusions on individual incentives

7.4.1 *Direct public subsidy for basic research*

For the future development of new antibiotics it is vital to address the decades-long exodus of specialist knowledge, skills and experience. Traditional tools, such as **grants** and **fellowships for training**, can help attract new scientists to the field. However, there should also be efforts to re-engage older researchers in order to avoid losing existing knowledge that has diverted to other areas over the past decades. Without public funding for capacity building and retraining it seems unlikely that even the most interested developers will be able to find the necessary human resources for basic research to expand work in antibiotics. Specifically, funding could be made available for **basic and translational research** into resistance and potential targets (biomarker discovery), gene identification, platform technologies and clinical development, as discussed in Section 6.1.3.

Support for open-access molecule libraries or open-access research more generally could also help remove barriers to participation and collaboration. Currently few of the requisite tools to support knowledge-sharing within the biomedical sciences are within the public domain and there is strong proprietary history in the field. However, open-access approaches should be publicly supported now in order to foster important developments in the (perhaps near) future. Indeed, the reshaping of the business environment through technology and the changing drug development landscape more generally, would suggest that open source approaches may provide important contributions to product development quite soon. Efforts to hasten this evolution could include mandatory free access to findings stemming from all publically-funded projects.

Despite their ability to foster creative accounting amongst companies (Kremer & Glennerster 2004), **tax incentives** have a successful record in stimulating innovation in the United States by effectively lowering the costs of drug development (Yin 2008). As the effectiveness of these tax credits depends in part on the revenue potential of the final product, it has been suggested that larger tax credits may be required to stimulate R&D for antibiotics as these lose value as resistance emerges (Yin 2008). In Europe, limiting consumption is an essential part of resistance control therefore tax incentives for antibiotics should not apply to post-approval, revenue-related activities such as marketing or sales volumes. Rather than using tax incentives as pull mechanisms, reliant on the lure of high volume sales, they should be used solely for push purposes. The level of the tax credit or rebate should reflect the amount of risk that the donor is willing to take on, as such arrangements place most of the risk of failure on the funder. Yet push tax incentives alone are unlikely to attract interest from developers. For antibiotics, they would need to be combined with a pull mechanism to increase the revenue potential of the drug and create a clearly defined market (Tickell 2005; Yin 2008). However, as the temporal dynamics of tax credits and capital allowances tend to benefit those with existing (upcoming in the case of deferrable credits) tax liabilities, SMEs with limited portfolios stand to gain very little unless the design takes account of their specific needs.

PDPs can provide a mechanism for greater collaboration. While very attractive in theory, it should be noted that complicated partnerships or shared rights can repel participants from any incentive scheme. Partnership arrangements for drugs developed for both developing and developed country markets are particularly difficult to negotiate, especially those surrounding IP rights and pricing (Pecoul 2009 [personal communication]). This is especially true of the traditionally autonomous and financially self-sufficient large companies. Antibiotics is a therapeutic area that lacks the positive public relations effect of neglected diseases and therefore is even less likely to compel large pharmaceutical companies to leave their IP comfort zones and accept shared rights agreements. One proposed solution is to separate the various stages of antibiotic development and licensing. A design option that deserves further exploration entails establishing a not-for-profit foundation for development stages up through Phase II trials. Products could then be licensed to commercial companies for completion of trials and sale in the industrialized market, while sales in the developing world would remain on a not-for-profit basis (Tickell 2005).

While not intended for full product development, the **IMI** is a specially designed PDP that is likely to foster essential collaboration between public and private entities and amongst traditionally competitive private entities in order to tackle key bottlenecks, thereby accelerating product development. While still in its infancy, the key to the IMI's success will likely be the focus on precompetitive technology (means for predicting safety and efficacy) which increases the chances for close collaboration and knowledge sharing amongst experts. The initiative has significant industry support and input. However, this industry support may also present drawbacks – it is yet to be seen whether chosen areas of work will derive from pure financial interest or rather reflect the most socially beneficial areas of therapeutic need, such as antibiotics. The inclusion of the topic of diagnostics (to improve trials for respiratory tract infections) in the recent second call is a positive sign for the tackling of resistance. In sum, the IMI should be considered as a promising collaboration to foster important developments in safety and efficacy in the long term. However, as with PDPs in general, such an arrangement is not likely to offer solutions to urgent development needs.

The pull effect produced by a prize-based incentive is dependent on an appropriate calculation of the reward (see Box 6.9 for discussion). If the magnitude of the prize is sufficiently large, sales can be decoupled from the recouping of R&D costs. In this case, **monetary prizes** can help prevent the overmarketing and subsequent overconsumption of an antibiotic product that is ultimately developed. However, the separation of sales from the amount of compensation the developer receives implies that continued product quality has no bearing on the magnitude of the reward. A multiple-winner approach may encourage a greater number of researchers to participate, thereby increasing the overall amount of research focused on a given issue. Naturally, conditions must be used to mitigate the risk of the funder paying more than once for a given development. Monetary prizes will only be attractive to SMEs if they already benefit from early stage funding in the form of venture capital or other forms of push funding. SMEs may also be attracted to this type of pull incentive if their strategy is to bring one product to market rather than develop a multiproduct portfolio. In addition, given the lower revenue requirements for SMEs, it is possible that smaller awards could be used.

Milestone monetary prizes reward developers for reaching certain stages within the product development process, e.g. completing Phase I and Phase II trials. The incremental nature of the reward allows developers to reduce risk by recouping investment costs earlier than under single post-development reward arrangements. Smaller companies likely are also more attracted to this scheme as development costs are reimbursed at an earlier stage of product development, potentially making it easier to attract venture capital for later stages of development. Milestone rewards have the disadvantage that the funding body will reward some research on products that never reach the market – a product that reaches the Phase I milestone may fail during Phase II trials. However, a significant proportion of molecules fail during Phase I therefore part of this weakness could be eliminated by setting the first milestone for successful Phase I trials. Also, as the most expensive stage of clinical trials occurs with Phase III testing, a milestone payment after Phase II could help SMEs to find the additional funds to conduct Phase III trials.

Optional reward systems (Shavell & van Ypersele 2001) can be more advantageous to developers than traditional prize systems as they allow more time to assess the value of the finished product within a more up-to-date economic and competitive environment and make the choice of reward accordingly. Therefore, the optional reward system reduces the developers' risk by passing it to the funders. Further, given the asymmetry of information and the required 10 to 15 years of development, developers are better able to understand the potential resistance profile of the product. Therefore, despite even the strictest criteria for granting of the reward, the risk to the funder is high if the criteria are established at the outset when little is known about the true duration of product effectiveness. Overall, the asymmetry of information combined with the uncertainty surrounding the growth of resistance suggest that this incentive would not be suitable for promoting R&D in antibiotics.

Research tournaments in which a sponsor rewards the developer who has progressed the furthest in research by a specified date (Kremer & Glennerster 2004). They are similar to monetary prizes in that they rely on a pull mechanism and reward to promote competition amongst developers. Their ability to promote development progress depends largely on the number of developers, as well as the level of collusion between them. The main advantage of this incentive design lies in its ability to attract developers who believe that they have a competitive advantage – in antibiotics this could be those with existing molecules that have been set aside. Developers most attracted to the competition would likely be those that have undertaken some discovery work and believe that they have found something promising. However, confidentiality fears could deter those with truly breakthrough technology. Another major disadvantage of this proposal is that sponsors would be obliged to pay the reward regardless of the actual level of overall progress or whether the product is likely to make it to market. Generally, such incentives should be seen as potential mechanisms to overcome specific bottlenecks within the development cycle or to help spur creation of follow-on products. Their suitability for promoting progress in the development of novel antibiotics appears limited.

A **patent buyout** takes place when a monetary award or fund is used to purchase the IP of a new product and secure it in the public domain. Awards that effectively buy the patent from the developer have the advantage of decoupling sales from recoupment of the R&D investment. In the case of antibiotics, this crucially eliminates the need for large-scale marketing and the related overuse of the product. If calculated appropriately, patent buyouts may elicit some interest from smaller companies, public researchers or PDPs that combine the two. They may be more attracted to a one-off payment and a single product development strategy that enables the concentration of limited resources. However, buying out the patent from the developer extinguishes the developer's incentive to produce follow-on generations of the product.[69] Any further exploration would therefore require the product to be licensed to developers[70] under new arrangements for rewarding the incremental innovation.

Kesselheim and Outterson (2010) suggest the use of a stockpile (Strategic Antibiotic Reserve) to boost sales of the first-in-class product purchased in

---

[69] Generally, follow-on products are not novel enough to avoid cross-resistance with earlier generation products over the long term but they can slow resistance in the short term.
[70] Of course, this could be the previous developer who has knowledge advantages in working with the product.

patent buyout, early on, when cheaper alternatives are likely to keep demand low. This certainly deserves further exploration but there is a concern that, over time and even while held largely in reserve, the first-in-class product could face decreased efficacy due to cross-resistance. Similar products may be developed over that period as the market may not remain completely static nor should it be encouraged to do so. Also, in order to qualify for stockpiling antibiotics will likely have to be formulated for simple consumption to ensure they can be disseminated widely to the public in an epidemic. Anecdotal evidence from the United States suggests that antibiotics in their originally marketed parenteral formulations are generally not considered for stockpiling and this may have cost implications for developers.

By specifying price and the number of doses to be purchased **AMCs** have the benefit of aligning incentives for the funder, developer and user early in the development process. These arrangements both reduce the risk to developers and potentially increase the size of the market for the eventual product. AMCs reward successful outputs with predetermined characteristics rather than reward inputs into research that may not succeed (Webber & Kremer 2001), allowing developers to pursue whichever R&D approach or mechanism appears likely to maximize their chances of success. They are seen to combine the incentives of patents and monetary prizes while eliminating the price distortions associated with patents as the profit-maximizing developer does not set the final price (Glennerster & Kremer 2001; Kremer 1998). AMCs applied to antibiotics would likely raise a few key challenges with product specification and quantity guarantee given the changes in the market and the unpredictability of resistance. One suggestion is to avoid establishing a contractual minimum threshold quantity thereby leaving the funder free to choose amongst all the products qualifying for the price guarantee (Barder 2005). This more closely mimics an actual market but substantially increases the risk to the developer. Pricing structure and IP arrangements also affect developer reward and hence risk. Another challenge in applying AMCs to antibiotics concerns the difficulty of determining the purchase volume given the changing epidemiological environment. One option would be for the government to commit to purchasing a certain amount and stockpile the product if too much is purchased. Again, this may have cost implications for developers and must be accounted for in AMC designs with high volume commitments. In addition, there may be substantial risks in committing to purchase large quantities of the developed product before its resistance profile is properly understood – cross-class resistance with the novel product could render it obsolete before the product is even fully marketed. In addition, elements of push funding are likely to be needed if the AMC is to attract SMEs or public sector participants.

A **patent pool** is a coordinating mechanism that enables the collective acquisition and management of IP for use by third parties for a fee. Patent holders from the public or private sector may contribute patents to the pool. A developer wanting to use the patent to develop a new product then seeks a licence from the pool against the payment of royalties to produce the medicines. Efficiency gains are made through the collective management structure which centralizes, simplifies and streamlines the administrative, legal and bureaucratic processes of obtaining and managing licences from a multitude of patent holders. The possibility of a one-stop-shop rather than multiple individual agreements reduces costs and market entry barriers to potential new developers or manufacturers ('t Hoen 2009). Further cost-savings may be achieved through the reduction of litigation costs for patent infringements. Also, perhaps more importantly, pools increase access to IP as developers and manufacturers no longer need to wait out the patent term. This can allow faster downstream innovation and technology transfer and scale-up if and when necessary ('t Hoen 2009). For antibiotics, patent pools may be useful for fostering innovation where developers have previously abandoned efforts. However, it could be argued that the pooled licences are unlikely to be those with the most promise as those would likely be pursued under normal IP arrangements. Therefore, it could be suggested that patent pools are more likely to foster incremental innovation than novel innovation, presenting significant advantages in terms of exploring fixed-dose combinations for creating new antibiotic treatments. Harmonization across all the licences within the pool may facilitate this exploration substantially.

In theory, the reduction of **clinical trial requirements** could help to speed authorization and lower costs associated with the development of new antibiotic products. As discussed, there may be scope for delaying Phase III trials until post-launch for drugs for very serious infections, as for certain HIV/AIDS drugs, or limiting liability through expanded indemnification insurance. Another possibility may be to accept more evidence based on modelling predictions (PK/PD). It is not within the remit of this report to comment definitively on the appropriateness of evidence requirements but it is hoped that they will receive serious analysis and consideration. However, it is strongly recommended that further progress be made towards providing developers with clear and consistent guidance for trials for relevant indications. It is hoped that the upcoming EMA guidelines will be more instructive and perhaps even indication-specific.[71] Whilst it may be necessary to alter regulatory requirements, given scientific understanding and biological evolution, there should be further efforts to maintain transparency and consistency vis-à-vis the demands on developers seeking regulatory approval.

---

71 FDA guidance is already indication specific but guidelines are not available for all relevant indications.

Incentives based on increasing the speed of regulatory review should not be regarded as sufficiently lucrative to stimulate the level of desired innovation in antibiotics. In principle, antibiotics for serious infection that fulfil certain criteria already qualify for **accelerated regulatory assessment** in both the United States and the EU. The existing empty pipeline therefore suggests that these mechanisms do not provide a sufficiently strong lure for developers. The introduction of a priority review voucher would make this privilege transferrable and increase the strength of the incentive in Europe but application of the voucher to another market would cause distortion. Perhaps most importantly, incentives based on the speed of regulatory review may not be suitable to promote R&D for antibiotics given the fragmented regulatory structures of the EU. Even if the scientific assessment is accelerated for priority medicines, post-authorization procedures that extend down to Member States are likely to remain time consuming without broader reforms. Better coordination of regulatory processes across European institutions and Member States (e.g. for HTAs) could help make incentives based on accelerated regulatory review a more viable option.

Unlike many therapeutic agents, antibiotics tend to be prescribed as short-course fully curative regimens. Their extensive use in clinical practice reflects the expedient and often life-saving nature of these drugs but their advantages are not fully acknowledged by **pricing and reimbursement** agencies. Indeed, pricing and reimbursement decisions appear minimally to reflect actual therapeutic benefits or cost savings that drugs provide. There are suggestions to tie pricing and reimbursement to the social value of the product. Measurement of a product's social value is challenging but even an imperfect metric such as the QALY[72] would likely suffice for such calculations in the short term. Limited pricing and reimbursement reform to better reflect therapeutic value may be possible in the short to medium term or while a more holistic social-value based system is developed. The (fulfilled) promise of higher prices would go far in luring developers to antibiotics. Further, in contrast to patent-term extensions, reimbursement incentives would allow developers to recoup R&D costs at an early stage (Outterson 2008) and reduce their amount of risk. Also, reimbursement incentives have a direct influence on prescribers and patients and in turn could provide positive knock-on effects on conservation efforts and resistance.

Reimbursement and price restructuring could have a significant impact on investment in R&D for antibiotics. However, within a European context, the success of this type of reform as an incentive would depend largely on the number of Member States adopting such an approach. A standardized

---

[72] The QALY design is currently under revision.

European approach to assessment would make the prioritization of antibiotics more credible and in turn contribute greatly to the strength of such an incentive. Such major reforms will undoubtedly take time and therefore reimbursement reforms should be perceived as a key approach for directing R&D investment towards long-term needs rather than a solution to fill urgent treatment gaps. However, in the short to medium term even minor price-restructuring within Member States could help start more appropriate prioritization of R&D investment.

In paying developers retrospectively according to the estimated health benefits derived from the use of their products, the **HIF** would initially produce much needed medicines for diseases that are concentrated amongst the poor – including those that are not currently lucrative (Hollis & Pogge 2008). It seems likely that the fund could help to spur innovation in therapeutic areas in which treatments are not available currently or are overpriced and needed by very large populations. This very interesting idea should be explored further even though the HIF is unlikely to meet the need to produce novel antibiotics for MDR bacterial infections in the necessary time frame. The curing of resistant bacterial infection would likely be associated with high QALY values but the existence of generic antibiotics that treat the majority of bacterial infections would not make antibiotics an obvious choice for early HIF registration.

The **ACE Programme** is so far the most holistic proposal aimed at solving the problems of AR and the lack of new product development. In offering rewards for conservation efforts and tying market exclusivity extensions to continued product efficacy, the proposal seeks to align incentives and thereby overcome key problems plaguing the market. Further, as mentioned above, the ACE Programme's proposed reimbursement reforms (tying reimbursement levels to social value) are badly needed to rectify the dissociation between therapeutic value and price. However, the proposal to create umbrella patents over resistance classes (forcing developers to internalize the cost of resistance, thereby producing a greater stake in maintaining product efficacy) raise the same questions of acceptability and practicality as the FRG proposal. It is hoped that the upcoming publication containing details of the ACE Programme will be seriously considered and spur much-needed discussion about the future of AR and the overall multisector incentive structures needed for conservation. However, the proposed ACE reforms should not be relied on to spark the levels of investment needed in the short term.

The process to obtain market authorization is usually long and reduces the effective life of a patent. Proponents of **IP extensions** suggest that a developer's profits from selling a product during the effective patent life may not be sufficient to justify the costs of R&D, particularly for treatments with high

R&D costs and/or lower revenue potential. The high level of interest that large companies demonstrate for IP extensions (for market exclusivity extensions in particular) suggests that they would be likely to continue or re-enter the search for new antibiotics if such lucrative incentives were in place. IP extensions have the advantage of avoiding the need for overt calculation of the amount of public subsidy required to reignite R&D and thus are more politically palatable as the high cost can be hidden. However, while extensions to IP protection may have significant appeal, it must be clear that the ultimate cost associated with these mechanisms will not necessarily be lower. Indeed, the extended monopoly status could impose a significant social cost – increasing IP protection for antibiotics will delay generic competition and postpone the availability of cheaper products. Without differential pricing strategies this will have major knock-on effects for developing countries that are already likely to face delays in accessing new drugs; in areas with high levels of MDR this delay could impose a significant human toll. Also, crucially, the offer of IP extensions for antibiotics risks signalling to industry that any drug category with similar underinvestment will ultimately be granted similar privileged status. Obviously the repercussions of such a message would translate to immense social loss in the longer term.

By allowing patent extension to be transferable across products and companies (wildcard patent extension) this incentive could be made even more powerful and more attractive to SMEs which could sell it on to companies with blockbuster drugs. However, there is a trade-off between luring SMEs to the scheme and minimizing the distortionary nature of the wildcard. Application of the extension to other entirely unrelated products risks severely disrupting the market in other therapeutic areas and also creates problems with equity and transparency (Kesselheim 2009). Further, the potential social loss could be high as the extension would likely be transferred to blockbuster products. Wildcard patent extensions should not be considered for promoting R&D in antibiotics.

Another variation of patent extension incentive involves applying patents over FRGs in order to reduce resistance arising from competition between drugs under different patents for the same condition (Laxminarayan et al. 2007). As mentioned, one firm's inability to control the sales of antibiotics by other companies creates a tragedy of the commons (Horowitz & Moehring 2004; Outterson 2005, 2008, 2009), potentially resulting in aggressive marketing of the drug and thereby accelerating the development and spread of resistance. The FRG scheme would relax antitrust laws to allow companies to sell the rights to their product to another company with a competing antibiotic in the same functional group, thereby creating monopolies through mergers. Patents could then be created for FRGs rather than individual drugs (see Boxes

6.11 and 6.12). Such broad patents will stop companies from competing for the same pool of effectiveness within an FRG and incentivize those without a patent for an FRG to develop new antibiotics outside of the patented classes (Laxminarayan & Brown 2001). This would force companies to better internalize the cost of resistance and to produce and sell antibiotics more closely to the socially optimal level by giving developers the incentive to manage sales and related consumption patterns (and resistance) (Laxminarayan & Brown 2001; Pray 2008).

The creation of FRGs would require reforms to current antitrust laws as they inherently require collaboration that would be interpreted as collusion. This would undoubtedly be seen to present the danger of setting precedents to justify non-competitive activities in other sectors. Aside from this immense challenge, the FRG proposal is fraught with numerous practical difficulties. The number of antibiotic patent owners, the number and variety of patents and their varying levels of remaining IP protection would make the creation of FRGs an extremely complicated process. Classification of the respective FRGs would likely need to be dynamic as resistance develops, given that resistance could emerge across seemingly unrelated classes. Also, the development of both new and follow-on antibiotics could be hindered if developers have no incentive to research drugs in other FRGs where patents already exist (Laxminarayan et al. 2007). In addition, many classes of antibiotics include drugs that are off-patent or have patents owned by different companies, necessitating the implementation of ***sui generis*** rights (Laxminarayan et al. 2007). A *sui generis* right would allow the original patent holder to produce the antibiotic in perpetuity, effectively eliminating the development of generics for off-patent drugs (Laxminarayan et al. 2007). A number of challenges arise from this proposal. For example, it is unclear who would receive rights for off-patent antibiotics – one proposed solution is to hold an auction for the rights over certain classes of antibiotic (Laxminarayan et al. 2007). Overall, and especially if they are considered for the long term, *sui generis* rights are likely to be politically contentious. At the time of writing, there is too little knowledge about tackling the practical challenges of FRGs to merit their recommendation. Significant research would be necessary to understand how to amalgamate new groups while adequately compensating developers within such a system.

Orphan drug legislation has proven to be very successful in promoting R&D for rare diseases. Through a combination of early push benefits and extended market exclusivity, it has appeal for both SMEs and large developers. In theory antibiotics can qualify for orphan status under the current legislation, indeed a few have already received orphan designation[73] and reached the market (e.g.

---

73 European Commission Enterprise and Industry. Register of designated orphan products available at: http://ec.europa.eu/enterprise/sectors/pharmaceuticals/documents/community-register/html/orphreg.htm, accessed 10 July 2010.

aztreonam). However, current legislation has several drawbacks and generally does not set out eligibility criteria in a manner designed for acute short-term conditions. The drafting of new antibiotic-specific legislation should be explored with the possibility of including provisions for desired pricing and volume measures.

The **COA** is a hybrid push-pull mechanism based on the principles of call options in equity markets and AMCs. The model allows an investor to purchase the right to buy something at a later time, in this case the right to purchase a specified amount of an antibiotic at a later date for a specified price. If the product does not reach the market, the purchaser has paid only the cost of the initial option contract and has no further obligations. If the project is terminated following problems during clinical trials, the purchaser retains access and joint ownership of the early findings of the research conducted using the funds from the option. Thus, the purchaser has joint rights to any later antibiotic based on that initial research. The COA model is like most pull mechanisms in that it gives only the option, rather than a commitment, to buy and thereby places substantial risk on the developer. However, the fact that the purchaser pays a premium early in the development phase compensates for some of this demand-side risk.

In providing early funding to developers, the COA may lower barriers to entry and provide crucial funding for SMEs. By spreading the cost of drug purchase it may be more fiscally feasible than other pull mechanisms (e.g. AMCs, prizes), likely producing knock-on effects that increase the credibility of the scheme by improving the funder's chances of compliance. The quality marker within the model crucially allows for the size of the reward to be determined as a function of the type of product developed – more for innovative therapies and less for me-too drugs. However, there are also some shortcomings. For example, the COA hinges on thorough evaluation of the potential drugs and therefore asymmetry of information may hinder efficient allocation of resources to different projects. The model allows potential gaming as developers could take early seed money and then prematurely terminate a project that became more expensive or less viable than expected. Reputational concerns are likely to be important in preventing such offences. Also, when the purchased number of call options has been used the antibiotics return to full price rather than the marginal cost of production. This could have a negative effect on antibiotic prices in developing countries which would only be part of the option scheme if developed and developing country markets were segmented appropriately. However, it could be argued that the higher prices in developed countries could help prevent overdiffusion and consumption of the product. Also, arrangements for joint ownership of early research findings in the event of product failure are likely to be difficult. Finally, the presence of sunk costs in certain projects may unduly influence organizations to purchase sub-par drugs when other better options may have become available in the interim. Yet despite these limitations, early analysis of the COA model suggests that it holds promise for making antibiotic research attractive.

Appendix A
EU Council conclusions on innovative incentives

Council conclusions of 1 December 2009 on innovative incentives for effective antibiotics

(2009/C 302/05)

Nota bene: In this document, the term 'antibiotics' encompasses medicinal products produced either synthetically or naturally used to kill or inhibit the growth of bacteria as well as those with alternative mechanisms of action, for example effect on bacterial virulence. In this context, alternative methods for prevention and control of infections should also be taken into account.

1. RECALLS the Community strategy against antimicrobial resistance (COM(2001) 0333).

2. RECALLS the Council Recommendation of 15 November 2001 on the prudent use of antimicrobial agents in human medicine [1].

3. RECALLS the Council conclusions on antimicrobial resistance of 10 June 2008 [2].

4. RECALLS the Council Recommendation of 9 June 2009 on patient safety, including the prevention and control of healthcare associated infections [3].

5. RECALLS the WHO report (2004) Priority Medicines for Europe and the World [4].

6. RECALLS the ECDC/EMEA joint technical report (2009) 'The bacterial challenge: time to react' on the gap between multi-drug-resistant bacteria in the EU and the development of new antibacterial agents [5].

7. RECOGNISES that the spread of antibiotic resistance is a major threat to public health security worldwide which requires action at all levels. The disease burden related to antibiotic resistant bacteria that cannot be effectively treated with first- or even second-line medicinal products, is rapidly increasing in the world.

8. RECOGNISES that antibiotic resistance could be the final consequence of several inadequacies occurring in the healthcare system and in animal husbandry, including those related to the prevention, management and treatment of infections.

lethal threats and many medical and therapeutic procedures, such as cancer treatments and transplantations, will carry high risks.

10. RECOGNISES that a wide range of measures is needed to ensure that currently available antibiotics remain effective for as long as possible such as effective vaccines to prevent infections, new diagnostic methods and greater awareness among the public, healthcare and veterinary professionals of the importance of rational use of antibiotics to prevent the spread of antibiotic resistance, in both the human and animal sector.

11. RECOGNISES that adequately resourced prevention and control of antibiotic resistance and healthcare associated infections is a cost-effective strategy which contributes to the overall financial sustainability of healthcare systems and ensures continuous quality and patient safety improvements.

12. RECOGNISES that research into and development of new effective antibiotics has significantly declined and probably will not provide sufficient new therapeutic alternatives to meet medical needs within the next 5–10 years. There is therefore an urgent need to create incentives for research and development of new antibiotics, especially in those areas where the need is greatest.

13. WELCOMES the outcome of the Conference on Innovative Incentives for Effective Antibacterials in Stockholm, 17 September 2009, which provided valuable input for further action to promote research and development of new effective antibiotic medicinal products and methods.

9. RECOGNISES that access to effective and rationally used antibiotics is essential to ensure a high level of public health and effective healthcare in both the developed and the developing countries. Without access to effective antibiotics, common infectious diseases may again become

---

(¹) OJ L 34, 5.2.2002, p. 13.
(²) 9637/08.
(³) OJ C 151, 3.7.2009, p. 1.
(⁴) http://whqlibdoc.who.int/hq/2004/WHO_EDM_PAR_2004.7.pdf
(⁵) http://www.nelm.nhs.uk/en/NeLM-Area/News/2009September/17/ECDCEMEA-joint-technical-report-The-bacterial-challengetime-to-react/

14. CALLS UPON THE MEMBER STATES to:

— develop and implement strategies to ensure awareness among the public and health professionals of the threat of antibiotic resistance and of the measures available to counter the problem;

— ensure the development and use of integrated strategies to diminish the development and spread of antibiotic resistance as well as healthcare-associated infections and their consequences, encourage healthcare institutions to have structures in place as well as ensuring effective coordination of programmes focusing on diagnosis, antibiotic stewardship and infection control;

Appendix B
US–EU joint declaration on creation of transatlantic taskforce on antimicrobial resistance

The White House

Office of the Press Secretary

For Immediate Release

November 03, 2009

U.S.-EU Joint Declaration and Annexes
2009 U.S.-EU Summit Declaration
November 3, 2009

We, the leaders of the United States and the European Union, met in Washington to renew our global partnership, and to set a course for enhanced cooperation that will address bilateral, regional and global challenges based on our shared values of freedom, democracy, respect for international law, human rights and the rule of law. Our goal is to ensure a more prosperous, healthy and secure future for our 800 million citizens, and for the world. We will build upon our strong partnership and work together to strengthen multilateral cooperation. As the EU strengthens as a global actor, we welcome the opportunity to broaden our work together, particularly in the areas of freedom, security and justice.

The United States and European Union economies make up over half of global GDP, account for over one third of world trade and are the leading providers of development assistance. The direct impact of our economic policies on the global economy has never been more apparent than over the past year, making the imperative of collaboration even greater. We recognize the importance of expanding our cooperation on issues of global concern, notably climate change, development, energy, cyber security and health. We therefore agree:

- To promote an ambitious and comprehensive international climate change agreement in Copenhagen. Together, we will work towards an agreement that will set the world on a path of low-carbon growth and development, aspires to a global goal of a 50% reduction of global emissions by 2050, and reflects the respective mid-term mitigation efforts of all major economies, both developed and emerging. We recognize the scientific view that the increase in average global temperature ought not to exceed 2 degrees Celsius above pre-industrial levels, as stated by the Leaders of the Major Economies Forum on Energy and Climate. All contributions to the global mitigation effort should be robust, recognizing that their specific features will need to be designed in the light of science and our respective capabilities. In the context of an ambitious agreement in Copenhagen, we are prepared to work to mobilize substantial financial resources to support adaptation for the most vulnerable and to support enhanced mitigation actions of developing countries.

- To strengthen efforts to develop strong and well-functioning carbon markets, which are essential to maximize climate finance and to engage emerging and developing countries in ambitious emissions reduction actions. We will therefore work together to expand carbon markets as we design and implement our cap and trade systems.

- To follow up on our Pittsburgh Summit commitment to implement the G-20 Framework for Strong, Sustainable and Balanced Growth. We commit to remain vigilant to take actions to assure a strong recovery and to plan for cooperative and coordinated exit strategies to be implemented once recovery is ensured. We further commit to undertake financial regulatory reforms to improve the resilience of our financial system to prevent future financial crises, create a 21st century international economic architecture, and address pressing global challenges including energy security and climate, unemployment and decent work. We will continue to fulfill commitments from the Pittsburgh, London and Washington Summits, including the creation of more resilient financial regulatory structures with an enhanced and expanded scope of regulation and oversight.

- To fight protectionism together, as the world's largest economies. We will lead by example by respecting our G-20 commitments to refrain from raising or imposing new barriers to trade and investment. We are committed to supporting efforts by the WTO and other international institutions to monitor new trade barriers with a view to increasing transparency in global trade.

- To make determined efforts to seek in 2010 the conclusion of a Doha Development Agenda agreement. We affirm our commitment to reach an ambitious, comprehensive and balanced agreement, based on the progress already made, including with regard to modalities.

- To intensify our work under the Framework for Advancing Transatlantic Economic Integration and the Transatlantic Economic Council, including through the formation of a high-level innovation dialogue, strengthened regulatory cooperation in key sectors leading to reduced barriers to trade, investment and economic activity. We aim to reach a second-stage air transport agreement in 2010 which includes benefits for both sides.

- To re-launch our dialogue on development [ref Annex 1: Statement on Development Dialogue and Cooperation] with an initial emphasis on sustainable global food security, including investing development assistance through country-led plans and processes, donor coordination and multilateral institutions, as well as to guide our cooperation at policy level. We will also support climate change mitigation and adaptation and will work together in preparation for the Millennium Development Goals Review in 2010. We will also renew our efforts to improve the quality and effectiveness of aid in accordance with the Paris Declaration on Aid Effectiveness and its implementation agreement, the Accra Agenda for Action. We intend to hold the first meeting of this renewed dialogue at ministerial level as soon as possible after the Summit.

- To establish a Ministerial-level U.S.-EU Energy Council [ref Annex 2: The U.S. EU Energy Council] that will improve energy security and contribute to achieving our ambitious climate change goals. The Council will promote new and ongoing cooperation on energy security and markets, energy policy, energy technologies research, and the deployment of clean and sustainable energy technologies which we agree are critical to sustainable economic growth and development.

- To strengthen our cybersecurity dialogue to identify and prioritize areas where we can work together to help build a reliable, resilient, trustworthy digital infrastructure for the future.

- To establish a transatlantic task force on urgent antimicrobial resistance issues focused on appropriate therapeutic use of antimicrobial drugs in the medical and veterinary communities, prevention of both healthcare- and community-associated drug-resistant infections, and strategies for improving the pipeline of new antimicrobial drugs, which could be better addressed by intensified cooperation between us.

We welcome the joint statement adopted by our Justice and Home Affairs Ministers on 28 October 2009, in which we commit to enhancing our policy and operational cooperation on Justice and Home Affairs matters. Our partnership will benefit our people and address our common challenges of maintaining security and individual rights while facilitating travel, business and communication. We face common threats from those who seek to commit acts of terrorism and transnational crime, including the challenge of terrorist travel. With this in mind, we:

- Welcome the ratification of the U.S.-EU Extradition and Mutual Legal Assistance Agreements and look forward soon to their entry into force.

- Welcome the completion of the High Level Contact Group's work to foster mutual understanding and identify a core set of common principles that unite our approaches to protecting personal data while processing and exchanging information. We have important commonalities and a deeply rooted commitment to the protection of personal data and privacy albeit there are differences in our approaches. The negotiation of a binding international agreement should serve as a solid basis for our law enforcement authorities to enhance cooperation, while ensuring full protection for our citizens.

- Will develop our working relationship on mobility and security matters, including border, readmission and travel document security policies. We welcome the signature of the working arrangement between the U.S. Department of Homeland Security and the EU border security agency Frontex and we will work closely to implement it.

- We acknowledge the social and economic benefits to our citizens from visa-free travel in a secure environment between our two continents. We will work together to complete visa-free travel between the U.S. and EU as soon as possible and increase security for travelers.

Reaffirming the necessity of working together on important regional and international issues, we:

- Agree to a joint declaration on nonproliferation and disarmament [ref Annex 3: Declaration on Non-proliferation and Disarmament] highlighting the need to preserve and strengthen the relevant multilateral measures and in particular the Nuclear Non-proliferation Treaty, expressing support for the entry into force of the Comprehensive Test Ban Treaty, and calling for the start of negotiations on the Fissile Material Cut-Off Treaty in January 2010.

The statement reiterates the necessity for Iran and the DPRK to fulfill their international nuclear obligations.

- Reiterate our commitment to seek a comprehensive, long-term and appropriate solution to the Iranian nuclear issue through dialogue and negotiation. This continues to be the objective of our dual-track approach and implies that Iran must fulfill its international obligations on its nuclear program. Iran has rights, but it also has responsibilities. In addition, we express our deep concern about the current human rights situation in the country.

- Declare our determination to achieve a comprehensive and lasting peace in the Middle East, including a two-state solution with Israel and Palestine living side-by-side in peace and security. We are working to remove obstacles and create the context for a prompt resumption of negotiations between the parties.

- Renew our commitments in Afghanistan and the region to initiatives that will increase the capacity of the Afghan government to take responsibility for delivering better security, stability and development for the Afghan people. We welcome in this context the recently adopted Plan for Strengthening EU Action in Afghanistan and Pakistan. We look forward to working with the new Afghan administration and renewing efforts to promote good governance, respect for human rights, gender equality and democratic development. These could be supported at an international conference, possibly in Kabul. We support the strengthening of the assistance and coordination role of the United Nations Assistance Mission in Afghanistan (UNAMA). We welcome the conclusion of the electoral process, and we congratulate President Hamid Karzai on his reelection. We look forward to the formation of a new government, representing the will of the Afghan people. We encourage the new government to swiftly develop an agenda focused on the serious challenges facing Afghanistan.

- Commit to continue to work, including through the Friends of Democratic Pakistan, to assist Pakistan's efforts to promote socio-economic development and respect for human rights and democratic values, to combat violent extremism and to address that country's energy crisis. We will support rehabilitation and reconstruction in Malakand, and target assistance to Pakistan's border regions through the World Bank-administered Multi-Donor Trust Fund agreed by the Friends.

- Will support the countries of Eastern Europe and the Southern Caucasus as they fulfill their great promise by working with them to build strong democracies and prosperous economies. We undertake to strengthen coordination and build on the work of our bilateral initiatives and the

European Union's Eastern Partnership as we work to strengthen these countries' ties to the EU and Euro-Atlantic institutions.

- Support the countries of Southeastern Europe as they advance on the path towards European and Euro-Atlantic integration and welcome progress made in implementing the necessary reforms, including in meeting the criteria set out in the visa liberalization roadmaps of the EU for the Western Balkan countries. We remain committed to the sovereignty and territorial integrity of Bosnia and Herzegovina; we are concerned about the current political situation and strongly urge its leaders to seize the opportunity afforded by the Butmir talks now to adopt the reforms needed to meet the conditions for an application of EU membership and conditions for the NATO Membership Action Plan. We remain committed to a stable, democratic, integrated and multi-ethnic Kosovo and commend the EU rule of Law Mission (EULEX) and KFOR for their role in promoting stability and the rule of law in Kosovo.

Annex 1
Statement on Development Dialogue and Cooperation

The United States and the European Union have agreed to reinvigorate our development dialogue and cooperation in order to improve the quality and effectiveness of our development assistance. In the face of growing challenges to efforts to achieve the Millennium Development Goals (MDGs), sustainable economic growth and poverty eradication, it is more important than ever for the U.S. and the EU, the leading providers of development assistance, to work together on some of the world's most pressing development issues.

We have therefore agreed to re-launch the High Level Consultative Group on Development and to hold annual meetings at ministerial level to advance and guide our cooperation at policy level as well as the achievement of results in the field. The High Level Consultative Group will convene as soon as possible following the Summit to identify and agree outputs under each of the three initial priority topics.

We want to intensify our development policy dialogue and increase cooperation in practical ways to achieve lasting results. In order to improve aid effectiveness, we will accelerate implementation of our commitments under the Paris Declaration and Accra Agenda for Action, with a strong focus on in-country implementation. We will focus our initial cooperative efforts on three common priorities: food security and agricultural development, climate change and the Millennium Development Goals.

Food Security & Agricultural Development: The initial focus of our joint efforts will be to improve global food security and revitalize agricultural development, with an initial focus on Africa. We will agree on a coordinated approach to identify and resource credible, country-owned food security plans through sustained commitments that advance the L'Aquila principles. In line with the Joint Statement on Food Security made by more than 25 countries and organizations at the July 2009 G-8 Summit in L'Aquila and the proposal from the UN Secretary-General and U.S. Secretary of State Clinton on September 26 in New York, and recognizing the importance of national, regional and global partnerships to advance the food security agenda, we agree to join our efforts and expertise in a Global Partnership for Agriculture, Food Security and Nutrition (GPAFSN). The immediate action is to organize key actors to work with host-country governments to support policy reforms, build public and private sector operational capacity, mobilize additional resources and align resources with country-based strategies. In the context of agricultural development in Africa, we will support country ownership in the framework of the Comprehensive African Agricultural Development Program (CAADP) and comparable consensus-building institutions. We will also work together to improve cooperation at regional and global levels in line with L'Aquila principles.

Climate Change: We will work to promote enhanced cooperation at the country level in developing countries of mutual interest to ensure effective and efficient actions to combat climate change. We will concentrate our efforts on the development aspects of climate change with particular focus on adaptation through an enhanced exchange of information on adaptation experiences and identifying opportunities for joint work in priority areas such as capacity building, financing of urgent adaptation needs, building on National Adaptation Plans of Action and other country-driven adaptation strategies and supporting the strategic integration of climate resilience in development policies. Furthermore, we will work together to assist developing countries to develop and implement effective low-carbon strategies and take ambitious actions to mitigate the effects of climate change, taking into account outcomes from the Fifteenth Conference of the Parties to the UN Framework Convention on Climate Change in Copenhagen.

Millennium Development Goals: Over the past nine years significant strides have been made towards most of the MDGs, especially the poverty goal, although progress has been uneven and Sub-Saharan Africa in particular is lagging behind. The economic and financial crisis is now not only threatening the achievement of the MDGs by 2015, but also risks undermining past progress. With only six years remaining before 2015, we recognize that a coordinated international effort is needed to assist developing countries accelerate progress towards the MDGs. Our initial focus will be to agree on a harmonized approach to the September 2010 UN High Level MDG Review. Alongside developing countries, we will focus our joint efforts on actions contributing to the achievement of the MDGs by 2015. On top of delivering on our official development assistance (ODA) commitments, we will concentrate on policy coherence for development and aid effectiveness as well as explore the potential of new innovative financing mechanisms, including new forms of voluntary contributions by citizens and corporations.

Annex 2
The U.S.-EU Energy Council

The United States and the European Union agree to establish the U.S.-EU Energy Council at ministers' level, in order to deepen the dialogue on strategic energy issues of mutual interest, foster cooperation on energy policies and further strengthen research collaboration on sustainable and clean energy technologies.

Members of the Council on the U.S. side are the Secretaries of State and of Energy, and on the EU side the Commissioners for External Relations, for Energy and for Science and Research, as well as the EU Presidency, assisted by the Secretary General/High Representative. It should meet annually, alternately in the U.S. and EU, and report to the U.S.-EU Summit. The Energy Council may decide to delegate preparatory work and follow-up to working groups at senior officials' level.

The Energy Council will study diversification of energy sources, such as through increased use of liquefied natural gas (LNG), solar power, wind power and biofuels, and the use of nuclear power. It will discuss how to effectively promote global energy security on the basis of transparent, stable and non-discriminatory global energy markets and diversified energy sources. Diverse supplies and sources, as well as enhanced energy efficiency and transparent markets, are the surest route to energy security. The Council will foster energy policy cooperation, bilaterally and with third countries, aimed at improving energy security, enhancing energy efficiency, and deepening research, development, demonstration and deployment of sustainable and clean energy technologies.

In particular, the Energy Council will:

- Support action to make energy markets stable, reliable and transparent, particularly in oil and gas and electricity supply.

- Promote the modernization of existing infrastructures wherever necessary and the diversification of energy routes and sources, including the

Euro-Mediterranean Gas and Electricity Ring and a Southern Corridor to Europe, in order to achieve enhanced global energy security.

- Work towards increasing energy efficiency, study expansion of the Energy Star agreement.
- Promote strengthened power grids to facilitate the deployment of renewable and low carbon sources of energy.
- Promote security of transit and key energy infrastructures that could improve energy security at a regional and global level
- Continue to deepen ongoing joint work on new and renewable technologies, and reinforce co-operation in new areas, in particular on smart grids, energy efficient building technologies and new materials for energy applications.
- Deepen collaboration on nuclear energy, both fusion and fission on safety, geological waste disposal and plant lifetime management.
- Support sustainable development of biofuels and biomass.
- Cooperate to develop and demonstrate technologies for carbon capture and storage
- Strengthen cooperation on international energy policy, and consult on an ad hoc basis on approaches to bilateral energy relations with third countries; encourage energy efficiency and low-carbon energy use in developing countries.
- Examine ways to promote partnering between U.S. and European companies and investors in green and sustainable technologies.

Annex 3
Declaration on Non-proliferation and Disarmament

We express our full support for action in the field of non-proliferation, disarmament, and arms control, including through various treaties and other multilateral instruments.

We reaffirm our commitment to seeking a safer world for all and to creating the conditions for a world without nuclear weapons, in accordance with the goals of the Nuclear Non-Proliferation Treaty (NPT). We are convinced that intermediate steps on our path towards this objective can also represent significant increases in security for all.

We welcome the outcome of the UN Security Council Summit on nuclear non-proliferation and nuclear disarmament, express support for UN Security Council Resolution 1887, and recognize the role of the Council in addressing threats to international peace and security arising from non-compliance with non-proliferation obligations.

We are committed to preserve and strengthen the authority and integrity of the NPT. The NPT, based on its three mutually reinforcing pillars of non-proliferation, disarmament, and peaceful uses of nuclear energy, represents a unique and irreplaceable framework for maintaining and strengthening international peace, security, and stability. We will work actively for the successful outcome of the 2010 Review Conference. We welcome the proposals on all three pillars of the NPT presented by the EU, which can inform our efforts to develop a forward looking action plan at the Review Conference. We call upon all States that are not Parties to the NPT to accede as non-nuclear-weapon States to achieve universality. We will also work with regional states to advance the objectives of the 1995 Middle East Resolution.

We welcome the commitment of the United States and the Russian Federation to the further reduction and limitation of their strategic offensive arms and to concluding, at an early date, a new legally binding agreement to replace the current Strategic Arms Reduction Treaty (START).

We express our support for entry into force of the Comprehensive Nuclear-Test-Ban Treaty (CTBT) at an early date, and in the meantime continued observance of moratoria on nuclear test explosions. We call for the immediate start of negotiations of a Fissile Material Cut-off Treaty (FMCT), including verification provisions, when the Conference on Disarmament (CD) reconvenes in January 2010, on the basis of the consensus agreement on a program of work in the CD in May 2009. In the meantime, we call on all states concerned to declare and uphold an immediate moratorium on the production of fissile materials for nuclear weapons or other nuclear explosive devices.

We support UNSCR 1540, welcome its recent comprehensive review, and will continue our consultations to better coordinate third country assistance that promotes adherence to the obligations imposed by 1540 as we work together towards full implementation of the Resolution, including in such areas as export controls and regional centers to promote cooperative efforts. We call on all states to implement the measures included in the Resolution and urge all states and regional and international organizations to cooperate with the Committee established by that Resolution.

We express our full support for the International Atomic Energy Agency (IAEA) and its important work in the field of nuclear safeguards, nuclear safety, and nuclear security. We endorse the Additional Protocol and comprehensive safeguards as the standard for NPT verification. We will work to ensure that the IAEA has the resources and authority to carry out its essential mandate.

We remain committed to ensuring responsible development of peaceful uses of nuclear energy, in the best safety, security, and non-proliferation conditions, by countries wishing to develop their capacities in this field. We encourage the work of the IAEA on multilateral approaches to the nuclear fuel cycle and appreciate ongoing initiatives in this regard. We also welcome research into technologies that will improve proliferation resistance in the nuclear fuel cycle. We also note with interest the initiative by France to convene an international conference on the peaceful uses of nuclear energy, in coordination with the IAEA.

We express our support for the convening of the April 2010 Nuclear Security Summit, recognizing that the unauthorized trade in and use of nuclear materials is an immediate and serious threat to global security. We look forward to concrete proposals to increase the security of vulnerable nuclear materials, which could include measures to effectively investigate and prosecute instances where material has been unlawfully diverted.

We remain fully committed to the fight against nuclear terrorism and support all measures designed to prevent terrorists from acquiring WMD, their means of delivery or related materials. We reiterate our support for the Global Initiative to Combat Nuclear Terrorism (GICNT) and the Proliferation Security Initiative (PSI). We will work together constructively on the possibilities for an expansion of the Global Partnership to new participants and new fields of cooperation and are ready to discuss the role the Global Partnership could play beyond 2012.

We recognize the importance of the IAEA Code of Conduct on the Safety and Security of Radioactive Sources and the associated Guidance on the Import and Export of Radioactive Sources in preventing a radiological attack and will work toward their global implementation.

We stress the importance of the full implementation of the provisions of the NPT. We emphasize that measures are needed to demonstrate that there will be real and immediate consequences for non-compliance with the Treaty or for abuse of its withdrawal provision, such as withdrawing while in violation of the Treaty. The proliferation of weapons of mass destruction and their means of delivery continues to represent a threat to international peace and security. The international non-proliferation regime faces major challenges. We are committed to continue to address them resolutely.

Iran's nuclear activities, in particular the recent revelation of Iran's construction of an undisclosed facility near Qom intended for enrichment, have reinforced the international community's concerns regarding the nature of its nuclear program. We stress that Iran has the responsibility to restore international confidence in this regard and must fulfill its international obligations in order to demonstrate the exclusively peaceful nature of its nuclear program. We urge Iran to engage seriously and constructively with China, France, Germany, the Russian Federation, the United Kingdom, and the United States with the support of the High Representative of the European Union (P-5+1) to advance the dialogue on the nuclear issue begun in Geneva on October 1. We reiterate our commitment to seek a comprehensive, long-term and appropriate solution to the Iranian nuclear issue through dialogue and negotiation based on Iran's compliance with UN Security Council resolutions. This continues to be the objective of our dual-track approach. Iran has rights, but it also has responsibilities. We remain unified in our support for the IAEA's draft agreement that responds to Iran's request for assistance in refueling the Tehran Research Reactor, which represents a confidence-building step, addresses Iran's need for medical isotopes, and creates an opportunity for further progress.

We support the IAEA's efforts to implement verification activities related to the Dair Alzour site in Syria. We call upon Syria to adopt promptly an Additional Protocol and provide, without further delay, access to additional information and sites as requested by the Agency to complete its ongoing assessment.

We call on the Democratic People's Republic of Korea (DPRK) to live up to its obligations as called for in the September 2005 Joint Statement, and to take steps toward irreversible verifiable denuclearization. We reiterate the importance of full and transparent implementation of UNSCRs 1718 and 1874 as tools to constrain the DPRK's proliferation activities and to convince the DPRK to return to the Six-Party Talks and denuclearization.

We will continue to work toward universalisation and full implementation of the Chemical Weapons Convention and we support, to this end, the work of the Organization for the Prohibition of Chemical Weapons.

We will also work for the universalisation and full implementation of the Biological and Toxin Weapons Convention (BTWC) and we encourage, in this regard, the work of the Implementation Support Unit. We continue to support the intersessional Program of Work, including efforts to improve the ability of all nations to recognize and respond to outbreaks of infectious disease. We will continue to work together to find ways to address the evolution of the biological weapon threat, and to promote compliance with the BTWC by greater transparency and effective implementation.

We appreciate our continued productive dialogue on verification and compliance, established at the EU-U.S. 2005 Summit.

We support the Hague Code of Conduct (HCoC) and other efforts to curb the proliferation of missile technology and will aim at universality and better implementation of HCoC provisions.

We recognize the importance of effective export controls, and we will work together to strengthen all multilateral export control regimes and to provide assistance to third countries in improving their export controls to international standards, as required by UNSCR 1540 obligations. We endorse efforts to reach agreement within the Nuclear Suppliers Group this year on strengthened export controls on enrichment and reprocessing technologies and on making the Additional Protocol a standard for nuclear supply.

We recognize the importance of using appropriate financial tools to strengthen the international framework to combat proliferation finance and will continue to work together on this issue in the Financial Action Task Force.

We support efforts to overcome the current issue with the Russian Federation with respect to the Treaty on Conventional Armed Forces in Europe in order to preserve its long term viability.

We welcome agreement to negotiate an Arms Trade Treaty (ATT) and urge that transfers of all conventional weapons be subject to the highest possible standards, so that they do not contribute to regional instability or support violations of human rights. We support the UN Program of Action to prevent, combat, and eradicate the illicit trade in Small Arms and Light Weapons in all its aspects.

We are convinced that working together in the area of non-proliferation, disarmament and arms control, and cooperating with all our partners, will significantly contribute to a safer world.

Appendix C
Global vaccine research

Table A *New vaccines against infectious diseases: R&D status as of February 2006*

Pathogen		Vaccine mechanism	Developer	Stage
Streptococcus	Group A (S. pyogenes)	26-valent M protein N-terminal epitopes + conserved protein Spa	ID Biomedical	Phase II
		J14 moiety fusion peptide combined with 7-valent determinants on polymer backbone	Queensland Institute of Medical Research, Australia	Ready to enter Phase I
		C-terminal part of M protein expressed as a fusion protein on surface of Streptococcus gordonii	Rockefeller University, New York/SIGA	Phase I
		Recombinant fusion peptide containing N-terminal M protein fragments from Group A Streptococcus serotypes 1, 3, 5, 6, 19, and 24	Center for Vaccine Development, Baltimore, USA	Phase I
Neisseria meningitidis	Groups A,C, Y, W135	Group A PS conjugate	Serum Institute of India	Phase I
		Trivalent A, C,W135 PS	GSK	Phase II
		Tetravalent PS conjugate	Sanofi Pasteur	Licensure
		Heptavalent DPT-HepB-Hib-MenA/C conjugate	GSK	Phase II
	Group B	NZ Por A outer membrane vesicles	GSK	Phase II
		New membrane protein subunit	Chiron/Auckland University	Phase III/IV
		New membrane protein subunit	Chiron/Microscience	Preclinical/Phase I

Pathogen	Vaccine mechanism	Developer	Stage
Streptococcus pneumoniae	Conjugate 13-valent (tridecavalent) vaccine containing serotypes 6A and 19A	Wyeth (Prevenar 13™)	13 March 2009 Biologic licence application (BLA) submitted to FDA. Fast-track status.
	Conjugate 9-valent vaccine	Wyeth (Prevenar)	End of Phase III
	Conjugate 11-valent vaccine	Sanofi Pasteur;	Phase III
		GSK Phase III completed (old formulation)	Phase II (improved formulation)
	BVH3/11V fusion protein	ID BioMedical	Phase I completed
	PspA+PsaA	Sanofi Pasteur	Phase I in adults
	Pneumolysin, PspA, adhesins, PiaA, PiuA, etc, subunit or DNA vaccines	Various academic institutions	Preclinical/Phase I
C. difficile	*C. difficile* candidate vaccine	Acambis, now part of Sanofi Pasteur	Phase II
Enterococcus	*E. faecalis* and *E. faecium* (enterococcus)	Vancomycin	
S. aureus		StaphVAX (Nabi Biopharmaceuticals) V710 (Merck & Co./Intercell) SA75 (VRi Plc)	StaphVAX, based on patented technology that Nabi licensed from the Public Health Service/NIH

Source: Adapted from WHO Initiative Vaccine Research (Special Programme for Research and Training in Tropical Diseases 2007).

Appendix D
Possible funding mechanisms for a COA scheme

The EC has mandated the European Investment Bank (EIB) and the European Investment Fund (EIF) to manage two financial tools aiming at supporting and encouraging innovation within the EU.

Risk-sharing finance facility (RSFF)

The EC and the EIB set up the RSFF under the umbrella of the knowledge economy to which the EIF also contributes. Intended partly to address the dearth of (particularly more high risk) funding for R&D in the EU area, the RSFF's supporting programme is the FP7, the main financial tool through which the EU supports R&D (European Investment Bank 2009). Like FP7, the RSFF runs from 2007 to 2013. Each party is expected to provide up to €1 billion which in turn is expected to attract four to six times the community funds provided to the facility, possibly up to €10 billion (European Investment Bank 2009). An average of 20% of the volume of each loan is set aside for risk coverage. For loans of less than €7.5 million the RSFF is available indirectly through intermediary banks (and other institutions) in Member States (European Investment Bank 2009) and therefore it is likely that the eligibility criteria for these smaller loans are even more stringent.

The requirement for loan beneficiaries to be creditworthy limits the eligibility of many smaller SMEs and biotechs that may not have revenue-yielding products already on the market or the capacity to carry out clinical trials within Europe. Research, Development and Innovation projects tend to be multi-annual (3–4 years) (European Investment Bank 2009). RSFF can support a range of these projects, from basic to applied research and from proof of concept to feasibility studies. Eligible investments can be tangible (construction and equipment) or intangible (salaries, operating cost, management and support staff, utilities, consumables, IP acquisition) assets and can cover up to 50% of eligible investments (European Investment Bank 2009).

Until the end of 2008, 23% of RSFF funds had been allocated to life sciences and predominantly to mid-cap companies such as Solvay and Teva. Very few SMEs or biotech companies have been successful in securing these loans but PharmaMar is a notable exception. This Spanish biotechnology company (with successful products launched and in pipeline) received a €30 million RSFF loan to assist continuation of their work on innovative anticancer treatments of marine origin (European Investment Bank 2009).

Competitiveness and Innovation Framework Programme

This programme is a €1.1 billion facility (of which €160 million is earmarked for eco-innovation) to encourage the competitiveness of European enterprises, support innovation and provide SMEs with better access to finance through a venture-capital style mechanism. The facility is split between venture capital and guarantees covering the period 2007–2013. The former capability is provided by the High Growth and Innovative SME Facility (GIF; €550 million) and the latter by the SME Guarantee Facility (SMEG; €506 million). The EU guarantees are provided by the EIF on behalf of the EC and cover a part of the risk of the financial intermediary relating to the relevant loans or lease transactions (European Investment Bank 2009).

- The GIF supports innovative SMEs by providing risk capital in their early stages through GIF1 (EIF investing 10–25% of total funds raised by the intermediary venture capital fund) and their expansion phase through GIF2 (EIF investing 7.5–15% by total funds raised). Additionally, investments in new funds likely to have a particularly strong catalytic role can be up to 50% in GIF1 and 25% in GIF2, to a maximum of €30 million. These provide important leverage for the supply of equity to these companies (European Investment Bank 2009).

- Through the SMEG the EIF supports SMEs by providing co-, counter and direct guarantees to financial intermediaries providing loans, mezzanine finance and equity to SMEs. The objective of the SMEG is to reduce the particular difficulties that SMEs face in accessing finance, due either to the perceived higher risk or to lack of sufficient collateral (European Investment Bank 2009).

References

Abramowicz M (2003). Perfecting patent prizes. *Vanderbilt Law Review*, 56:115–236.

Adams C, Brantner V (2006). Estimating the cost of new drug development: is it really $802 million? *Health Affairs*, 25:420–428.

Aiello A et al. (2006). Ethical conflicts in public health research and practice: antimicrobial resistance and the ethics of drug development. *American Journal of Public Health*, 96:1910–1914.

Allerberger F et al. (2008). Antibiotic stewardship through the EU project – ABS international. *Wiener Klinische Wochenschrift*, 120:256–263.

Alliance for the Prudent Use of Antibiotics (1999). *Questions and answers about antibiotics and resistance*. Boston, MA, Alliance for the Prudent Use of Antibiotics (http://www.tufts.edu/med/apua/Q&A/Q&A.html, accessed 12 November 2008).

Alliance for the Prudent Use of Antibiotics (2005). Executive summary: global antimicrobial resistance and implications. *Clinical Infectious Diseases*, 41:S221–S223.

Anderson T (2009). Novartis under fire for accepting new reward for old drug. *Lancet*, 373:1414.

André F (2002). How the research-based industry approaches vaccine development and establishes priorities. *Developments in Biologicals*, 110:25–29.

Arias C, Murray B (2009). Antibiotic-resistant bugs in the 21st century – a clinical super-challenge. *New England Journal of Medicine*, 360:439–443.

Arnold S, Straus S (2005). Interventions to improve antibiotic prescribing practices in ambulatory care. *Cochrane Database of Systematic Reviews*, 4:CD003539.

Ball P (2000). Quinolone-induced QT interval prolongation: a not-so-unexpected class effect. *Journal of Antimicrobial Chemotherapy*, 45:557–559.

Bancroft E (2007). Antimicrobial resistance: it's not just for hospitals. *JAMA*, 298:1803–1804.

Barder O, ed. (2005). *Making markets for vaccines: a practical plan*. Washington, DC, Center for Global Development and Global Health Policy Research Network (http://www.who.int/intellectualproperty/news/en/SubmissionBarder1.pdf, accessed 23 February 2009).

Barlam T, DiVall M (2006). Antibiotic-stewardship practices at top academic centers throughout the United States and at hospitals throughout Massachusetts. *Infection Control and Hospital Epidemiology*, 27:695–703.

Barquet N, Domingo P (1997). Smallpox: the triumph over the most terrible of the ministers of death. *Annals of Internal Medicine*, 127:635–642.

Barrett C, Barrett J (2003). Antibacterials: are the new entries enough to deal with emerging resistance problems? *Current Opinion in Biotechnology*, 14:621–626.

Barrett J (2005). Can biotech deliver new antibiotics? *Current Opinion in Microbiology*, 8:498–503.

Battista R, Hodge M (1999). The evolving paradigm of health technology assessment: reflections for the Millennium. *Journal of the Canadian Medical Association*, 160:1464–1467.

Bauraind I et al. (2004). Association between antibiotic sales and public campaigns for their appropriate use. *JAMA*, 292:2468–2470.

Berndt E, Hurvitz J (2005). Vaccine advance-purchase agreements for low-income countries: practical issues. *Health Affairs*, 24:653–665.

Berndt E et al. (2005a). *Advanced purchase commitments for a malaria vaccine: estimating costs and effectiveness*. Cambridge, MA, National Bureau of Economic Research (NBER Working Paper No. 11288).

Berndt E et al. (2005b). Industry funding of the FDA: effects of PDUFA on approval times and withdrawal rates. *Nature Reviews Drug Discovery*, 4:545–554.

Berndt E et al. (2007). Advance market commitments for vaccines against neglected diseases: estimating costs and effectiveness. *Health Economics*, 16:491–511.

Bhattaram V et al. (2005). Impact of pharmacometrics on drug approval and labeling decisions: a survey of 42 new drug applications. *AAPS Journal*, 7:E503–E512.

Biotechnology Industry Organization (2009). *Press release: Biotech funding crisis*. Washington, DC, Biotechnology Industry Organization (http://bio.org/news/pressreleases/newsarchive.asp?year=2009, accessed March 2009).

Boissinot M, Bergeron M (2002). Toward rapid real-time molecular diagnostic to guide smart use of antimicrobials. *Current Opinion in Microbiology*, 5:478–482.

Boucher H et al. (2009). Bad bugs, no drugs: no ESKAPE! An update from the Infectious Diseases Society of America. *Clinical Infectious Diseases*, 48:1–12.

Bradley J et al. (2007). Anti-infective research and development – problems, challenges, and solutions. *Lancet Infectious Diseases*, 7:68–78.

Braine T (2008). Controversial funding mechanism to fight pneumonia. *Bulletin of the World Health Organization*, 86:321–416.

Brogan D, Mossialos E (2006). Applying the concepts of financial options to stimulate vaccine development. *Nature Reviews Drug Discovery*, 5:641–647.

Brown S (2006). *Global public-private partnerships for pharmaceuticals: operational and normative features, challenges, and prospects*. Ottawa, Canadian Political Science Association (http://www.cpsa-acsp.ca/papers-2006/Brown.pdf, accessed 13 March 2009).

Bryce E, Kerschbaumer V (2000). The cost of doing business – managing MRSA and VRE. *Infection Control and Hospital Epidemiology*, 21:119.

Buse K (2003). *Governing partnership – a comparative analysis of the organizational and managerial arrangements of 18 global public-private partnerships*. Geneva, Initiative for Public-Private Partnerships for Health.

Buse K, Harmer A (2007). Seven habits of highly effective global public-private health partnerships: practice and potential. *Social Science and Medicine*, 64:259–271.

Buse K, Walt G (2000). The United Nations and public-private partnerships: in search of 'good' global governance. *Workshop on Public-Private Partnerships in Public Health, Dedham, MA, 7–8 April 2000*.

Carroll K (2008). Rapid diagnostics for methicillin-resistant *Staphylococcus aureus*: current status. *Molecular Diagnosis and Therapy*, 12:15–24.

Cars O et al. (2008). Meeting the challenge of antibiotic resistance. *BMJ*, 337:726–728.

Caves R et al. (1991). *Patent expiration, entry, and competition in the US pharmaceutical industry*. Washington, DC, Brookings Institution Press.

Centers for Disease Control and Prevention (CDC) (2008). *If you have a cold or flu, antibiotics won't work for you!* Atlanta, GA, Centers for Disease Control and Prevention (http://www.cdc.gov/Features/getSmart/, accessed 23 February 2009).

Chapman S, Durieux P, Walley T (2004). Good prescribing practice. In: Mossialos E, Mrazek M, Walley T, eds. *Regulating pharmaceuticals in Europe: striving for efficiency, equity and quality*. Maidenhead, Open University Press:144–157.

Charles P, Grayson M (2004). The dearth of new antibiotic development: why we should be worried and what we can do about it. *Medical Journal of Australia*, 181:549–553.

Chopra I et al. (2008). Treatment of health-care-associated infections caused by Gram-negative bacteria: a consensus statement. *Lancet Infectious Diseases*, 8:133–139.

Coast J et al. (1998). An economic perspective on policy to reduce antimicrobial resistance. *Social Science and Medicine*, 46:29–38.

Coenen S et al. (2001). Variation in European antibiotic use. *Lancet*, 358:1272.

Community Research and Development Information Service (CORDIS) (2009) [web site]. New project to create pan-European network of microbiological resources. Luxembourg, Publications Office of the European Union (http://cordis.europa.eu/fetch?CALLER=FP7_NEWS&ACTION=D&RCN=30592, accessed 7 April 2009).

Congressional Budget Office (1998). *How increased competition from generic drugs has affected prices and returns in the pharmaceutical industry*. Washington, DC, U.S. Department of Health & Human Services (http://www.fda.gov/ohrms/DOCKETS/dailys/04/June04/061404/03p-0029-bkg0001-Ref-15-vol3.pdf, accessed 27 March 2009).

Cosgrove S (2006). The relationship between antimicrobial resistance and patient outcomes: mortality, length of stay, and health care costs. *Clinical Infectious Diseases*, 42:S82–S89.

Cosgrove S, Carmeli S (2003). The impact of antimicrobial resistance on health and economic outcomes. *Clinical Infectious Diseases*, 36:1433–1437.

Cosgrove S et al. (2003). Comparison of mortality associated with methicillin-resistant and methicillin-susceptible *Staphylococcus aureus* bacteremia: a meta-analysis. *Clinical Infectious Diseases*, 36:53–59.

Council of the European Union (2009). *Council conclusions on innovative incentives for effective antibiotics*. Brussels, Council of the European Union.

Croft S (2005). Public-private partnership: from there to here. *Transactions of the Royal Society of Tropical Medicine and Hygiene*, 99:S9–S14.

Croft S, Engel J (2006). Miltefosine – discovery of the antileishmanial activity of phospholipid derivatives. *Transactions of the Royal Society of Tropical Medicine and Hygiene*, 100:S4–S8.

Croghan T, Pittman P (2004). The medicine cabinet: what's in it, why, and can we change the contents? *Health Affairs*, 23:23–33.

Dagan R, Klugman K (2008). Impact of conjugate pneumococcal vaccines on antibiotic resistance. *Lancet Infectious Diseases*, 8:785–795.

Danzon PM et al. (2003). *Productivity in pharmaceutical biotechnology R&D: the role of experience and alliances*. Cambridge, MA, National Bureau of Economic Research (NBER Working Paper No. 9615).

Datamonitor (2003). *Strategic perspectives: vaccines – optimum growth in a crowded market place*. New York, NY, Datamonitor (ID: DFMN886361).

Davey P et al. (2005). Interventions to improve antibiotic prescribing practices for hospital inpatients. *Cochrane Database of Systematic Reviews*, 4:CD003543.

Davin-Regli A, Pegis J (2007). Regulation of efflux pumps in Enterobacteriaceae: genetic and chemical effectors. In: Amabile-Cuevas C, ed. *The threat of antibiotic-resistant bacteria and the development of new antibiotics*. Norwich, Horizon BioScience:55–75.

Davis L (2004). How effective are prizes as incentives to innovation? Evidence from three 20th century contests. *DRUID Summer Conference 2004 on Industrial Dynamics, Innovation and Development, Elsinore, Denmark, 14–16 June 2004* (http://www2.druid.dk/conferences/viewpaper.php?id=2387&cf=16, accessed 26 April 2010).

de Pastors A (1995). Supplementary protection certificates. Situation after two years of operation of the EC1768/92 SPC Regulation. *World Patent Information*, 17:189–192.

de Varax A et al. (2008). *Study on orphan drugs. Phase 1: overview of the conditions for marketing orphan drugs in Europe.* Paris, ALCIMED (http://ec.europa.eu/enterprise/sectors/pharmaceuticals/files/orphanmp/doc/pricestudy/final_final_report_part_1_web_en.pdf, accessed 24 May 2010).

Deasy J (2009). Antibiotic resistance: the ongoing challenge for effective drug therapy. *Journal of the American Academy of Physician Assistants*, 22:18–22.

DeBresson C, Amesse F (1991). Networks of innovators: a review and introduction to the issue. *Research Policy*, 20:363–379.

Dellit T et al. (2007). Infectious Diseases Society of America and the Society for Healthcare Epidemiology of America guidelines for developing an institutional program to enhance antimicrobial stewardship. *Clinical Infectious Diseases*, 44:159–177.

Demain A, Sanchez S (2009). Microbial drug discovery: 80 years of progress. *Journal of Antibiotics*, 62:5–16.

Dentico N, Ford N (2005). The courage to change the rules: a proposal for an essential health R&D treaty. *PLoS Medicine*, 2:e14.

Derbyshire K, Bardarov S (2000). DNA transfer in mycobacteria: conjugation and transduction. In: Hatfull G, Jacobs W, eds. *Molecular genetics of mycobacteria.* Washington, DC, ASM Press:93–107.

DiMasi J et al. (2003). The price of innovation: new estimates of drug development costs. *Journal of Health Economics*, 22:151–185.

DiMasi J et al. (2004). *Assessing claims about the cost of new drug development: a critique of the public citizen and TB Alliance reports.* Boston, MA, Tufts Center for the Study of Drug Development, Tufts University (http://csdd.tufts.edu/files/uploads/assessing_claims.pdf, accessed 26 April 2010).

Dorlo T et al. (2008). Pharmacokinetics of miltefosine in old world cutaneous leishmaniasis patients. *Antimicrobial Agents and Chemotherapy*, 52:2855–2860.

Dove A (2007). Biomedical research faces flat budget for 2008. *Nature Medicine*, 13:228–229.

Drusano G (2004). Antimicrobial pharmacodynamics: critical interactions of 'bug and drug'. *Nature Reviews Microbiology*, 2:289–300.

Durieux P et al. (2008). Computerized advice on drug dosage to improve prescribing practice. *Cochrane Database of Systematic Reviews*, 3:CD002894.

Edgar T et al. (2009). Sustainability for behaviour change in the fight against antibiotic resistance: a social marketing framework. *Journal of Antimicrobial Chemotherapy*, 63:230–237.

Elbasha, E (2003). Deadweight loss of bacterial resistance due to overtreatment. *Health Economics*, 12:125–138.

Engemann J et al. (2003). Adverse clinical and economic outcomes attributable to methicillin resistance among patients with *Staphylococcus aureus* surgical site infection. *Clinical Infectious Diseases*, 36:592–598.

European Academies Science Advisory Council (2007). *Tackling antibiotic resistance in Europe.* London, The Royal Society (http://www.knaw.nl/pdf/EASAC_Antibacterial_resistance.pdf, accessed 23 February 2009).

European Agency for the Evaluation of Medicinal Products (1999). *Public statement on Trovan/Trovan IV/Turvel/Turvel IV (trovafloxacin/alatrofloxacin). Recommendation to suspend the marketing authorisation in the European Union*. London, European Agency for the Evaluation of Medicinal Products (EMEA/18046/99).

European Agency for the Evaluation of Medicinal Products (2000). *Points to consider on pharmacokinetics and pharmacodynamics in the development of antibacterial medicinal products*. London, European Agency for the Evaluation of Medicinal Products (CPMP/EWP/2655/99).

European Agency for the Evaluation of Medicinal Products (2004). *Note for guidance on evaluation of medicinal products indicated for treatment of bacterial infections*. London, European Agency for the Evaluation of Medicinal Products (CPMP/EWP/558/95 rev 1).

European Antimicrobial Resistance Surveillance System (2007). *EARSS Annual Report 2006*. Bilthoven, European Antimicrobial Resistance Surveillance System.

European Antimicrobial Resistance Surveillance System (2008). *EARSS Annual Report 2007*. Bilthoven, European Antimicrobial Resistance Surveillance System.

European Commission (2009) [web site]. FP7 *Health budget 2007–2013*. Brussels, European Commission (http://ec.europa.eu/research/fp7/index_en.cfm?pg=health, accessed 13 March 2009).

European Generic Medicines Association (2001). *Data exclusivity and the 2001 review*. Brussels, European Generic Medicines Association (EGA Discussion Paper) (http://www.egagenerics.com/doc/ega_dataex-2001-07.pdf, accessed 26 April 2010).

European Generic Medicines Association (2007) [web site]. Data exclusivity. Brussels, European Generic Medicines Association (http://198.170.119.137/gen-dataex.htm, accessed 24 May 2010).

European Investment Bank (2009). *Banking on research, banking for research. Risk-sharing finance facility (RSFF)*. Brussels, European Commission (http://ec.europa.eu/invest-in-research/pdf/download_en/rssfb_brochure.pdf, accessed 26 April 2010).

European Medicines Agency (2008). *Public statement on Levviax (telithromycin). Withdrawal of the marketing authorization in the European Union*. London, European Medicines Agency (EMEA/CHMP/26421/2008).

European Medicines Agency (2009a). *Survey 2008 on the performance of EMEA scientific procedures for medicinal products for human use*. London, European Medicines Agency (EMEA/MB/30754/2009).

European Medicines Agency (2009b). *Follow-up recommendations from CHMP on novel influenza (H1N1) outbreak, Tamiflu (oseltamivir), Relenza (zanamivir)*. London, European Medicines Agency (EMEA/CHMP/326095/2009).

European Medicines Agency (2009c) [web site]. Press release – Relenza to be distributed with Rotacap/Rotahaler inhalation device during influenza pandemic. London, European Medicines Agency (http://www.ema.europa.eu/influenza/newsroom/newsroom.html, accessed 26 April 2010).

European Medicines Agency and the European Centre for Disease Prevention and Control (2009). *The bacterial challenge – time to react. A call to narrow the gap between multidrug-resistant bacteria in the EU and development of new antibacterial agents*. London, European Medicines Agency (http://www.ema.europa.eu/pdfs/human/antimicrobial_resistance/53394009en.pdf, accessed 26 April 2010).

European Parliament (1999). *Orphan drugs*. Brussels, STOA Publications (PE 167 780/Fin. St.).

European Parliament (2005). *Antibiotic resistance*. Brussels, European Parliament, Policy Department, Economic and Scientific Policy (http://www.europarl.europa.eu/stoa/publications/studies/stoa173_en.pdf, accessed 31 October 2008).

Fasihul A et al. (2009). The additional costs of antibiotics and re-consultations for antibiotic-resistant *Escherichia coli* urinary tract infections managed in general practice. *International Journal of Antimicrobial Agents*, 33:255–257.

Ferech M et al. (2006). European surveillance of antimicrobial consumption (ESAC): outpatient antibiotic use in Europe. *Journal of Antimicrobial Chemotherapy,* 58:401–407.

Finch R (2007). Innovation – drugs and diagnostics. *Journal of Antimicrobial Chemotherapy*, 60:i79–i82.

Finch R, Hunter P (2006). Antibiotic resistance – action to promote new technologies: report of an EU Intergovernmental Conference held in Birmingham, UK, 12–13 December 2005. *Journal of Antimicrobial Chemotherapy*, 58:3–22.

Finkelstein A (2004). Static and dynamic effects of health policy: evidence from the vaccine industry. *Quarterly Journal of Economics*, 119:527–564.

Fireman B et al. (2003). Impact of the pneumococcal conjugate vaccine on otitis media. *Pediatric Infectious Disease Journal*, 22:10–16.

Fishman N (2006). Antimicrobial stewardship. *American Journal of Infection Control*, 34:S55–S63.

Food and Drug Administration (FDA) (1992). Press release: 5 June 1992. Silver Spring, MD, U.S. Food and Drug Administration (http://www.fda.gov/bbs/topics/NEWS/NEW00279.html, accessed December 2008).

Food and Drug Administration (FDA) (2005). *Animation of antimicrobial resistance.* Silver Spring, MD, U.S. Food and Drug Administration (http://www.fda.gov/cvm/antiresistvideo.htm, accessed 22 November 2008).

Foster S (2010). Economic consequences of antibiotic resistance. *2010 Annual Conference on Antimicrobial Resistance, Bethesda, MD, 1–3 February 2010.*

Frank RG (2003). New estimates of drug development costs. *Journal of Health Economics*, 22:325–330.

Frazee B et al. (2005). High prevalence of methicillin-resistant *Staphylococcus aureus* in emergency department skin and soft tissue infections. *Annals of Emergency Medicine*, 45:311–320.

French H (2005). Maximizing exclusivity for drug products. *Nature Reviews Drug Discovery*, 4:709.

Friedrich A et al. (2008). EUREGIO MRSA-net Twente/Munsterland – a Dutch-German cross-border network for the prevention and control of infections caused by methicillin-resistant Staphylococcus aureus. *EuroSurveillance*, 13(35).

Galambos L (2008). What are the prospects for a new golden era in vaccines? *Eurohealth*, 14:12–14.

GAVI Alliance (2009) [web site]. Press release: GAVI partners fulfil promise to fight pneumococcal disease: advance market commitment could save 7 million infants by 2030. Geneva, GAVI Alliance (http://www.gavialliance.org/media_centre/press_releases/2009_06_12_AMC_lecce_kick_off.php, accessed 26 April 2010).

GlaxoSmithKline (2007) [web site]. Press release: GSK awarded US Department of Defense contract to pursue novel antibacterial research program. Philadelphia, PA, GlaxoSmithKline (http://us.gsk.com/ControllerServlet?appId=4&pageId=402&newsid=1146, accessed 26 April 2010).

GlaxoSmithKline (2008) [web site]. Press release: GSK and Mpex Pharmaceuticals form alliance to develop novel efflux pump inhibitors for use against serious gram-negative infections. Brentford, GlaxoSmithKline (http://www.gsk.com/media/pressreleases/2008/2008_pressrelease_10066.htm, accessed 26 April 2009).

GlaxoSmithKline (2009a) [web site]. Press release: Creating a pool of intellectual property to fight neglected tropical diseases. Brentford, GlaxoSmithKline (http://www.gsk.com/research/patent-pool.htm, accessed 26 April 2010).

GlaxoSmithKline (2009b) [web site]. Press release: Alnylam joins GSK in donating intellectual property to patent pool for neglected tropical diseases. Brentford, GlaxoSmithKline (http://www.gsk.com/media/pressreleases/2009/2009_pressrelease_10071.htm, accessed 26 April 2010).

Glennerster R, Kremer M (2001). A better way to spur medical research and development. *Regulation*, 23:34–39.

Global Alliance for TB Drug Development (2001). *The economics of TB drug development*. New York, NY, Global Alliance for TB Drug Development (http://www.tballiance.org/downloads/publications/TBA_Economics_Report.pdf, accessed 26 April 2010).

Goossens H (2009). Antibiotic consumption and link to resistance. *Clinical Microbiology and Infection*, 15:12–15.

Goossens H et al. (2005). Outpatient antibiotic use in Europe and association with resistance: a cross-national database study. *Lancet*, 365:579–587.

Goossens H et al. (2006). National campaigns to improve antibiotic use. *European Journal of Clinical Pharmacology*, 62:373–379.

Graves N, McGowan J Jr. (2008). Nosocomial infection, the Deficit Reduction Act, and incentives for hospitals. *JAMA*, 300:1577–1579.

Grijalva C et al. (2007). Pneumococcal vaccination and public health. *Lancet*, 369:1144–1145.

Grossman M (1972). *The demand for health: a theoretical and empirical investigation*. New York, NY, Columbia University Press.

Heemstra H et al. (2008). Orphan drug development across Europe: bottlenecks and opportunities. *Drug Discovery Today*, 13(15–16):670–676.

Her Majesty's Revenue and Customs (2006). *HMRC sets up specialist units for R&D tax credit claims* (http://www.hmrc.gov.uk/randd/special-units.htm, accessed 26 April 2010).

Her Majesty's Revenue and Customs (2009) [web site]. Tax allowances and reliefs – employees or directors (http://www.hmrc.gov.uk/incometax/tax-allow-ees.htm#2, accessed 26 April 2010).

Herrling P (2009). Financing R&D for neglected diseases. *Nature Reviews Drug Discovery*, 8:91.

Hollingsworth R, Hollingsworth E (2000). Major discoveries and biomedical research organizations: perspectives on interdisciplinarity, nurturing leadership, and integrated structure and cultures. In: Stehr N, Weingart P, eds. *Practicing interdisciplinarity*. Ontario, University of Toronto Press:215–244.

Hollis A (2005). *An efficient reward system for pharmaceutical innovation*. Alberta, Department of Economics, University of Calgary, Institute of Health Economics.

Hollis A, Pogge T (2008). *The Health Impact Fund: making new medicines accessible for all*. New Haven, Incentives for Global Health.

Hopenhayn H et al. (2006). Rewarding sequential innovators: prizes, patents and buyouts. *Journal of Political Economy*, 114:1041–1068.

Horowitz J, Moehring H (2004). How property rights and patents affect antibiotic resistance. *Health Economics*, 13:575–583.

Houck P et al. (2004). Timing of antibiotic administration and outcomes for Medicare patients hospitalized with community-acquired pneumonia. *Archives of Internal Medicine*, 164:637–644.

Howard D (2004). Resistance-induced antibiotic substitution. *Health Economics*, 13:585–595.

Howard D et al. (2003). The global impact of drug resistance. *Clinical Infectious Diseases*, 36:S4–S10.

Hsu J, Schwartz E (2003). *A model of R&D valuation and the design of research incentives*. Cambridge, MA, National Bureau of Economic Research (NBER Working Paper No. 10041).

IMS Health (2001). Data exclusivity – the generics market's third hurdle. Quoted in: Pugatch M (2004). *Intellectual property and pharmaceutical data exclusivity in the context of innovation and market access*. Geneva, International Centre for Trade and Sustainable Development:13.

IMS LifeCycle™ (2008). IMS Health Limited Database. All rights reserved. Norwalk, IMS Health Inc.

Infectious Diseases Society of America (2004) [web site]. Bad bugs, no drugs: as antibiotic discovery stagnates ... a public health crisis brews. Arlington, VA, Infectious Diseases Society of America (http://www.idsociety.org/badbugsnodrugs.html, accessed 26 April 2010).

Initiative for Open Innovation (2009) [web site]. Why do we need the Initiative for Open Innovation? Cambia, Queensland University of Technology, Brisbane (http://www.openinnovation.org/daisy/ioi/about.html, accessed 24 May 2010).

Innovative Medicines Initiative (2009) [web site]. IMI 2nd call 2009: announcement of the topics to be included in the IMI JU 2nd call. Brussels, Innovative Medicines Initiative (http://imi.europa.eu/calls-02_en.html, accessed 9 March 2010).

International Expert Group on Biotechnology, Innovation and Intellectual Property (2008). *Toward a new era of intellectual property: from confrontation to negotiation.* Montreal, International Expert Group on Biotechnology, Innovation and Intellectual Property (http://www.theinnovationpartnership.org/data/ieg/documents/report/TIP_Report_E.pdf, accessed 26 April 2010).

International Federation of Pharmaceutical Manufacturers and Associations [web site] (2005). R&D for neglected diseases: lessons learned and remaining challenges. Geneva, International Federation of Pharmaceutical Manufacturers and Associations (http://www.ifpma.org/News/NewsReleaseDetail.aspx?nID=4762, accessed May 2009).

Jayaraman R (2009). Antibiotic resistance: an overview of mechanisms and a paradigm shift. *Current Science*, 96:1475–1484.

Kades E (2005). Preserving a precious resource: rationalizing the use of antibiotics. *Northwestern University Law Review*, 99:611–676.

Kahlmeter G (2003). An international survey of the antimicrobial susceptibility of pathogens from uncomplicated urinary tract infections: the ECO-SENS project. *Journal of Antimicrobial Chemotherapy*, 51(1):69–76.

Kapczynski, A (2009). Commentary: innovation policy for a new era. *Journal of Law, Medicine & Ethics*, 37:264–268.

Kaplan S et al. (2004). Decrease of invasive pneumococcal infections in children among 8 children's hospitals in the United States after the introduction of the 7-valent pneumococcal conjugate vaccine. *Pediatrics*, 113:443–449.

Kaplan W, Laing R (2004). *Priority medicines for Europe and the world.* Geneva, World Health Organization, Department of Essential Drugs and Medicines Policy.

Karlowsky J, Sahm D (2002). Antibiotic resistance – is resistance detected by surveillance relevant to predicting resistance in the clinical setting? *Current Opinion in Pharmacology*, 2:487–492.

Kawamoto K et al. (2005). Improving clinical practice using clinical decision support systems: a systematic review of trials to identify features critical to success. *BMJ*, 330:765.

Kesselheim A (2009). Drug development for neglected diseases – the trouble with FDA review vouchers. *New England Journal of Medicine*, 359:1981–1983.

Kesselheim A, Outterson K (2010). Improving antibiotic markets. *Yale Journal of Health Policy, Law & Ethics*, 31 (in press).

Klein E et al. (2007). Hospitalizations and deaths caused by methicillin-resistant *Staphylococcus aureus*, United States, 1999–2005. *Emerging Infectious Diseases*, 13:1840–1846.

Klevens R et al. (2007). Invasive methicillin-resistant *Staphylococcus aureus* infections in the United States. *JAMA*, 298:1763–1771.

Kölch M et al. (2007). The EU-regulation on medicinal products for paediatric use: impacts on child and adolescent psychiatry and clinical research with minors. *European Child & Adolescent Psychiatry*, 16:229–235.

Kollef M, Micek S (2005). Staphylococcus aureus pneumonia: a "superbug" infection in community and hospital settings. *Chest*, 128:1093–1097.

Kosikowski A (2009). Achaogen signs $26.6 million contract with NIAID for development of new therapy to treat resistant strains of NIAID category A and B priority pathogens. *Business Wire*, 3 March 2009.

Kremer M (1998). Patent buyouts: a mechanism for encouraging innovation. *Quarterly Journal of Economics*, 113:1137–1167.

Kremer M, Glennerster R (2004). *Strong medicine: creating incentives for pharmaceutical research on neglected diseases*. Princeton, NJ, Princeton University Press.

Kremer M, Snyder C (2003). *Why are drugs more profitable than vaccines?* Cambridge, MA, National Bureau of Economic Research (NBER Working Paper No. 9833).

Kremer M et al. (2005). *Briefing note on advance purchase commitments*. London, DFID Health Systems Resource Centre. (http://www.who.int/intellectualproperty/submissions/MichealKremerKTW_CIPIH_submit_2.pdf, accessed 26 April 2010).

Krohmal B (2007). *Prominent innovation prizes and reward programs*. Washington, DC, Knowledge Ecology International (KEI Research Note 2007:1).

Lancet Infectious Diseases (2008). Laying down the law on healthcare-associated infections. *Lancet Infectious Diseases*, 8:583.

Lawton R et al. (2000). Practices to improve antimicrobial use at 47 US hospitals: the status of the 1997 SHEA/IDSA position paper recommendations. *Infection Control and Hospital Epidemiology*, 21:256–259.

Laxminarayan R (2002). How broad should the scope of antibiotic patents be? *American Journal of Agricultural Economics*, 84:1287–1292.

Laxminarayan R, Brown G (2001). Economics of antibiotic resistance: a theory of optimal use. *Journal of Environmental Economics and Management*, 42:183–206.

Laxminarayan R et al. (2007). *Extending the cure: policy responses to the growing threat of antibiotic resistance*. Washington, DC, Resources for the Future (RFF Report).

Levin A et al. (1999). Intravenous colistin as therapy for nosocomial infections caused by multi-drug resistant *Pseudomonas aeruginosa* and *Acinetobacter baumannii*. *Clinical Infectious Diseases*, 28:1008–1011.

Levine M, Sztein M (2004). Vaccine development strategies for improving immunization: the role of modern immunology. *Nature Immunology*, 5:460–464.

Levy S (1998). The challenge of antibiotic resistance. *Scientific American*, 278:46–54.

Levy S (2002). *The antibiotic paradox. How the misuse of antibiotics destroys their curative powers*. Cambridge, MA, Perseus.

Levy S, Marshall B (2004). Antibacterial resistance worldwide: causes, challenges and responses. *Nature Medicine*, 10:S122–S129.

Li J et al. (2007). Economic return of clinical trials performed under the Pediatric Exclusivity Program. *JAMA*, 297:480–488.

Light D (2009). *Advanced market commitments: current realities and alternate approaches*. Amsterdam, Health Action International Europe, Frankfurt am Main, Medico International (http://www.haiweb.org/31032009/27%20Mar%202009%20AMC%20Current%20Realities%20&%20Alternate%20Approaches%20FINAL.pdf, accessed 6 April 2009).

Light D et al. (2009). Estimated research and development costs of rotavirus vaccines. *Vaccine*, 27:6627–6633.

Lodise T, McKinnon PS (2007). Burden of methicillin-resistant *Staphylococcus aureus*: focus on clinical and economic outcomes. *Pharmacotherapy*, 27:1001–1012.

Lodise T et al. (2003). Outcomes analysis of delayed antibiotic treatment for hospital-acquired *Staphylococcus aureus* bacteremia. *Clinical Infectious Diseases*, 36:1418–1423.

Love J (1997). Health registration data exclusivity, biomedical research, and restrictions on the introduction of generic drugs. *Statement before Subcommittee on Labor, Health and Human Services and Education and Related Agencies Committee on Appropriations US Senate.* Washington DC, Consumer Project on Technology (http://www.cptech.org/pharm/senhregd.html, accessed 26 April 2010).

Love J (2003). *Evidence regarding research and development investments in innovative and non-innovative medicines*. Washington, DC, Consumer Project on Technology.

Love J (2007). Would cash prizes promote cheap drugs? *New Scientist*, 2629:24.

Love J (2008). *Annex 1 – cost benefit analysis for UNITAID patent pool*. Washington, DC, and Geneva, Knowledge Ecology International (http://www.keionline.org/misc-docs/1/cost_benefit_UNITAID_patent_pool.pdf, accessed 26 April 2010).

Love J, Hubbard T (2007). *The big idea: prizes to stimulate R&D for new medicines*. Washington, DC, and Geneva, Knowledge Ecology International (http://www.keionline.org/misc-docs/bigidea-prizes.pdf, accessed 23 February 2009).

Lowy F (1998). *Staphylococcus aureus* infections. *New England Journal of Medicine*, 339:520–532.

Lowy F (2003). Antimicrobial resistance: the example of *Staphylococcus aureus*. *Journal of Clinical Investigation*, 111:1265–1273.

Luehrman TA (1997). What's it worth? A general manager's guide to valuation. *Harvard Business Review*, 75:132–142.

Lybecker K, Freeman R (2007). Funding pharmaceutical innovation through direct tax credits. *Health Economics, Policy and Law*, 2:267–284.

MacCara M et al. (2001). Impact of a limited fluoroquinolone reimbursement policy on antimicrobial prescription claims. *Annals of Pharmacotherapy*, 35:852–858.

MacCoss M, Baillie T (2004). Organic chemistry in drug discovery. *Science*, 303(5665):1810–1813.

McDonnell Norms Group (2008). Antibiotic overuse: the influence of social norms. *Journal of the American College of Surgeons*, 207:265–275.

MacDougall C, Polk R (2005). Antimicrobial stewardship programs in health care systems. *Clinical Microbiology Reviews*, 18:638–656.

McGowan J Jr. (2001). Economic impact of antimicrobial resistance. *Emerging Infectious Diseases*, 7:286–292.

McGuire A, Drummond M, Rutten F (2004). Reimbursement of pharmaceuticals in the European Union. In: Mossialos E, Mrazek M, Walley T, eds. *Regulating pharmaceuticals in Europe: striving for efficiency, equity and quality*. Maidenhead, Open University Press:130–143.

Maeder T (2003). The orphan drug backlash. *Scientific American*, 288:80–87.

Mainous A III et al. (2000). An evaluation of statewide strategies to reduce antibiotic overuse. *Family Medicine*, 32:22–29.

Mandelbaum-Schmid J (2004). New generation of non-profit initiatives tackles world's "neglected" diseases. *Bulletin of the World Health Organization*, 82:395–396.

Maragakis L et al. (2008). Clinical and economic burden of antimicrobial resistance. *Expert Review of Anti-Infective Therapy*, 6:751–763.

Martin JB, Kasper DL (2000). In whose best interest? Breaching the academic-industrial wall. *New England Journal of Medicine*, 343(22):1646–1649.

Masterton R (2000). Surveillance studies: how can they help the management of infection? *Journal of Antimicrobial Chemotherapy*, 46:53–58.

Mauldin P et al. (2010). Attributable hospital cost and length of stay associated with health care-associated infections caused by antibiotic-resistant Gram-negative bacteria. *Antimicrobial Agents and Chemotherapy*, 54:109–115.

Maurer S et al. (2004). Finding cures for tropical diseases: is open source an answer? *PLoS Medicine*, 1:183–186.

Mayer L (2007). Immunity for immunizations: tort liability, biodefense, and Bioshield II. *Stanford Law Review*, 59:1753.

Metersky M et al. (2009). Antibiotic timing and diagnostic uncertainty in Medicare patients with pneumonia: is it reasonable to expect all patients to receive antibiotics within 4 hours? *Chest*, 130:16–21.

Metz-Gercek S, Mittermayer H (2008). The European surveillance activities EARSS and ESAC in the context of ABS International. *Wiener Klinische Wochenschrift*, 120:264–267.

Meurer M (2003). *Pharmacogenomics, genetic tests, and patent-based incentives*. Boston, MA, Boston University School of Law (Working Paper No. 03-09).

Milstien J et al. (2006). The impact of globalization on vaccine development and availability. *Health Affairs*, 25:1061–1069.

Moellering R Jr. (2006). The growing menace of community-acquired methicillin-resistant *Staphylococcus aureus*. *Annals of Internal Medicine*, 144:368–370.

Molstad S et al. (2008). Sustained reduction of antibiotic use and low bacterial resistance: 10-year follow-up of the Swedish STRAMA programme. *Lancet Infectious Diseases*, 8:125–132.

Monaghan R, Barret J (2006). Antibacterial drug discovery – then, now and the genomics future. *Biochemical Pharmacology*, 7:901–909.

Monnet D (2005). Antibiotic development and the changing role of the pharmaceutical industry. *International Journal of Risk & Safety in Medicine*, 17:133–145.

Moran M (2005). A breakthrough in R&D for neglected diseases: new ways to get the drugs we need. *PLoS Medicine*, 2:828–832.

Moran M et al. (2005). *Executive summary for the new landscape of neglected disease drug development: pharmaceutical R&D policy project*. London, Wellcome Trust (http://www.wellcome.ac.uk/stellent/groups/corporatesite/@msh_publishing_group/documents/web_document/wtx026593.pdf, accessed 3 December 2008).

Moreno F et al. (1995). Methicillin-resistant *Staphylococcus aureus* as a community organism. *Clinical Infectious Diseases*, 21:1308–1312.

Moritz E, Hergenrother P (2007). The prevalence of plasmids and other mobile genetic elements in clinically important drug-resistant bacteria. In: Amabile-Cuevas C, ed. *Antimicrobial resistance in bacteria*. Norwich, Horizon BioScience:25–53.

Munos B (2006). Can open-source R&D reinvigorate drug research? *Nature Reviews Drug Discovery*, 5:723–729.

Murphy D, Albrecht R (2001). *Background material for the September 13, 2001, Advisory Committee Meeting*. Silver Spring, MD, US Food and Drug Administration (www.fda.gov/ohrms/dockets/ac/02/briefing/3837b1_01_Intro.doc, accessed 26 April 2010).

Nathan C, Goldberg F (2005). The profit problem in antibiotic R&D. *Nature Reviews Drug Discovery*, 4:887–891.

National Institutes of Health (NIH) (2007) [web site]. Re-engineering the clinical research enterprise: translational research. Bethesda, MA, National Institutes of Health (http://nihroadmap.nih.gov/clinicalresearchtheme/, accessed 17 November 2007).

National Nosocomial Infections Surveillance System (2004). National Nosocomial Infections Surveillance System Report – data summary from January 1992 through June 2004. *American Journal of Infection Control*, 32:470–485.

Nemet, G (2009). Demand-pull, technology-push, and government-led incentives for non-incremental technical change. *Research Policy*, 38:700–709.

NIH Record (2009). *ARRA results in unprecedented boost for NIH budget*. Bethesda, MA, National Institutes of Health (http://nihrecord.od.nih.gov/newsletters/2009/03_20_2009/story1.htm, accessed 7 April 2009).

Nordberg P et al. (2004). *Antibacterial drug resistance*. Background document to Priority Medicines for Europe and the World. (http://soapimg.icecube.snowfall.se/stopresistance/Priority_Medicine_Antibacterial_background_docs_final.pdf, accessed 26 April 2010).

Nordmann P et al. (2007). Superbugs in the coming new decade; multidrug resistance and prospects for treatment of *Staphylococcus aureus*, *Enterococcus spp.* and *Pseudomonas aeruginosa* in 2010. *Current Opinion in Microbiology*, 10:436–440.

Norrby S et al. (2005). Lack of development of new antimicrobial drugs: a potential serious threat to public health. *Lancet Infectious Diseases*, 5:115–119.

Nulens E et al. (2008). Cost of the methicillin-resistant *Staphylococcus aureus* search and destroy policy in a Dutch university hospital. *Journal of Hospital Infection*, 68:301–307.

O'Brien M et al. (2007). Educational outreach visits: effects on professional practice and health care outcomes. *Cochrane Database of Systematic Reviews*, 4:CD000409.

Organisation for Economic Co-operation and Development (2002). *Tax incentives for research and development: trends and issues*. Paris, Organisation for Economic Co-operation and Development.

Organisation for Economic Co-operation and Development (2009). *Coherence for health: innovation for new medicines for infectious diseases*. Paris, Organisation for Economic Co-operation and Development.

Okeke IN et al. (2005). Antimicrobial resistance in developing countries. Part I: recent trends and current status. *Lancet Infectious Diseases*, 5:481–493.

Olesen O et al. (2009). Human vaccine research in the European Union. *Vaccine*, 27:640–645.

Olson M (2008). The risk we bear: the effects of review speed and industry user fees on new drug safety. *Journal of Health Economics*, 27:175–200.

Outterson K (2005). The vanishing public domain: antibiotic resistance, pharmaceutical innovation and global public health. *University of Pittsburgh Law Review*, 67:67–123.

Outterson K (2008). Author's reply. *Lancet Infectious Diseases*, 8:212–214.

Outterson K (2009). The legal ecology of resistance: the role of antibiotic resistance in pharmaceutical innovation. *Cardozo Law Review*, 31:613–678.

Outterson K et al. (2007). Will longer antimicrobial patents improve general global public health? *Lancet Infectious Diseases*, 7:559–566.

Oxfam International (2008). *Ending the R&D crisis in public health: promoting pro-poor medical innovation*. Oxfam Briefing Paper. Oxford, Oxfam International (http://www.oxfam.org/sites/www.oxfam.org/files/bp122-randd-crisis-public-health.pdf, accessed 26 April 2010).

Parks M, Disis M (2004). Conflicts of interest in translational research. *Journal of Translational Medicine*, 2:28.

Parmet W (2007). Legal power and legal rights – isolation and quarantine in the case of drug-resistant tuberculosis. *New England Journal of Medicine*, 357:433–435.

Payne D et al. (2007). Drugs for bad bugs: confronting the challenges of antibacterial discovery. *Nature Reviews Drug Discovery*, 6:29–40.

Peters N et al. (2008). The research agenda of the National Institute of Allergy and Infectious Diseases for antimicrobial resistance. *Journal of Infectious Diseases*, 197:1087–1093.

Pham P, Bartlett J (2008). *Miltefosine*. Baltimore, MD, Johns Hopkins POC-IT Center (http://prod.hopkins-abxguide.org/antibiotics/antiparasitic/miltefosine.html?contentInstanceId=254945, accessed 13 March 2009).

Phelps C (1989). Bug/drug resistance. Sometimes less is more. *Medical Care*, 27:194–203.

Philipson T et al. (2005). *Assessing the safety and efficacy of the FDA: the case of the Prescription Drug User Fee Acts.* Cambridge, MA, National Bureau of Economic Research (NBER Working Paper No. 11724).

Pirson M et al. (2008). Financial consequences of hospital-acquired bacteraemia in three Belgian hospitals in 2003 and 2004. *Journal of Hospital Infection*, 68:9–16.

Poupard J (2006). Is the pharmaceutical industry responding to the challenge of increasing bacterial resistance? *Clinical Microbiology Newsletter*, 28:13–15.

Power E (2006). Impact of antibiotic restrictions: the pharmaceutical perspective. *Clinical Microbiology and Infection*, 12:25–34.

Powers J (2004). Antimicrobial drug development – the past, the present, and the future. *Clinical Microbiology and Infection*, 10:23–31.

PR9.net (2004). *Visiongain predicts by 2009 orphan drugs will grow to be worth almost $65 million.* San Francisco CA, PR9.net (http://www.pr9.net/pdf/1373december.pdf, accessed 24 May 2010).

Pray L (2008). *Antibiotic R&D: resolving the paradox between unmet medical need and commercial incentive.* Needham, MA, Cambridge Healthtech Institute (Insight Pharma Reports).

Prins J et al. (2008). Experiences with the Dutch working party on antibiotic policy (SWAB). *Eurosurveillance*, 13(46) pii=19037.

Projan S (2003). Why is big pharma getting out of antibacterial drug discovery? *Current Opinion in Microbiology*, 6:427–430.

Projan S, Bradford P (2007). Late stage antibacterial drugs in the clinical pipeline. *Current Opinion in Microbiology*, 10:441–446.

Public Citizen's Congress Watch (2002). *America's other drug problem: a briefing book on the Rx drug debate.* Washington, DC, Public Citizen's Congress Watch.

ReAct – Action on Antibiotic Resistance (2007). *Cure with care: understanding antibiotic resistance.* Uppsala, ReAct – Action on Antibiotic Resistance, Uppsala University (http://soapimg.icecube.snowfall.se/stopresistance/cure_with_care.pdf, accessed 26 April 2010).

Reed S (2002). Economic issues and antibiotic resistance in the community. *Annals of Pharmacotherapy*, 36:148–154.

Rice L (2003). Do we really need new anti-infective drugs? *Current Opinion in Pharmacology*, 3:459–463.

Rice L (2006). Unmet medical needs in antibacterial therapy. *Biochemical Pharmacology*, 71:991–995.

Richet H, Fournier P (2006). Nosocomial infections caused by *Acinetobacter baumannii*: a major threat worldwide. *Infection Control Hospital Epidemiology*, 27:645–646.

Ridley D et al. (2006). Developing drugs for developing countries. *Health Affairs*, 25:313–324.

Rinaldi A (2005). Adopting an orphan. *EMBO Reports*, 6:507–510.

Roberts R et al. (2009). Hospital and societal costs of antimicrobial-resistance infections in a Chicago teaching hospital: implications for antibiotic stewardship. *Clinical Infectious Diseases*, 49:1175–1184.

Rohde D (2000). The Orphan Drug Act: an engine of innovation? At what cost? *Food and Drug Law Journal*, 55:125–143.

Rosdahl V, Pedersen K, eds. (1998). *The Copenhagen recommendations. Report from the Invitational EU Conference on the Microbial Threat, Copenhagen, 9–10 September 1998*. Copenhagen, Danish Ministry of Health and Danish Ministry of Food, Agriculture and Fisheries.

Ross D (2007). The FDA and the case of Ketek. *New England Journal of Medicine*, 356:1601–1604.

Royal Society (2008). *Innovative mechanisms for tackling antibacterial resistance*. London, The Royal Society (RS Policy Document 14/08) (http://www.bsac.org.uk/_db/_documents/Innovative_mechanisms_for_tackling_antibacterial_resistance.pdf, accessed 26 April 2010).

Rubin P (2004). The FDA's antibiotic resistance. *Regulation*, 27:34–37.

Sakoulas G et al. (2004). Relationship of MIC and bactericidal activity to efficacy of vancomycin for treatment of methicillin-resistant *Staphylococcus aureus* bacteremia. *Journal of Clinical Microbiology*, 46:2398–2402.

Saver R (2008). In tepid defense of population health: physicians and antibiotic resistance. *American Journal of Law and Medicine*, 34:431–491.

Sellers L (2003). Big pharma bails on anti-infectives research. *Pharmaceutical Executive*, 23:22.

Shavell S, van Ypersele T (2001). Rewards versus intellectual property rights. *Journal of Law and Economics*, 44:525–547.

Shillcutt S (2008). Cost-effectiveness of malaria diagnostic methods in sub-Saharan Africa in an era of combination therapy. *Bulletin of the World Health Organization*, 86:81–160.

Shlaes D, Moellering R Jr. (2002). The United States Food and Drug Administration and the end of antibiotics. *Clinical Infectious Diseases*, 34:420–422.

Shlaes D et al. (1991). Antimicrobial resistance: new directions. *American Society of Microbiology News*, 57:455–458.

Singh M, Greenstein M (2000). Antibacterial leads from microbial natural products discovery. *Current Opinion in Drug Discovery & Development*, 3:167–176.

Sloan F, Hsieh C, eds. (2006). *Pharmaceutical innovation: incentives, competition, and cost-benefit analysis in international perspective*. Cambridge, Cambridge University Press.

Smart T (2005). TB treatment and diagnostics pipeline: once empty, suddenly offers new hope for TB care. *National Aids Manual, Aidsmap news, 2 December 2005*. London, NAM (http://www.aidsmap.com/en/news/3E8441AA-7034-4C5A-BCF9-6776081A5E19.asp, accessed 13 March 2009).

Smith RD et al. (2005). Assessing the macroeconomic impact of a healthcare problem: the application of computable general equilibrium analysis to antimicrobial resistance. *Journal of Health Economics*, 24:1055–1075.

Snapinn S (2000). Noninferiority trials. *Current Controlled Trials in Cardiovascular Medicine*, 1:19–21.

Sonderholm J (2009). Wild-card patent extensions as a means to incentivize research and development of antibiotics. *Journal of Law, Medicine, and Ethics*, 37:240–246.

Sorenson C, Drummond M, Kanavos P (2008). *Ensuring value for money in health care: the role of health technology assessment in the European Union*. Copenhagen, WHO Regional Office for Europe on behalf of the European Observatory on Health Systems and Policies.

Special Programme for Research and Training in Tropical Diseases (2007). *Making a difference: 30 years of research and capacity building in tropical diseases*. Geneva, World Health Organization (http://www.who.int/tdr/svc/publications/about-tdr/30-year-history/making-difference, accessed 13 March 2009).

Special Programme for Research and Training in Tropical Diseases (2008). *Laboratory-based evaluation of 19 commercially available rapid diagnostic tests for tuberculosis*. Geneva, World Health Organization (http://www.who.int/tdr/publications/tdr-research-publications/diagnostics-evaluation-2/pdf/diagnostic-evaluation-2.pdf, accessed 30 March 2009).

Spellberg B (2008a). Trials and tribulations of antibiotic development. *Lancet Infectious Diseases*, 8:209.

Spellberg B (2008b). Antibiotic resistance and antibiotic development. *Lancet Infectious Diseases*, 8:211–212.

Spellberg B et al. (2004). Trends in antimicrobial drug development: implications for the future. *Clinical Infectious Diseases*, 38:1279–1286.

Spellberg B et al. (2007). Societal costs versus savings from wild-card patent extension legislation to spur critically needed antibiotic development. *Infection*, 35:167–174.

Spellberg B et al. (2008a). The epidemic of antibiotic resistant infections: a call to action for the medical community from the Infectious Diseases Society of America. *Clinical Infectious Diseases*, 46:155–164.

Spellberg B et al. (2008b). Position paper: recommended design features of future clinical trials of antibacterial agents for community-acquired pneumonia. *Clinical Infectious Diseases*, 47:S249–S265.

Spurling G et al. (2007). Delayed antibiotics for respiratory infections. *Cochrane Database of Systematic Reviews*, 3:CD004417.

Stewart P, Costerton J (2001). Antibiotic resistance of bacteria in biofilms. *Lancet*, 358:135–138.

Stolk P et al. (2005). Rare essentials: drugs for rare diseases as essential medicines. *Bulletin of the World Health Organization*, 84(9):745–751.

Struck M (1996). Vaccine R&D success rates and development times. *Nature Biotechnology*, 14:591–593.

Swanick M, Le Claire L (2008). The new French R&D tax credit system gives a good signal. *Pharma and Life Sciences Tax News*, 7(5).

Swedish Presidency of the European Union (2009) [web site]. Press release – EU and USA initiate cooperation against resistant bacteria. (http://www.se2009.eu/en/2.543/2.578/2.737/2.741/1.22026, accessed 26 April 2010).

't Hoen EF (2009). *The global politics of pharmaceutical monopoly power: drug patents, access, innovation and the application of the WTO Doha Declaration on TRIPS and Public Health*. Diemen, AMB Publishers (http://www.msfaccess.org/fileadmin/user_upload/medinnov_accesspatents/01-05_BOOK_tHoen_PoliticsofPharmaPower_defnet.pdf, accessed 26 April 2010).

Taubes G (2008). The bacteria fight back. *Science*, 321:356–361.

Tegnell A et al. (2002). BICHAT: an EU initiative to improve preparedness and response to bioterrorism. *Eurosurveillance*, 6(28) pii=020711.

Thompson C et al. (2004). Antibacterial research and development in the 21st century – an industry perspective of the challenges. *Current Opinion in Microbiology*, 7:445–450.

Tickell S (2005). *The Antibiotic Innovation Study: expert voices on a critical need*. Uppsala, ReAct – Action on Antibiotic Resistance. (http://soapimg.icecube.snowfall.se/strama/AIS%20Report%20React.pdf, accessed 23 February 2009).

Tillotson G, Echols R (2008). Clinical trial design and consequences for drug development for community-acquired pneumonia: an industry perspective. *Clinical Infectious Diseases*, 47:S237–S240.

Towse A, Kettler H (2005). Advance price or purchase commitments to create markets for treatments for disease of poverty: lessons from three policies. *Bulletin of the World Health Organization*, 83:301–307.

Trull M et al. (2007). Turning biodefense dollars into products. *Nature Biotechnology*, 25:179–184.

Tufts Center for the Study of Drug Development (2005). Drug safety withdrawals in the US not linked to speed of FDA approval. *Tufts CSDD Impact Report*, 7:1–4.

UK National Health Service (2003). *NIHR health technology assessment programme*. Southampton, NIHR Evaluation, Trials and Studies Coordination Centre, University of Southampton (http://www.hta.ac.uk/, accessed 26 April 2010).

Ultra-Sensitive Diagnosis for Emerging Pathogens (2007) [web site]. Summary. (http://www.usdep.eu/project, accessed 26 April 2010).

UNITAID (2009). *The Medicines Patent Pool initiative: fact sheet*. Geneva World Health Organization (www.who.int/hiv/amds/unitaid_patent_pool2_2009.pdf, accessed 26 April 2010).

US Congress, Office of Technology Assessment (1995). *Impacts of antibiotic-resistant bacteria*. Washington, DC, US Government Printing Office.

US Department of Health and Human Services (2007). *Project BioShield Annual Report to Congress: August 2006 – July 2007*. Washington, DC, US Department of Health and Human Services (http://www.hhs.gov/aspr/barda/documents/bioshieldannualreport2006.pdf, accessed 27 March 2009).

US Office of Orphan Products Development [web site] http://www.fda.gov/orphan, accessed 10 July 2010.

Vergidis P, Falagas M (2008). Multidrug-resistant Gram-negative bacterial infections: the emerging threat and potential novel treatment options. *Current Opinion in Investigational Drugs*, 9:176–183.

Vicente M et al. (2006). The fallacies of hope: will we discover new antibiotics to combat pathogenic bacteria in time? *FEMS Microbiology Reviews*, 30:841–852.

von Schoen-Angerer T (2008). Questioning the 1.5 billion dollar vaccine deal. *Development Today*, 25 April 2008.

Walker A et al. (2008). Fairness of financial penalties to improve control of Clostridium difficile. *BMJ*, 337:a2097.

Waltz E (2008). FDA launches priority vouchers for neglected-disease drugs. *Nature Biotechnology*, 26:1315–1316.

Warner S (2005). The return of vaccines: why is big pharma investing in a market they once spurned? *Scientist*, 19:28.

Webber D, Kremer M (2001). Perspectives on stimulating industrial research and development for neglected infectious diseases. *Bulletin of the World Health Organization*, 79:735–741.

Webber D, Piddock L (2003). The importance of efflux pumps in bacterial antibiotic resistance. *Journal of Antimicrobial Chemotherapy*, 51:9–11.

Wellcome Trust (2005). *Antibiotic resistance an unwinnable war?* London, Wellcome Trust (http://www.wellcome.ac.uk/stellent/groups/corporatesite/@msh_publishing_group/documents/web_document/wtx026231.pdf, accessed 26 April 2010).

Wellcome Trust (2007) [web site]. Press release – Wellcome Trust and GlaxoSmithKline announce partnership to target drug-resistant hospital infections. London, Wellcome Trust (http://www.wellcome.ac.uk/News/Mediaoffice/Pressreleases/2007/WTX037132.htm, accessed 26 April 2010).

Wellcome Trust (2008a). *Annual report and financial statements 2008*. London, Wellcome Trust (http://www.wellcome.ac.uk/stellent/groups/corporatesite/@msh_publishing_group/documents/web_document/wtx052796.pdf, accessed 24 May 2010).

Wellcome Trust (2008b) [web site]. Press release – Development of a new class of antibiotics to treat MRSA. London, Wellcome Trust (http://www.wellcome.ac.uk/News/Media-office/Press-releases/2008/WTX050499.htm, accessed 26 April 2010).

Wellcome Trust (2009a) [web site]. Press release – New seeding drug discovery award will help develop new antibiotics. London, Wellcome Trust (http://www.wellcome.ac.uk/News/2009/News/WTX052832.htm, accessed 26 April 2010).

Wellcome Trust (2009b). *Wellcome Trust Strategic Plan 2005–2010*. London, Wellcome Trust.

Wertheim H et al. (2004). Low prevalence of methicillin-resistant Staphylococcus aureus (MRSA) at hospital admission in the Netherlands: the value of search and destroy and restrictive antibiotic use. *Journal of Hospital Infection*, 56:321–325.

Whitby M et al. (2001). Risk of death from methicillin-resistant Staphylococcus aureus bacteraemia: a meta-analysis. *Medical Journal of Australia*, 175:264–267.

Widdus R (2005). Public-private partnerships: an overview. *Transactions of the Royal Society of Tropical Medicine and Hygiene*, 99:S1–S8.

Woolf S (2008). The meaning of translational research and why it matters. *JAMA*, 299:211–213.

WHO (2002). *Antimicrobial resistance*. Geneva, World Health Organization Fact sheet No 194. (http://www.who.int/mediacentre/factsheets/fs194/en/, accessed 26 April 2010).

WHO (2006). *New vaccines against infectious diseases: research and development status*. Geneva, World Health Organization (http://www.who.int/vaccine_research/documents/en/Status_Table.pdf, accessed 26 April 2010).

WHO (2009). *World health statistics 2009*. Geneva, World Health Organization (http://www.who.int/whosis/whostat/EN_WHS09_Full.pdf, accessed 26 April 2010).

WHO Commission on Intellectual Property Rights (2006). *Intellectual property rights: Commission on Intellectual Property Rights, Innovation and Public Health: report*. Geneva, World Health Organization.

Yin W (2008). Market incentives and pharmaceutical innovation. *Journal of Health Economics*, 27:1060–1077.

Zaidi A et al. (2005). Hospital-acquired neonatal infections in developing countries. *Lancet*, 365:1175–1188.

Zaoutis T (2009). Antibiotic resistance: who will pay the bills? *Clinical Infectious Diseases*, 49:1185–1186.

Zentner A et al. (2005). Methods for the comparative evaluation of pharmaceuticals. *GMS Health Technology Assessment*, 1.